The Verse of Asaph

D1044379

C. DANIEL KOON

The Verse of Asaph

POETIC RENDITIONS OF BIBLE STORIES

Copyright © 2021 C. Daniel Koon

All rights reserved. No portion of this book may be reproduced or transmitted in any form or by any means, electronic or mechanical, including photocopying, recording, or any information storage and retrieval system, without written permission from the publisher.

Published by CDK ·

Cover design by Mikhail Starikov

Book Design by Kory Kirby
SET IN PERPETUA

ISBN 978-1-7375991-0-4 (Paperback)
ISBN 978-1-7375991-1-1 (eBook)

Printed in the United States of America

Bench of Innards

May I, with witty lines and candid tones,
Retell the Bible stories you have known
Since you've had hairless pits. You see, I fear
You've missed their main intent. Come, lend an ear
And exercise that bootless organ lodged
Behind your nose, the one you've camouflaged
With corny facts for Trivial Pursuit,
What game night rosters dictate you compute
In place of wisdom gained. I mean to reach
Beyond the bones and grab the soul, beseech
The question more than answers had. I hope
To give you fresh perspectives—broader scope
Than what you've had before. It's to this end
(And for the Kingdom) that my verse is penned.

Proem

A word on the poem

The Verse of Asaph is a poetic representation of Bible stories, and it elaborates on certain narratives in an attempt to explore details our Biblical text omits. I'm reading between the lines, as it were, and having fun with the text to facilitate a more palpable grasp of what's really going on in these tales. My desire is to paint poetic portraits in which not only revelation is amusing to read but also the colors of honest inference are stark and lurid enough to upstage our sugarcoated glaze. I intend to get down to the marrow of these stories and will not be deterred with the bones of creed or the obscene flavor of sticky things. There is a balance I want to maintain, not wanting to push too close to sacrilege, but I will ensure common sense conjectures have their say. And all of this is accomplished in poetic verse. Don't get contemptuous if the poem doesn't match the Biblical text perfectly, because it doesn't. Let the work speak for itself. It is not the Bible; it is *The Verse of Asaph*. I trust it will restore some raw vitality to aid us on our individual pilgrimages, the zest of which is too often muddled by dogma and line memorization. That said, it's also possible I'll be the prophet not accepted in his hometown, or maybe even his own generation.

A word on form

For centuries, it has been the practice of English poets to pen in verse, even fashionable to imitate the work of Homer, Virgil, and Ovid—men who had created work in hexameter. Chaucer spearheaded this imitation for the English language and developed a five-stress, decasyllabic line. This structure later became the standard for Milton, Marlowe, Shakespeare, and Pope. These men wrote mostly in what is known as iambic pentameter, a term used to describe a type of uniform for a line in poetry. The line must have ten syllables, and the line must have five feet, each foot consisting of two syllables. And lastly, the feet should have the stress on the second beat, thus producing a marching sound when read:

> With <u>stone</u> / of <u>flint</u> / he <u>kept</u> / the <u>bloo</u> / dy <u>pledge</u>
> And <u>tithed</u> / his <u>phal</u> / lus <u>tip</u> / with <u>sick</u> / le's <u>edge</u>.

The Verse of Asaph is written in iambic pentameter with rhyming couplets. It seemed the best fit for my epopee, and I thought I'd give Chaucer a run for his money. When it comes to a word's syllables, I tried to stick with what is in the *norma loquendi*. Initially, I thought it would be helpful to add apostrophes to certain words to eliminate syllables, but I decided that probably wasn't the way to go. My poem had the look of a seventeenth-century work by Milton:

> Then swoll'n with pride into the snare I fell
> Of fair fallacious looks, venereal trains,
> Softn'd with pleasure and voluptuous life;
> At length to lay my head and hallow'd pledge[1]

This is great stuff, but I ultimately decided against making such apostrophic shortenings in the text to eliminate syllables. May you, reader, be gracious in your assessment of my pentameter. Perhaps one day I will look at you through a book.

You may wonder why I'd willingly submit myself to such an exacting ambition as writing in verse. Has it not become the standard in the post-modern era to write what is commonly called "free verse"? I would say that it has—to our shame. "Free verse" is a bit of an oxymoron, though, and such styles of writing would probably be better named "prose poetry." To say that something is verse is to suggest it has structure, order, and rules. We call someone a skilled musician because they understand the chords, bars, and notes of their trade. They may vary from these slightly, as in jazz, but even the variance is dependent on the law. You might argue that "free verse" is a

---

1 Milton, John. Samson Agonistes, Lines 532 - 535

law to itself whose only rule is no rule. I will leave you to your literary anarchy. To be fair, I still write "prose poetry" on occasion when thoughts have trouble fitting the suit of verse. But I believe poetry, like any art, must adhere to some kind of discipline, not simply be a splotch of emotion on a page. I really think the English-speaking world must give up its love affair with the strumpet of "free verse." I propose we let the king know he hasn't a stitch on his bare rump.

A word on rhyme

Milton stuffily asserted in the opening remarks for *Paradise Lost* that rhyme is nothing more than constraint, calling it trivial and of no musical delight. He further states that the deficiency of rhyme is only exacerbated in longer works of epic poetry. He then goes on to excuse himself from the wretched vexation of such adjuncts and says his work would "rime not." I suspect he was disenchanted by the unpalatable lines of poets like Samuel Johnson, specifically in his work *The Vanity of Human Wishes.* Johnson wrote in a very mechanical manner, and one can hear the clanking ascent of his first ten syllables and the inevitable descent of the following ten, again and again. I find the same monotonous tenor in Alexander Pope. Having written one or two lines myself, I've determined the characteristic of tedious rhyming is a product of the push, forcing poems to marry rhymes before they've time to court. One need only pick two rhyming words and invert the sentences to couple them. It is also the simplest way of making verses rhyme. But too often the output of such mass production is a cryptic enigma, and comprehension becomes something the poet shares alone. But if it's done with skill, rhyme can provide the panache that is the hallmark of good poetry.

There is a sense in which I agree with Milton. No one wants to read an epic poem and have to stop every twenty syllables to ponder the poet's meaning; one or two lines, fine—but not the whole book. And yet, there exists a poet who has written a rhyming epic that is not a tedious trudge. Chaucer was able to pull it off because of the conversational nature of *The Canterbury Tales.* He also utilized unexceptional words for an accessible means of communication. He draws readers in with droll anecdotes and, much like Catullus, flavors his work with dirt to hold the traction of his audience. Because of this, his rhyme does not annoy; rather, it tickles us with wit. Although I've followed Chaucer's tutelage and pungently seasoned this poem with licentiousness, I remain a didactic poet in the order of Hesiod. "My epic poem," I'm calling it, with Aristotle's approval: he said that epic poems are verse representations of noble men and noble deeds. So yes, my epic poem "does rime."

A word on dedication, appreciation, and supplication

This work is for my daughters. May your blessings be to a thousand generations. Special thanks to Shannan Zerance, Bailey Jarvis, Christine LePorte, and Ramona Freeman for their encouraging and patient edits. Extra special thanks to Rosebud; you've given the emperor a new groove. And may I, with the imagination of Milton, the innovation of Ovid, the candor of Chaucer, and by the Muses of Mount Helicon, create what will be more durable than stone, more gripping than Gorilla Glue, and more potent than ignorance.

My heart is always stirred by noble themes
As I, before the King, this verse recite.
My tongue, though ever proved of meager means,
Now sounds the words a skillful pen could write.
(Psalm 45:1)

BOOK 1
The Promise

Come, tell me—is your god in mortal guise,
No more than just a man whose lies deceive,
Or son of such, unable to advise
About a future he has not perceived?

CHAPTER 1

Proto-Evangel

"Let Us," They said, "continue with Our plan.
This chaos let Our revelation span."
(From self-existence, all the rest began.)

A Carpenter of old had built His shop
On wooded land. Each morning He would stop
His work and walk among the trees and stream,
Meandering the forest grounds and dream-
Ing how it'd look in years to come. For though
His land was rife with trees, the kind that grow
Like pillars for the sky, the whole was dark
And overgrown. For round the trunks and bark
Of each his trees were gripping on and wound
The creeper vines of poison leaves. From ground
To highest branch, these hairy vines had clung
And further climbed by twisting upward—strung
Themselves like leeches made of rope until

They joined and knotted in the heights. Their will
Was greed, and so they robbed the trees of light,
Distorting their magnificence, and might
Have killed them if they would have been allowed.
For stem and bine and poison leaf did shroud
And strangle out the sun. So, as the Man
Would walk, He (careful not to touch) would plan
How He would rid the forest of those vines
And welcome in the sun again to shine.
He'd shape the forest into something that
Was pleasant to the eye, a land grown fat
On rays of beaming sun and breezy shade
That rustles through the leaves to serenade.
When winter's chill had come—when all the leaves
Of vine and tree alike had dropped to grieve
Beneath a covering of snow—the Man
Had marked it time to carry out His plan.
And each new day, with axe in hand, He'd slash
A vine in turn. The steel would sink and gash
The bark beneath as well-aimed, weighty chops
Would cut the creeping things in half. The tops
Were grabbed, and firmly He would snap and rip
The vines in upward jerk. Deprived of grip,
They dangled on the gallows, there untaxed
Of life and its demands. So all He axed
Each day would hang upon the heights and limbs
Above, now terminal and spitting grim
And poison juice against the snow. Like so,
He grabbed the bottom half, as well, and slow-
Ly pulled them off the base of each His trees—
Pulled more and more until the Man could see
Their roots in cold, disrupted earth. He'd take
His axe and cut the roots, and then He'd shake
The chunks of dirt from off those harmless sticks,
The hairy sides still holding mud in thick
And frozen fists. He'd smack them hard against
The trunks as if He swung a bat—dispensed
The hanging mud across the forest floor!
Then, all the vines were gathered up (no more

The great imposers stealing life) and tossed
Atop a compost pile to rot the frost-
Y elements of Old Man Winter's bag.
In time, the spring returned! The youthful flags
Of budding green could wave each thawing twig;
The adolescent strived in every sprig.
By then the Carpenter could walk along
And feel the rays of sun—could hear the song
The leaves would sing with unimpeded breeze.
For poison vines had been suppressed and trees
Could breathe again.

Our God now works the same—
A little more each day, each day to claim
A little more. He works to clean His land,
Subject it to His will; at least, He's planned
And promised so to do. But what's the phrase
For female ears, the one we're meant to graze
Upon to feed a sacred hope? Oh, yes!
I'll paraphrase the phrase for you, I guess:
"Between your seed and his will always be
A nasty open cut, an injury,
And so, until it's all restored, you'll feel
The serpent's fangs embedded in your heel.
One day, the woman's Seed will stand your stead;
His foot, in lofty stomp, shall crush its head!"   (GENESIS 3:15)
How's that for cryptic promises to sip
Beside your tea? Now, whether you can grip
The implications of this text in full
Has no import. It's simply just a tool
To help you know God has our backs. I mean,
The ending's written out; it's been foreseen.
But what are we to do now as we wait—
Go twiddle thumbs or try to contemplate
What's coming down the pike, what can be read
From signs of times or public watersheds,
What's hot upon the press and sits the stand?
No—let me try and help you understand.
It isn't your concern how all this ends.

Just know it ends and ends for good. So, lend
Your efforts elsewhere, or, much like Voltaire,
Go tend the garden given to your care.
"Candide said that," you say? Oh, I'm unmanned!
I needed it to rhyme, you understand?
So go and cut the grass or trim your hair—
Just tend the garden given to your care!
Meander your own woods in stewardship,
For life is marked by change. I think I'll skip
The arguments that have *immutable*
Addressed. We'll skip for now; our plate is full.
But, as I said and say, all life is change
Because it's moving, and it grows, exchange-
Ing old for new one second at a time.
Consult old Heraclitus. In his prime,
He said that all is in a constant flux.
He told about the river, with its ducks
And fish—that always it was moving, and
That twice one river you could never stand.
The current changes it. Look, here's the point:
If things are always growing and disjoint
From any constancy or permanence,
Then always they'll need tending to. The fence
Needs fresher paint; the leaves must rake to curb.
So, steward what is in our care and verb
Your lives as such till what is not is seen.
Yes—trim your beards and mow your lawns; go clean
A toilet bowl, ye prophets of the LORD!
For such will see a paradise restored.

CHAPTER 2

Two Brothers

Our epic journey has begun! And though
We've passed the start, a bellowed "tallyho"
Still in the air, I'd like to halt the race
A moment here to catch our breath. This pace
Is just too fast to suit my taste. Come, sit—
Pull up a stone with me, and for a bit
I'll bend your ear with what we have in store.
I'm sure you've heard the story told before,
But not like this. That said, you will be pleased
With what we have ahead, for I have seized
Upon perspectives that provoke and on
Deductions that disrupt the Parthenon
Of comfort zones; and these I consummate
With my poetic flare. How's that for bait?
We'll take the scenic route, and I would say
You should enjoy the view we have. You may
Just want to smell a rose or two. So pick

A languid speed; backpack and walking stick
I see you have. But here's a friendly tip
As we go on: be careful not to slip
Upon the rocks that jut the path. We'll treat
These parts with caution, though, for they secrete
A ribald steam—a fog that some will stum-
Ble in. Resign these things to heathendom
If you so wish, but they are really gems
For those of you with ears. Perhaps they stem
From primal urges, but they are the grit
We find our traction on. Why, then, omit
Such treasures from the trail? Keep both eyes peeled
So you don't trip. There're other things concealed
Here, too, so watch and heed. Pick either word,
I guess, but I would really like to gird
Your expectations with some thoughts about
The text we aim to scale. Some themes stand out
To me that are the common threads, if I
Might be so bold to bind and unify
Each story with the next. A spoiler, you
Might ask? No, no, my canny buckaroo;
It's more a whiff than any taste. We'll sniff
Our fill and leave the kitchen, not to miff
The cook. I'm sure the salivation wets
Your whistle now. How could it not? So, let's
Proceed with what's the first I'll set before
Your nose, and that is barren wife. What's more
Is when that wife conceives a son. You'll see
This soft motif takes many shapes, so be
Upon the watch. The second is don't spill
The seed. The scent of this feels overkill
At times, but there behind the smoke are flames
That burn to see an infant born. This frames
A couple stories more than most and seems
To moralize at times. The third of themes
Is that of younger son, and how those born
After the elder soon become a thorn
In that one's side. That's it! Remember these
As we go on, and all will be a breez-

Y walk in parks. Lord willing and the creek
Don't rise, we'll get this done. Hold your critique
A moment and imagine you're about
To see a play in Barrymore—devout
In your attendance to such cultural
Affairs, I'd never doubt. The air is dull,
And all the suits, from storage to display,
Have mothball residue in their bouquet.
But then, the curtain's pulled, the backdrop lit;
The audience applauds as players hit
The stage. Then, clapping dwindles down to nil
As all anticipation, all the thrill,
Resigns to judgments eyes and ears have weighed—
Determines if it's worth admission paid.
I've heard the strength of Shakespeare is the script.
That is to say, it can be played unzipped
Of pantaloons and priggish English drawl,
For it's the script that beams as light. Let all
The clouds of heaven push against the sky
To keep away the sun; I dare them, try.
It will peek through each shoddy weld, each roll
That's been discharged of storm; even the whole
Will warm to lighter blues. The script comes through
The less-than-perfect acts, the ill-timed cues,
The costume flops, the stage prop tragedies.
And Shakespeare's words are portable; they're free
Of time. Pick any place or social norm
You like and plug them in. His words conform
And fit the robes of ancient Rome as well
As suits from Saks on Fifth, and tickets sell,
Regardless of the scene, like hotcakes glazed
With butter cream. So, let the set be praised
Or tossed, for it's the words we come to see—
If words were ever heard by sight. For me,
The script is juice, the best our squeeze can get;
It's golden fruits on silver platters set.
You all may disagree, but just don't pass
A flippant wave at this or spew some crass
And artless jeer. Consider my next point:

The actors play the script; they can anoint
It with impromptu tears, yet still they're tied
To what the author wrote. Set that aside
And think about the texts you know by heart.
Who in this world has never heard that part
Where Cain shouts out, after young Abel's dead,
"Am I my brother's keeper?" Not a shred
Of guilt. "But wait," you say. "I've heard it, yes,
But he spoke not from script!" I'll acquiesce
For now; it would not do to have a brawl
Here at the start. But grab your shoes and all
Your gear, for we are on our way. There are
Those words we speak in daily life (on par
With what is tailored for routine) and those
That sound a deeper chord. Who really knows
Or could discern those deep from those that smack
Of what the mill might run? Words sometimes lack
In luster till old Hindsight hits the day;
Then cat will mew and dog will have his say.
Let's bridge this into lives, for lives are made
From words—each syllable a brick that's laid
Atop the next. The mortar of intent
Holds each one in its place. Then supplement
The rule with Moral Code; she'll keep it plumb
And see it well erect. We'll overcome
The urge for hay and sticks. The little pig
Who built his house of bricks was thought a prig,
But what he built no one could penetrate—
Made big bad wolves to hyperventilate.
Again, we build our house with what we've said,
And contemplating minds can go and spread
Their bricks judiciously; but thoughtless maws
Will see a house, a life, that's made of straw.
I'm working to this end: if words can speak
In double-meaning, puns, or tongue-in-cheek,
Then so can lives, and these perhaps the more
Will louder sound in tones of metaphor.
But look back at our play: it has begun.
So, one last thought on this I'll beg—just one.

Has not our God been called an author, too?
I'll spare you from suspense, for you are blue
About the lips with thought. Yes, it's a name
Ascribed to God. And it, as others, claims
To stamp an action with its dubbing ink—
Not in some hope to change by primp and prink
The nature by the name. No, at the core
Our God is One who writes and, furthermore,
Is said to write our faith. Now, faith is based
On acts: the acts of One. But He was placed
Among the lives of other men who spoke,
You say, apart from script. Oh, what a stroke
Of brilliance, then, to know how they would act,
How they would plot, what they would say—in fact,
To even know that they would kill. *Oh, how*
That older brother does behave! But now,
Let's watch the play. We have two brothers, mined
From out the stuff that makes a will, defined
By living out a tale of fratricide.
Those brothers both inadequately tried
To represent God's promise, still unseen:
The elder marred, the younger squeaky clean.
Kind Abel had his flocks that grazed the plain,
While all the fruit of harvest came from Cain.
And from these, both made sacrifice to God
And hoped their toil would meet approving nods.
But God had not been pleased with spoils of earth;
He liked the brother more of second birth.
Of course, young Abel's offerings were from
The herds he raised, and his great requiem
Would so be sung by shepherds all. Yet, gifts
Should not be circumscribed by any thrift
Or gain for self, especially when they
Are gifts for God. Well, Cain made his display
Of sacrifice, but God just wasn't pleased,
And God had let him know. So, Cain was seized
With anger and resentment then. He went
About his day with downcast eyes and spent
His time on brewing in that hate. He said,

"Are not these crops a sacrifice, this bread
And grain I've tilled from out Your fruitful land?
I grow the seeds You give and use my hands
To plow them up. Or maybe it just takes
An offering of blood? Perhaps that slakes
Your twisted thirst? Come, answer me and tell
How such things work!" God gave reply, "Expel
These rebel thoughts. Though I might seem unkind,
The error sits alone within your mind.
Your brother's gift was not by greed deterred;
He brought from better samples in his herd."
God saw Cain wouldn't let it go and told
The elder one (it was a tender scold),
"You know, you shouldn't let your loathing breed
Into an act. It's in your head, take heed!
The beast of sin waits crouching at the door,   (GENESIS 4:7)
And violent ways into your mind will pour.
It seeks to master you by vicious wit,
But you must stop its mouth and conquer it!"
Cain's constant meditation fed on hate,
And God's rebuke did nothing to abate
His rage. He nursed at it until the day
Had come at last, and thought demanded pay-
Ment of an act. Cain found his brother tend-
Ing to his flocks and, like a kindred friend,
Suggested Abel walk a distant field.
Cain's mother wouldn't see, their shapes concealed
By hills. When he and Abel were alone,
He crushed his brother's skull upon a stone.
Blood splattered on the dirt, and more it seeped
From unrelenting blows that Cain's wrath heaped.
Yet Cain's depravity ran deeper still,
And blood from Abel's veins that didn't spill
Was goblet-dripped; he'd down the ruddy pulp
And finish off the last with thirsty gulp.
Still, Abel propped his head to stave off death
And begged of Cain, the last his flagging breath
To spend, "Come, won't you leave a little bit?"
Cain answered him, mouth filled with gory spit,

"It's sweet, my brother, to this thirst of mine
To drink upon the blood that smiles Divine."
He sucked the final drop—left Abel dry—
Then, wrenching gut, concealment gone awry,
Spewed out the righteous blood in heaving thrust—
A crimson witness scattered on the dust!
That foul, malicious deed would be his bane:
An unsuspecting brother he had slain.
But when the sun was down, the cool of day
Then moving in, and Cain had made his way
Back to his hut, he waited for his God.
The LORD made often habit then to trod
The earth at eventide. He'd amble, then,
Among the trees and fields—confide with men
About a better life, what's good and true.
So, at Cain's hut, the LORD arrived on cue.
"Where is your brother Abel?" God then asked.
Cain knew his hidden act would be unmasked.
Then God went on: "I'm sure I heard it speak,
The blood upon the stones and on your cheek.
Where is your brother Abel—does he rest?
Don't hide your shifty eyes from my request!"
But Cain, with itchy conscience, only spurned
The voice of God. The rage in him still burned!
Cain asked, "Smell not the meat of his sweet gift?
I think he's nodding off to sleep. Be swift
And You might catch him, though. But as to where
He rests? I couldn't say, nor do I care!
I'm not a babysitter and, what's more,
To be my brother's keeper, never swore!"
The LORD of earth was grieved when He soon found
Poor Abel lying in his blood, a mound
Of body empty of its soul. God clutched
The second brother in His arms and touched
His face, a pose pietàs try to show
By stone and granite formed. God wept to know
That Abel had been killed. He wept to see
This favored brother so deformed and free
Of any life. But when this flow of tears

Had dried, He had to act. That much was clear.
He found the brother Cain then at his crops,
His hands still red and both his eyes still mop-
Ping at the ground. God spoke these fitting words
To Cain: He said, "Because of what I've heard
And what I've seen, I know what you have done.
There's no use arguing. You've killed the son
Your mother bore. He lies there in the field
Without a home, exposed and unconcealed
From wind and rain, from roving beasts and vul-
Tures of the air. You even crushed his skull
And staved it in; your stone has left a mark
Of death. But now your rebel ears will hark-
En to My words! I will not have this act
Unmet, nor will I have some reenact-
Ment in your punishment. No, I won't kill
You, Cain. You're going to live, and I will fill
Your days with restless wandering. You left
Your brother there without a home, bereft
Of any shelter from the sun—exposed.
The same will serve for you!" Then, quite composed,
The LORD knelt down and dug His hands into
The dirt. God said, "This dirt has given you
A livelihood. Your mattock and your plow
Have had success up to this point. But now
You'll vainly till for crops down in the mud
Because it has received your brother's blood.
The thorns and brittle twigs will fill your bush-
El baskets now! You'll have to sweat and push
Yourself to finish out your day." Then God
Began to root around there in the sod
Until He found a rock with sharpened point.
"You see this rock?" God asked. "I will anoint
Your head with such a mark, a mark of stone,
So all will know to leave you well alone
And cast you out. As vagrant you will roam—
A plague among mankind without a home."
God pulled Cain down and knelt upon his chest.
He scraped his forehead with the stone and pressed

Until the blood was running red into
Cain's ears. God pushed that dirty rock down through
The skin till it had reached the bone beneath.
Cain screamed and squirmed and clenched his marble teeth!
They shattered in his mouth; so tightly clamped
That jaw had been. When God had fully stamped
The older brother with that spectacle,
He let him up. Cain held his branded skull
Beneath the palms of both his hands and fled
His God, unsure about the path ahead.
So, hounded by the Furies, Cain would run—
A blood-crime violator all could shun.

CHAPTER 3

Water Wasted

O Muse, come sing and tell of when the last
Of days arrived, when unrelenting blasts
Of heaven's wrath turned wet. Yes, come and speak
Of when the storms had first made bold to streak
The hopeful skies with portents black as coal,
When massing billows snuffed the sun with roll-
Ing auguries. What were they filled with, Muse?
What omens would those sullied clouds suffuse
From off their scaffolds in the sky? "Some ven-
Geance might be hidden there," the councilmen
Had warned. They urged, "Perhaps the darkness wept
(Or soon would weep) out punishments long kept
Behind indulging eyes." But were they tears
Of some reluctant act or atmospheres
Prepared to waterboard the mouths still filled
With scoff? The rage of God would soon be spilled,
And, had they eyes, they'd see the spigot Wrath

Was filling buckets at. He'd pour a bath
Of recompense. But tell me of the rain
That fell, O Muse—what of that great campaign
To soak the earth? Tell when that rain had pulsed
The dwelling place of mortal men, convulsed
The ground beneath its force, when earth was plunged
To crushing depths. Tell when the dirt had sponged
That salty swill of heaven's cup and drank
It off to nausea. Tell how they sank
Like weighty stones, forever down to sound
The floor of Ocean's realm, how they were drowned
Beneath the din of those staccato drops,
Cacophonies of drips and constant plops
That had eclipsed all else from off the stage
Of noise. Come, speak on that, O Muse, God's rage.
They say it is a peaceful way to die
When someone drowns. You might just classify
A water death humane. The same was said
Each time Madame la Guillotine took heads
From off the shoulders of some poor Pierre
Or Jacqueline. That razor of despair
Was thought a quick and easy way to send
A person packing heavenward to wend
Until they reached Elysium. Of course,
They went without a noggin, sad divorce
Of body and of mind. Think of the Sea's
Extent. Think of the wrecks and casualties
That executioner has blankly notched
Upon her stock, that female so debauched
In flagrant fits that match with monthly moons.
What cities has she buried with monsoons
And tidal waves? What stones of Mu now wait
In murky depths, more vanquished than the Straits
Gibraltar kissed goodbye? Tell me, what more
Has she concealed away beyond the shore
And diver's gaze? What great Atlantis sits
To gather dust in boxes that admit
No key to probe? What counts the hours of time
With waves for minute-hands and surfs for chime?

Such places are forgotten, wholly lost
Beneath her weighty folds. They're always tossed
By swaying tantrums, ever monitored
By fish that are the warden mockingbirds.
They watch the dim-lit streets with eyes that dare
Not blink, with mouths that never close on air.
The murder done by Cain, that barbarous,
Appalling act, had served as stimulus
For all who followed in his wake. The earth
Was filled with rowdy miscreants. From birth
Until their death, they sought a worthy pyre
That matched in flame to their untamed desire.
You see, the race of giant men had made
A hash of things. Yes, after they surveyed
The maidens born of men and then discerned
Their charms was when they felt their yearnings churned.
They had the itch; their ornaments were blue
And leaking sap that smelled of honeydew.
Those hooligans had seen the girls in bloom
And had to have a taste! At length, their wombs
Were filled with tainted seed, abnormal mix
For ugly kids. Those Sons of God, unfixed
To what was right and higher rule, behaved
For selfish wants and strange attractions craved.
They treated virtue as disposable,
A means to serve their ends. Incapable
Of empathy, those Sons of God were mutts
Who squatted God's green earth—expatriates
Who stuffed their maws with fat the land would lend.
It was not hard to fathom God would send
A judgment down on them. It's how He sought
To amputate the limb, the gangrene rot
Past remedy. He'd slice that cheesecloth flesh
And toss it on the compost pile, start fresh
And clean. His cup of tolerance would hold
No more; that mug was full, and so He told
One man to pack up shop—told him to brace
For hell and for high water. Not a trace
Of all that sullied mess would stay. From out

The water new birth would arise. A stout
And sturdy Anabaptist dunk was in
The works. Oh, sprinkle on your brass and tin,
Your copper tools for holy festivals
And for your feasts. Or go and sprinkle skulls;
Set these apart for holy use. A soak
Both washes filth and also can evoke
A sense of holiness. The flood would kill
Two birds with just one boulder flung, a mill-
Stone where a pebble might suffice. But cast
Your rock of choice, for I will speak at last
About that noble idiot, that ripe
Old fool, an Adam-and-a-half. Don't gripe
To me about your woe as if I've nev-
Er seen a world destroyed. But you, howev-
Er, got to build a boat. It only took
A hundred years to do the job; the book
Records your speed the same way Ussher logged
The Annals of your dragging days and bogged
His readers down with stodgy figures for
A yawn. Back to the boat, decked with décor
Of that diluvian demand—you know,
Like mud and dried up grass. Then sloppy-joe
It all with pitch to stuff the paneling
Of gopher sticks and stud with shells for bling.
The Woodie station wagon of its time!
I see you tripping on your beard to climb
The finished work, that floating litterbox,
As giddy as that girl called Goldilocks,
Desiring with animals to bed.
I want to bring the Minotaur to wed
This lecture but will keep him to the side.
A massive ark, and if you should decide
To see it in the flesh, then by all means—
A reproduction sits among the greens
Of Cincinnati's flanks. By Amish hands
And Amish beards, she'll ever sail the land.
Imagine now the feathered violins
Of Bach and Brandenburg as safe within

That uterus of wood they all had sat.
The rain began, like fairy acrobats
With nimble feet. It echoed through the whole,
More as a touch than any knock—a stroll
More than a stomp—the orchestra to warm
Its strings and wet its reeds. They would perform
A harmony of hums and lullabies
To cradle some to sleep but euthanize
The rest. How happily oblivious
The boatless ones had been. They made no fuss
When clouds were turned to lofty showerheads,
When public bathhouse propaganda spread
Around the towns, when floating noodles soon
Were all the rave. But like a honeymoon
Of marriage ill-advised, it would be short
And sweet, the novelty to end in court
Or at each other's throats. But, for that horde
About to take the pulverizing sword
Of God, the rain felt rather nice at first.
They opened up their mouths and quenched their thirst
By catching drops on tongues. They never dreamed
The downfall it'd become. That rain was deemed
A kind anomaly as round they ran
And passed out snorkels like the frenzied clan
Of Bacchus passing sticks and clubs. And poor
Old Pentheus, to catch a peek of more
Than lingerie, paid hefty fees of en-
Trails disemboweled by his own mother hen
Dressed up in furs. Such are poetic ends
For those who raise their dander and suspend
Their disbelief for some façade. The sleight
Of hand in Daylight Savings twice rewrites
The books of Father Time each year. I guess
It's easier to change a clock than dress
When up the sun decides to come. Back to
Those puddle-stomping lemmings who were too
Enthralled with dancing at their funerals
To care—aquarium confessionals
And ordained mackerels about to bear

Their souls to Peter's lock and key. I swear,
This stuff just comes right out of me. Some hold
The flood to be the first, the grand unfold
Of rain, or what we know as rain today.
These ones believe the firmament would spray
A daily dole of measured dew—that things
Were only watered when the land would bring
This bit of moisture in the morn. Oh, fit
Your squares in round-shaped holes or counterfeit
Some bills to hide beneath your box of springs.
What do I care? Let paupers and let kings
Dress up and play their roles, for are we not
Just kindergarten kids who wipe their snot
On toys of coveted demand? And Time's
A curtain change, a backdrop swap when rhymes
Of intermission songs are played. Think what
You want, for your belief can make you strut
Or crawl. It's in your head, my friend. I'm done
With that for now. Just take your role as son,
As wife, as daughter; wear your robes—be crowned.
By God above the sky, assume the ground
Was how the water came! Think of the shock,
The flabbergasted blurting "poppycock"
In disbelief when something more than dew
Arrived. Napoleon at Waterloo
Had not been more surprised. The dew's the thing
By which we give the plants a watering.
Oh, nurse that mushy manna off the sponge
Each time the cock and crow get up; make lunge
Into the day, or into whatsoev-
Er just might lie beside you then. Yes, nev-
Er fail to work your plow while God still gives
Ability. Such are comparatives
Within my mind. Back to the rain, the sky
To sprinkle hemlock down. *I wonder why*
God didn't choose a plague. It seems a more
Efficient way to get it done, ignore
The huge amount of water poured to fill
The tub of all the earth. I'm sure the bill

Was through the roof. For forty days and nights
The rain came down, a pace the Israelites
Could tramp a wilderness patrol or song
By Jars of Clay could run repeat. Yes, long
And hard it fell like cats and dogs. Who knows
How many days until the boat that No-
Ah built had lost all contact with the ground,
How long until the people came to sound
His door with their petitions, soaking wet?
"Oh, let us in!" they said. "We brought baguettes,
A cheeseboard, and that casserole you al-
Ways liked. We also brought some games: Dodgeball
And Chutes and Ladders, too." But Noah glued
His eyes against his hands, not to be rude
But to pretend he didn't hear their knocks.
I'm sure they gripped on hard, that cracker box
Of Animals then passing splinters while
They waited, passing also stink from piles
Of excrement that motion sickness got
Them to release.

A cemetery plot
Will shift and move in time. The once-smooth ground
Becomes uneven with the woodchuck mounds
And burrowed caves and coffin sinkholes when
The rot has done its work. The tombstones men
Have set atop these graves move too. They tilt
The more the ground moves underneath. It jilts
That resting place when trees push up their mar-
Ble weight, commanding roots that would disbar
Them from their bed of dirt. So then, dislodged
From off their grip of earth and sabotaged
By gravity, those gravestones slant oblique,
Precariously holding ground with weak
And fading strength.

Like so, the people held
Their grip to what remained of life, compelled
To grab at straws or wish on stars gone dim.

It was their final stand—their final swim,
To speak more to the point and less to paint
This story with a verbalized restraint.
It rained until the corners-four were filled
With swaying waves; a heaving force that chilled
The dead had sent them belly up and plunged
Them down like doornails to the depths, expunged
All breath from out their coughing lungs. And still,
In spite of all this wash—this overkill
Of resources to scrub the filthy mess—
Man's heart was still unclean! Yet one success
That enterprise achieved was in the great
Amounts of water wasted. Fascinate
Me with your estimates on just how much
It took to get it done. Statistics such
As these I long to hear; I'll dub them stale
And pigeon-toed, bowlegged Chippendales
Of proof and fact. They miss the mark like cross-
Eyed archers miss their bales of straw. We toss
Aside the juicy meat to lick at bones,
At poultry bags of giblets, kidney stones
And necks. The facts—O precious things—the bits
That claim they're all that is. You hypocrites!
Go pull them from the rear of some dead hen
About to soup, or have them dressed like men
And women—mannequins for masquerades.
But if I had my way, I'd see them made
To take first place in line when jumping cliffs,
Or I would have them used for handkerchiefs
When flu bugs come to call. Who cares how much
It took to fill the earth? Go chuck the crutch
Of needing to explain things all the time.
It will not do, especially when rhymes
Of Asaph play upon your ear. Just say
It was enough to have old Atlas sway
And stagger with the weight of soggy con-
Tinents, his Titan back the thing whereon
The globe does rest. Say Retribution had
His fill and couldn't even think to add

Another bite into his snapping gob.
Or even say Poseidon knelt to swab
The decks of earth until His fingers pruned.
That's when the breath of God, the *Ruach*, crooned
Above the chaos and the great expanse
Of wet. Then, much by lucky happenstance,
Did Noah's boat touch bottom on the peak
Of Ararat; a little hide-and-seek
Had mountains played beneath the thrashing waves,
Titanic sailing skills, for sure, to stave
The boat you worked on for a hundred years
Against a mountain peak. Go for careers
In crashing things to test how durable
They are, or maybe something practical
Like how to be a vet. *I heard there was*
An opening. But first things first—the laws
That all receding water must obey:
The grueling drip to dry and file away
That takes so very long. Oh, yes—that's right,
The breath of God was there, and from the heights
A cosmic turbine dryer blew until
The earth was waterless. Give me the thrill
Of paper towels to dry my hands; I'm more
Of an old-fashioned chap and troubadour.
But all the pouring rage was made to cease
When bows of war were changed to ones of peace.
By then the passengers had had enough,
And every paw had turned to fisticuffs
Before the end, the natives growing rest-
Less, beating drums and stamping feet, protest-
Ing stink and claustrophobic cells then caked
With crap. Go charter Hercules: he raked
Augean stables in a single day!
A thousand cows for thirty years, they say,
Had trampled down their shit till it was crust
For years and years. One thinks the walls would bust
From all those mud pies underfoot and flies
Smooshed in for added grit. Throw down some lye
Or light a match to muck it out, then down

To pub we'll make our way. Have lager crown
Our day's work done; head home for soap and rinse.
I hear my wife: "What is that smell, my prince?"
She then escorts me out of doors; a bag
Of ice she gives to rest my head and nags
Me that my snoring is a bit too loud.
Well, back to Noah now: his well-endowed
And able wood, the tinder box he parked
Along a mountainside. All disembarked
That ride with Noah nodding proud, a rough
And tough swashbuckler then. That kind of stuff
Will make a man feel confident, to know
His purpose and to see it done; not so
For bards of doggerel in birthday suits
They purchased on their mother's card. Those brutes
And anarchists have all the sturdy back-
Bone of a jellyfish. Just paddywhack
Their naked bums and send them off to play.
Their stanzas need to shock; therefore, they say
(Or rather, blurt) some ostentatious rot!
I ask for verse and get lame duck—no pot
For piss or window for the chuck. Just rest
Your bromides for a sec. I'm not impressed
With macaroni art, with cotton swabs,
With sticks from Popsicles used to kebab
Your paper shapes. You are not Raphael,
And no one will remember you; none tell
Their kids to read your books, make pilgrimage
Unto your shrine, or pay their peonage
By spilling out their wine. You'll go the way
You came into this world. So keep cliché
Comparisons behind your teeth. Come see
Me when experience lends potency
Unto your views—when Wisdom deems it fit
To crinkle up your eyes and fills your wit
With something more than wind. Until that time,
Just be content to pay with Yankee dimes;
Your bag of bull has lost its credit here.
I'm straying off the mark. That gondolier

Called Noah needs regard, and here I am
Just going on about the flim and flam
Of poetry that marks our day and age.
Make it political to reengage
My interest? Oh, I think not. For now,
Let's focus on our text: ahead we'll plow.
The whole of life had been reborn by flood.
All that was new was eager. Every bud
Was filled with optimism and vivac-
Ity. They felt it in their veins! The grass
Was greener basking in the sun. Indeed,
The earth was fertile then, and males would seed
That ample Shangri-la. Oh, she was taut
And waiting there, as perky and unthought
As any pushup bra. Her nipples pressed
Against the camisole of Flora's chest.
It was a lovely sight! O Noah, do
You see? Or maybe you can smell the dew
That drips now off the muff? Oh, stiffen out
Your pole! A call for duty, little scout,
Was just announced. Where is that great buffoon?
Oh, there he is: he's on his knees. *A swoon*
Has taken him? No, no, he's planting seeds!
He needs to have a drink, to bottle-feed
The droning afternoons. It's clearly no
Concern to keep up with the Joneses. Throw
Your apprehension to the wind. We'll plant
A vineyard, let fermented grapes enchant
Our better moods until we're rolling robe-
Less round our tents where nosy sons might probe
Our naked arse. Good stuff. We'll come to that.
But first, we'll want to play the diplomat
And talk about the altar Noah built
And how he made a sacrifice—no guilt
In that. He paid his proper thanks to God,
The saint, by rounding up some birds, unflawed
By feathers in their place. Then to a crisp   (Genesis 8:20)
He burnt the birds atop his stones. No wisp
Of anything but soot remained. With meat

And bones still smoldering *(such things smell sweet
To God on High)*, old Noah hit it hard—
The wine, that is. For once the birds were charred,
He deemed it time to pound the sauce, and pound
He did. He drank in ways the Church has frowned
Upon since Jesus made a tasty vin-
Tage for some drunkards years ago. A sin
They call it now. *Oh, don't you know, to drink
In any excess, God forbids? I think
We shouldn't take a sip, it's better safe
Than sorry, don't you know?* Such caution chafes
My sitting apparatus to no end!
Let these ones pass us by; let them bartend
Their water made from wine, explain a drunk-
En fit from Welch's grapes, and stuff their trunks
With prude Victorian attire. Wake up
And smell the coffee brewing here! *Your cup
Needs more. I'd better add a shot.* Don't twist
A text to make it civilized, persist
That something is when it is not. It was
Real booze back then! Perhaps you should Lamaze
Your breathing to a steady pace; 'twill be
Okay. Back to the text: for here we see
That Noah had a taste for top-shelf stuff.
It took the edges off then grabbed his scruff
And lifted him to higher grounds. I ought
To know, I've had the wine this little plot
Of land will yield, the region Omar knew
And penned his verse about—a hedon who
Was fashioned after my own heart. My young
Sirrah, Syrah will see our verses sung.
Be wary of that Muse, though: she's a minx
Who gives us lavish lines when just two drinks
Have passed our lips; yet, when we go for three,
Prolonging buzz to write our epopee,
She'll mock us winos, call us derelict,
Kick us to curb and see our pockets picked.
Such gentle flowers, all. Well, Noah, too,
Would drink his sorrows dead. He took the cue

From God above: that is, to rather drown
An inconvenient truth than have to clown
Around with fixing it. He drank alone
Awhile until the clothes his wife had sewn
Were tossed outside his tent. We take our clothes
Off when we drink, from coats to pantyhose.
Again, I'm speaking from experience;
Our clothes become less help than hind-er-ance
When one is tanked. I only point this out
So that we grasp what Noah was about
There in his tent. He really looked the part,
Like he had been some Bacchant in the art
Produced by Rubens in his painting prime—
A chubby little cherub in the lime-
Light there or Bacchus drunk upon the floor.
A muslin rag of overlay he wore
Around his neck, while all his unders aired
The breeze of Middle Eastern clime. He spared
No passerby the pleasure of a peek,
Full glory and three sheets into the reek.
Let's turn him over; don't you know he'll barf
And choke that way? Hand me that muslin scarf;
We'll roll him like a log. My grandad taught
Me how it's done. You take one end and knot
It just like so. But wait! I think I hear
The villain in our play—he's coming near
And whistling a tune. He's chewing at
A jimsonweed, I see. That meddling cat
Is bound to find his father in this state.
We cannot stop him now; he has a date
With kith and kin. You've seen *Deliverance,*
I'm sure. So much for twisted prurience;
It feeds a burning urge within our core.
When push meets shove, we all are carnivores
That feed the meat of want! Back to our tale,
Before my huff-and-puff works to derail
The sweetest part. Well, Ham, the youngest son,
Looked in to view the show. It didn't stun
The lad but more enticed, as if he just

Had found Diana at her bath. He thrust
His peeping head a little further in
To get a better look. A sneaky grin
Was on his face when hungry eyes were met
With pallid rolls of flesh, a silhouette
Of secrets that were begging to be found.
"He'll never know." This thought began to pound
Within his head until his smirking lips
Were watering. Then, like a frat boy slips
A roofie to a drink, he made his way
Across the tent with stealth, intent to play
A naughty little game of poke the bear
Upon his father's naked derrière.
You might just want to cover up your eyes
For what comes next; he's gonna bastardize
His father's rear. Go take a leak or snoop
What snack bars have to peddle here. Regroup
And come back when the scene has changed. I'll take
One for the team and ride this out. Pete's sake!
It's shot in amateur! One needs more light
To see, though I admit my appetite
Is lost on manly tits. But in the morn,
That time of day when all regrets are born
From out a flashback's mouth, remorse set in.
Old Noah knew he drank too much: wineskin
Was empty on the floor, and all his head
Was throbbing still. But something more—a shred
Of memory that gave the man a tear.
Perhaps it was a dream? Oh, no—his rear
Was sore enough to tell another tale.
The man got hot; it turned him red! All hail
The temper unrestrained. He knew at once
The details of the night. With resonance
And clarity, the smutty scene came back
Into his mind, and all his gunnysack-
Ing did no good. *Oh, don't you know you'll give*
Yourself an ulcer, friend. Preventative
Is breathing through the nose. My wife says count
To ten with five deep breaths. It's paramount

You lift the arms; this spreads the diaphragm.
Here, let me help. So, Noah called for Ham,
His youngest son. He called the man by name.
Ham gave the shaft and now he'd get the same.
Hell hath no fury like a father porned!
He brandished off his belt, and so unwarned
The blows were dealt. Oh, for the love of types
And mysteries, you're cursing kids to wipe
Up milk their father's hands have spilled. *The hands?*
Perhaps it was another limb that stands
As culprit here. But either way, Ham spilled
The milk, and Canaan's children would be billed
For it. *Oh, that seems fair as love and war—*
To curse a child to pay his father's score.
Oh, yes—about as fair it is for them
To reap the blessing off the Son of Shem.

CHAPTER 4

Babel

In time, the sons of men in strength were blessed,
And so they thought it no strange thing to test
The limits of their might and aptitude—
For they were men and thought to build. They chewed
Against the cud of spunk and pondered on
The form of ingenuity. Each dawn,
They'd rise and put their hands to work, unchain
Their budding minds to fold their paper planes.
Such epoch saw the mighty Nimrod's skill—
A paragon of men, a man whose will
Did not know borders, knew no hint of fear.
He was a master of the bow, austere
And confident to hunt each beast he found.
Bravado such as his would seed the ground
Of Babel tilled. And so, it happened there
Upon great Shinar's verdant plain, right where
Two rivers meet, that men laid Babel's brick.

It was the glue of craftsmanship, the stick-
Y bond of unity—a common goal
That drove them on, a purpose that the whole
Could get behind. They would God's plan defy
By stacking mortared dust up to the sky.
The call to fill the earth would there be done,
Not scattered all abroad. They'd be as one
In constant labor; with their hearts aflame,
They'd build a lofty city for their name.
The sinews of their passions were entwined
And all imaginations of one mind.
The smoke of that commotion filled the air
With clouds that reeked of vanity, fanfare
Of man's quick mortal stint of eighty years.
It rose upon the swirling winds that steer
Their way above the mountain peaks to lift
The soaring falcon in his easy drift.

A field of yellow grass that's parched with heat
Will rage when bit with flame. It blindly meets
All else with its consuming burn and chokes
The very air with suffocating smoke.

So God, in heaven's height, coughed from the stench
That rode the wind. It was enough to wrench
His gut, the carbon stink, and jostle Him
From off the throne—reluctant stir. His limbs
Were stiff and ached while stomping to the clouds
Of heaven's floor, His voice, as breakers, loud
To sound the hallowed depths and echo through
The halls of time! "What's this?" He stormed and blew
The soot from out His nostrils filled. The veil
Of smoke was scudding round His waist—a pale,
Opaque, accumulated mass. "This stems
From Man's ambitious wish and stratagems,
No doubt!" He fumed and waved His hand to clear
The air, the starry arc and chandelier
Of heaven's dome. But then He mused, "This reek
Would stage a coup and Our eviction seek."

This thought unsettled His eternal mind.
He'd done so much; ungrateful humankind
Were at their wily tricks again. He took
Then to His balcony to have a look.
And so, He spied down from His bower—high,
Intrepid lean—His fists clenched tight with sky
And folds of tuft. He leveled out His gaze
Into a razor squint that cut the haze
Of smoke between the heaven's crescent loft
And earth's low floor so far beneath. "How oft,"
He said, "I've peered down from this attic on
The ways of man, on how between each dawn
And rosy sunset at the close of day
They choose to occupy their time. They stray
From off the humble path, go left and right;
The peace of well-enough is never-quite.
How willingly they break their backs to cast
Off My restraint, pretend to be harassed
By law." He hushed to stare as if He were
Some critic or some prudish connoisseur,
His probing gaze to pester earth. He passed
The morning by observing them and cast
His spying gaze, examining their deeds.
And then He said unto Himself, "We need
To see this for Ourselves, this spectacle
That stirs the dust and would Our rule annul.
I want to see the knowledge they engage   (GENESIS 11:5)
Firsthand." And so, with speed, He left the stage
Of stars' imposing height, the tippy-top
Of all creation made—so steep the drop
To basements of the earth. So many times
He'd made the trip, so many times He'd climb
From off His lofty throne at eventide
To talk with men, to reason and confide
About the better life. These trips were made
The swifter by His chariot inlaid
With flame. Upon its sides hung tapestries
Of golden thread, the woven artistry
Of skill Divine. The first of these portrayed

A field of grain, and in it every blade
Of wheat swayed low before the sun that rose
Against an azure sky. The form and pose
Of this was strung as might a puppeteer
String out his mannequins to help one peer
Into a deeper theme. Upon the field
Were birds that grazed on fallen seeds, the yield
Of all that grain. And there were beasts as well
That fed, from turtle to the swift gazelle.
Each had their place and simple station to
Obey. Innate their will, somehow they knew
What was expected, how to live. Around
That picture, burnished bronze was richly bound
And showed the hue of every season in
Its turn. But on the other side, the twin
Of that first natal scene, the counterweight
Of ordered good, was shown—the free estate
Of man. And woven there, a twisted ebb
And flow—chaotic thread and tangled web
Of will. For will is free, but not without
The taint of what does serve our wants. That spout
Doth pour its yearnings all day long! So, when
We speak about a will as free in men,
We must not think it ever goes beyond
What deeper hunger's claws allow. We're conned
To think of choice as some impartial thing
And not a motive pleaser that will bring
Its own concerns to every crossroad met.
No, no. A choice not free but much in debt!
So, if not willy-nilly we decide,
The question begs what moral code provides
Unto our reasoned choice. But let us get
Back to that tapestry, a mess and yet
The balance to the ordered good. For plots
Won't serve without a hook; no Camelot
Would rivet us without licentious knights
Like Lancelot, whose randy appetites
Present conflicted choice. And so, that shag,
That golden-woven tapestry, that swag

Of abstract cloth that hung the carriage cart
Of God's own chariot—that piece of art
Was spun in tightly overlapping knots.
The twining thread was gaunt and showed all thoughts
Behind an act: a ratty nest, and one
That would not see its tangles soon undone.
From center to circumference, it went
And linked all acts to habits, lifetimes spent
Immorally. At last, if I might end
This section on the tapestries and send
A stitch of closure through the whole, between
The first and second hung a third—a scene
More terrible and filled with dread. For it,
That final cloth, was of the One who sits
In judgment on it all. It hung the rail
As did the others, but the size and scale
Of this was grander more by far. It was
So woven that it looked to move, no pause
But constant motion, almost like a wave
That surges in and runs retreat to lave
Against a dirty shore. This last cloth served
To so portray God's judgment, which reserved
The rule Creator to creation holds.
It showed a flood—a crushing blow to scold
For crimes, a fitting way He might suppress
Men's excesses by Nature's own excess.
The chariot was drawn by seraph steeds,
Pectoral bulge and brawn equipped—a breed
Majestic, nourished on the barley oats
That God's own pastures yield, quite free to bloat
Themselves for days that have no end. But when
They are corralled to stables there, again
To see God's coach with speed to earth, a bit
Is lodged between their jaws—just adequate
To guide those restless brutes of jerking tug.
No human strength would soon restrain; all shrug
To think upon the task. But God was quick
And harnessed both; the bellybands were thick
And looped beneath the girth unto the breech—

The tug saw saddle-strap to crupper reach
And then the buckle drawn. The chariot
Was shuddering behind the stomping strut
Of both those brawny steeds, and foamy drool
Was frothing down their flanks. Their hooves dealt cruel,
Repeated blows against the stable boards
As on He climbed, the highest Lord of lords.
The canvases were flapping in the wind
And beat the carriage cart; momentum grinned
Upon the plummeting descent as down
The LORD dropped like a bird—the Holy Crown
Of heaven to the floor of Shinar's stage.

A shooting star will light the sky and rage
Against the darkened night. It's only seen
By eyes already lifted, ones with keen
Attention paid. That flash is bright but fades
A moment after into nightly shades.

God's throbbing chariot then halted to
A stop upon the plain. The chilly dew
Squeezed in between His toes as down He leapt
To earthen dust. All else seemed still and slept
Beneath the cloak of night. He pulled a hood
Atop His head and for a moment stood
To let His eyes into the pitch adjust.
Those eyes were in a simmer-glow and must
Have looked like amber coals beneath some soot
When flames of strength and vigor are kaput.

When all within a house are sound asleep,
A thief will come. He moves in stealth to reap
What was not properly secured or locked.

So God, under the dark of night, then stalked
Around to spy the ways of men, to glean
An understanding and to intervene
If need demand. Adopting then a stride
Meander-like, He paced the riverside

Until He reached the gates of Babel's wall.
He pulled his cloak up close, the protocol
Of any traveler who'd rather not
Be seen and, after gone, be all forgot.
The forges cooled and dozed beneath their slim
And ashen quilts; the daily hurried hymn
Of furtherance still lingered in the air
As on He strolled the dusty thoroughfare.
He walked sometime that way until he found
The obelisk erected from the ground
Unto the sky. It all had Him impressed!
Then to Himself He half-remarked, "The zest
They show in building this, the skill and art,
The craftsmanship they use—it warms My heart
To see it all so well constructed. Still,
It goes against Our deeper plan and will.
They don't intend to flourish in the land
Or spread the pure dominion as We've planned.
Design to fill the earth they will askew;
As one, they'll finish all they set to do."
But then, He thought, "We could destroy this breed
Again; that would ensure they won't succeed
In what they plan to do." With caution then,
And crossing T's with conscientious pens,
He said, "We vowed We would not crush mankind
Again by surging flood. Perhaps We'll bind
Their progress by another means." And then,
He smiled; a clever way to limit men
Had dawned upon His mind. At last, He said,
"Destruction will not serve Our ends; instead,
We'll plague confounded language on their nest!
This will unwanted purposes arrest!"
When morning came—when all had stirred from out
Their beds and pulled their tunics roundabout
Their waists—they stepped into the day. None felt
Or could suspect the artful card God dealt
Their way. They only knew the sun was hot;
They didn't sense their ears to be untaught.
The first to hear his fellowman come greet

With just a "Hi," "Hello," or "Pleased to meet"
On hearing the address was quite perplexed.
For though the other's mouth was posed and flexed
To speak as it had always done before,
The words that dribbled out were little more
Than gibberish to hear, and no one could
Make blubbering to something understood.
No ASL was there to meet the need,
And each, in their own language, disagreed.
They firstly thought a dream was still in play
And pinched themselves to curtly cast away
The frightful hold of sleep—to no avail.
And struggle as they might by tooth and nail,
They only to themselves could words address;
When speaking to their neighbors, spoke a mess.
So Babel's busy streets were soon dispersed,
For men in others' meanings were unversed.
But this confusion God would someday mend
With welding tongues of flame that He would send.

CHAPTER 5

Father Liar

A character we meet of consequence
Within our sacred text: when we dispense
With those who are the better understood
In allegoric terms, agree we should
That Abram is the first we are to find.
His mint-condition plays are countersigned
With signatures from dirty inkwells dipped.
And so, he is convincing in his script!
For which of you believes in spotless saints
Who've tasted only fruit without the taint
Of greediness? Or, for that matter, who
Thinks villains to be evil through and through,
Without at least just one redeeming trait
That virtue adds (not vice) to his estate?
Let me assure my readers that our bread
Has on it both some good and evil spread,
And people aren't completely one alone.

So, view all with a salted eye; condone,
Condemn, but always understand. Now to
The first my verse will seek to overview.
From out the realm of Ur he had been called
To up and move, a man who had been mauled
By age, by disappointment, by despair;
For he approached his end without an heir.
A barren wife he had and loved, no doubt,
Despite her failed attempts to carry out
Her function as the mother of the house:
Producing children. For herself and spouse,
Those years were labor-like and surely rife
With stoic resolutions formed. Then, wife
And childless graybeard got the call to leave
Their home of birth; to nomad life they'd cleave
Till afterlife—they'd bid a fond farewell
Unto their land of comforts known. They'd dwell
The land of Cain in tents. Oh, yes—the land
Of Cain, that rebel one whose head God's hand
Had marked with such a stigma so that all
Who saw the man would make a quick withdrawal.
The call for them to leave was brief and not
Some cryptic thing to ponder or a knot
That prying fingertips could ne'er undo.
God said, "Get up and leave this land. From you
I'll make a mighty nation be. I'll bless
The ones who bless you, too, for their success
Is in My hands. I'll also reimburse
The ones who think to shame you with a curse.
From out your seed, My plan will find its goal:
The nations of the world from chains parole."
I'll rest here just a moment with my quill.
Consider now with me the eerie thrill
That comes when we awake within the dead
Of night: perhaps we've heard a noise and dread
What might be in the house with us. Or it
Could easily have been a dream (gambit
Of fact in motley-fiction dressed). Forget
How we have woken up and that our sweat

Has served to wet our pillows cold. Our mind
And ears are sharp, but other senses find
This not the case; our touch is numb with rest
And taste is often acrid-glazed at best,
And darkness sees our eyes to be inept.
Around we feel with toes to intercept
All obstacles unseen. But ears—well they
Are stretched, as taut as skin on drums; they play
Each noise as loud as cannons sound. We hear
Not only noises that another's ear
Could verify as true but also those
Our fancy sings like Siren songs. Who knows
How they have come to be? And are they real?
Sometimes we simply want them so and peel
Our reason off the pith of thought. But let
Us all look over our own lives; I bet
We each could think of one—and if not just
A single time, then many times I trust
We could recall when we had broken sleep
And felt we must get up. As mourners weep
Compelled by grief, so we are like compelled.
We've heard a voice within our souls; it's yelled
Or whispered—either way, we've heard the call—
And us, from bed, that inspiration hauls.
Oh, feckless we would be if we ignore
That waking voice. For we should underscore
Those moments with a pen or say a prayer,
At least. Reflection, that's a gem! But spare
Me your excuses why you sleep away
Your life when you've been called. But now I stray
Too far from off my mark. Old Abram heard,
Upon the dust of Moreh's plain, God's word:
"Unto your sundry seed I'll give this place.
By faith, these words of promise must embrace."
God said this while the old man looked upon
The land of Canaan broad. Then, in the dawn,
The old man gathered stones to mark the site.
He built an altar there so that he might
Remember where the LORD had spoken clear.

Soon after this a famine quite severe
Had struck the land wherein they roamed. It had
Been said that Egypt's land had food; nomads
From all around were headed there to buy
The grain they had—great Goshen's grand supply.
But Abram, being ever one to work
Some kind of edge, great father of the kirk,
Had told his wife to keep it under wraps
That they gave marriage vows. He said, "Perhaps
They'll look upon your pretty face, those shaved
Egyptian men, and they will have me graved
To sample out your charms." For he was old,   (GENESIS 12:12)
That man of Ur, and Sarah, truth be told,
Had started as his sister (really niece).
But still, she played along to keep the peace
And told each one they met along the pike
To Egypt's sand that she was sister, like
Her husband said to do. She really thought
The whole thing nonsense, though; she had been taught
To tell the truth. But who would care? What's more,
Who would find out? That little lie would score
No gadabout. To her, it seemed a game—
A silly one, for still she felt the same:
Old Abram was her husband. Nothing changed,
Just roles of wife and sister rearranged.
Well, when they got there, even on the road
Egyptian men were speedy to decode
The appetizing beauty Sarah held.
Some princes (cronies close to Pharaoh) smelled
An opportunity. Advised the high-
One, "Snatch her up, before some passerby
Gets to the hottie first!" And so that king
Sent hurried word for those same men to bring
The girl to him. Who knows what Abram feared
When they arrived? He hadn't volunteered
The truth, that much we know, but off they rode
With his own loving wife. That episode
Would serve as what is known to be a type,
A glimpse that shows what's coming down the pipe

Of providential plan. Though still unknown
To them, the seed of Abraham would groan
Beneath Egyptian lash for many years.
Debate it all you like—God interferes
In daily life for larger plots, it's true.
If true it's not, He would have none to do
With prophecies or any future pledge;
They'd just be speculations on the ledge
Of chance. Where is free will in this, you ask?
Well, mysteries like that will wear a mask,
Probe as I might. Let's rest this mental churn
For now and call both true as we return
Unto our tale. We left poor Sarah on
Her way to meet the Pharaoh—paragon
Of men upon the earth, great keeper of
The wonders of the world—a man whose love
For women was insatiable and still
An appetite that he searched hard to fill.
The horses towing on the chariot
That Sarah rode were more than adequate
To get that pearl unto the king with speed.
They halted, panting, dust still canopied
Like dirty clouds and sticking to their flanks.
Then down the girl was pulled with hurried yanks
And off escorted to the royal soak—
There pampered with perfume of gentlefolk.
So, wiped and clean from all that herdsmen reek,
Sweet Sarah wore new silken robes; her cheeks
Were blushed with clay and henna painted thick
Around her eyes to shade. It all was quick,
That sanitizing purge, for Egypt loathed
All shepherds in their livestock's odor clothed!
But Abram sat at home; he was concerned
With how to save his skin, and wife returned
Was trivial at best. Yet when his mail
Was getting filled with what the Bloomingdale   (GENESIS 12:16)
Of Egypt could provide, he had to think
It pimping, in a sense. How could he wink
At someone with his wife (his wife!) to mate

While he's receiving gifts to compensate
The whole affair? The dirt is there when we
Let go our euphemistic lens to see
Without the candy-coat we blindly grant
To stories Biblical. Here ends my rant.
So, Sarah, after preened Egyptian style,
Was sent to meet the keeper of the Nile.
And Pharaoh, looking on that pleasing frame,
Thought surely it a pity not to claim
A comely girl like that. And still a maid—
Amazing! She was up for grabs! Afraid
And sweating bullets, Sarah went to meet
That Pharaoh in his all-inclusive suite.
When she walked in and shut the door behind,
She saw him in the bed, there intertwined
With pillows and with blankets loosely wrapped.
The Pharaoh's hand was tapping, then he snapped
His fingers for the timid girl to come
And join him on the bed. Her mind felt numb
As into bed she crawled; the sheets were soft
Against her skin, but then she gulped and coughed
At what was coming next. For Pharaoh took
To lift the sheets and pull her close. She shook,
And for a moment—just a fleeting sec—
She thought to tell the truth. But that would wreck
Her husband's credibility; they might
Be put to death for it! And so, despite
Her deeper impulse to come clean, she kept
Her mouth secure and sealed, chose to accept
The aftermath of lies. And lying there—
With Pharaoh's hands still groping round her hair
And lower to her curves and tender parts—
She played the canvas; Pharaoh brushed his arts.
But then, at length, he noticed something odd.
For though the woman was a gem, unflawed
In every way and really his to claim,
Rub as he might, his instrument was lame.
He tried to concentrate and kissed her on
The neck and closed his eyes. He felt his brawn
Encouraging his member to enjoin,

But blood rushed everywhere except the groin!
Embarrassed then, his royal cheeks were flushed—
His impotence made cold, his yearning crushed.
Each night then after, more he felt the wimp,
For his virility persisted limp.
Around the palace word began to spread
How every man, when they were in their bed,
Could not perform the function of a man.
They later then discerned it all began
When Sarah had arrived. Oh, this was it!
Those omen-readers knew how to outwit
A fibber in their camp. So, Sarah then
Was pulled aside and, 'fore the noblemen,
Was spotlight-questioned on her husband's tale.
And that girl talked: said she was not for sale
But married to the graybeard on the plain.
(She was his sister, too, tried to explain.)
Oh, he was mad to hear he had been duped!
"How low!" the Pharaoh raged. "How low they've stooped
To lie to me!" He gave the girl a frown
And scowled. In bed with her, he'd seemed a clown,
And if that were not bad enough, there was
A plague upon his house—and all because
Of codes he'd broke unwittingly. He snatched
Her arm, not lovingly but cold, detached,
And dragged her out into the light. Her God
Would surely see his efforts and applaud
At such transparency. He ready made
The chariots, the guard and cavalcade.
Then, with the girl beside, they charged and beat
The dusty plain like millstones grinding wheat.
They reached old Abram's hut in no time flat,
And that old graybeard then was busy at
The grooming of the livestock just received
As gifts from Pharaoh—Pharaoh when deceived.
Dismounting then, that king with all his guard
Took to release the man his wife, unmarred
And well—but her head hung in shame. She walked
To meet old Abram's side. He stood defrocked
Of credibility, but rightly so.

For all in this wide world innately know
You are to tell the truth. And when we fail
To tell the truth so falsehoods might prevail,
We'll wear an egg of shame upon our face
When truth comes out—and out it will by grace.
Old Abram stood there mopping up the sand
With both his eyes, and both his wrinkled hands
Were shoved into his pockets, deep. He found
The silence hard to bear with just the sound
Of wind to fill his ears; but still, he could
Not stand to lift his head. He understood
What he had done and knew he had been in
The wrong. The Pharaoh, though, his patience thin,
Was thinking how he might be done with that
Old man, not tyrant-like but diplomat
In style. He could have seen them both be put
To death; he didn't have to pussyfoot
Around. But still, he feared that God. If He
Could smite his household with impotency
As easy as He had, what else could their
Almighty God then conjure out of air?
Oh, no—he'd wash his hands of it and send
The pair away, not wanting to offend
Their nomad God a smidgen or a shred
More than he had already done. He said,
"Just take your wife and leave without delay!
And keep the gifts, as well, but you won't stay
A moment longer in my realm; your guile
Has ruined things!" The Pharaoh of the Nile
Made off, his guard left trailing in the rear.
Old Abram breathed in some relief. He near
Had seen a blade against his wrinkled throat.
But now he got to leave—and with the goats
And sheep he just received as gifts! His spouse
Just looked at him and moseyed to the house
To pack their things. Yes, Abram had his flaws,
But blessings find not better deeds as cause.
Almighty's vow does not on acts depend;
God's promise foolish actions will transcend.

CHAPTER 6

Greener Grass

And so, that aged graybeard made his way
To Bethel once again, wanting to pray
Right where he'd left an altar stand. His tent
Was in the spot it was before he went
To Egypt's land and knocked on Pharaoh's door
For food. He knew he had done wrong; therefore,
He'd pray at Bethel, strange in its mystique—
For in that place, by mouth he'd heard God speak.
He'd seek his grounding, center, and his core,
And to the left and right he'd look no more.
Before too long, he settled in the groove
Of daily life. He pitched his camp to move
When need demanded it—the need for more
To graze, that is. For he had sheep galore!
And no small task it proved to move those herds
From here to there. It really was absurd
How much he had; his wealth was then untold,

And lands found it a straining task to hold
That man with all his livestock gained. Well, add
His nephew Lot into the mix. *Egad,*
That was a lot of mouths to feed! The flocks
Of both combined consumed each leafy stock
And greener tuft they'd find. But food and drink
Were limited, and tempers flared. Just think
About the brawls between the teamster heads
And how they clashed about whose flocks could tread
And graze before the other one's. All moods
Had reached the boiling point, and attitudes
Were at their worst. Both Abraham and Lot
Knew that they could, or more so that they ought,
Soon seek a compromise and part their ways,
For their heyday had seen its better days.
So, Abram said, "Let strife from us be far,
For brethren of our father's tribe, we are.
From land that sits before us, you may choose:
Pick either right or left, I won't refuse."
Now Lot had always had a little itch
To see the land of Sodom, famed for rich
And lavish shows—all lecherously decked.
In short, the sex was free and ran unchecked.
The truth was, Mrs. Lot could not entice
Him anymore. His palate needed spice!
The taste of daily life was simply bland;
Variety, he felt, was in demand.
An urge inside was burning at his chest
And pushing him to go; he was possessed
To put his hand to something new, to try
An act that might his mojo vivify.
He had the curiosity, the thirst,
To drink forbidden cups, though he be cursed.
And Mrs. Lot had felt the same, that spark
Within her breast. Her flaccid patriarch
No longer stirred her blood or flutters wrought.
"That man would rather count the sheep," she thought,
"Than cherish his own wife within the bed.
In Sodom, I could paint the town and spread

My wings a bit. We have the money now,
And I am getting old. Time will allow
A few more years of beauty on my face."
She pondered more, that wife of Lot. "The place
Would surely better suit both him and I
Than does this roaming with the herds. I'll die
To spend another year this way! How grim—
To live a life led by his uncle's whim."
Well, Lot was versed with all his wife's complaints;
He also had his own. In truth, restraint
Was not a concept either of them liked.
And so, to hear the choice, young Lot was psyched!
His uncle offered it as simple stuff:
"Pick this or that, the greener land or rough."
And Lot, in mustered calm—his best to hold
That eagerness inside the feigning mold
Of somber thought—then tried his best to swab
The merry grin from off his smirking gob.
So, what was really music to his ears
Became a dirge sung with befitting tears.
He lifted up his eyes to Jordan's plain
And thought it fresh as Eden's lush terrain.
His miser mind was fixed; his will was bent,
And he from selfish course would not relent.
Survival of the shrewd had been his creed;
He was a wolf, and he had learned to feed
Upon the weak and feeble, like it's told
By Virgil: "Fortune sits upon the bold."
Lot looked at Abram then—just standing there,
A paltry thing, disheveled—and his hair
Was gray as any common stone beneath
The currents of the river Time. His teeth
Were gaunt and hardly apt enough to chew!
"Out with the old," Lot thought, "in with the new."
The future was a game that's simply for
The ones who have and take so they have more.
"It's right that we should part," Lot slyly shammed.
But then he clarified, "For I'll be damned
If uncle, honest Abe, I ever see

Live out the last his days in strife for me."
Old Abraham seemed pleased by that façade;
He pursed his lips in pride. Then, with a nod,
He urged the younger, "Choose what land you'll take."
Lot said, "I will take Sodom for your sake."
So, Lot had journeyed then to Sodom's gate
And in Gomorrah's grip would situate.
As Abram watched his nephew's train depart,
Distress for Lot's wellbeing vexed his heart.
For Sodom's men were famed for twisted taste;
Unnatural use of functions they all chased.
But more than this, the old man was concerned
With who would carry on his line. He yearned
And would have loved to have a son. His God
Had promised it to him, and so he pawed
At his remaining years to grip that word.
But still he questioned, "Have I really heard?
Perhaps I've just imagined it's a call,
And really it's my fancy, after all."
But God, Who sees His servants when distressed,
Some words of ease to Abraham addressed:
"Look north to south and from the east to west,
For all this land, by you, shall be possessed.
Lean down and fill your fists with gritty sand.
Just so, your seed will populate the land.
Wherever you might tread, there they will dwell—
And to their children, of you they will tell.
Your fruitful line will span eternity,
And then your seed, like sand, shall countless be."   (GENESIS 13:16)

CHAPTER 7

Melchizedek

Before too many sands had made the pass
Into and through the skinny-waisted glass
Of Time, it had occurred. And hardly dry
(Or so we speak when synonyms we try),
Yes, ink was hardly dry upon the deed
Of separation. For they both agreed
By parting ways was lesser evil bought.
Well, not long after, Abram's ears had caught
The winds of rumor drifting from the land
Of Sodom's green that there had been a band
Of kings deciding to rebel against
Some tyranny for years endured. Incensed,
They joined their forces, four kings fighting five,
And made a stand—all servitude deprived—
In Siddim's tar; that sticky battle might
Prove man from boy, prove brute from catamite.
And in that salty basin, battles waged;

Along with loot of Sodom, Lot was caged.

Imagine there's a boy upon a hill.
He watches from that height the brawn and skill
Of men then playing games upon the plain
Below. They swing their eager bats and strain
Themselves to strike a ball, to send it sail-
Ing past a crescent fence. Each time they nail
A hit, the boy can see the bat and ball
Connect before the noise of it can fall
Upon his ears. The sound is on delay;
That simple distance holds his ears at bay.

Like so, the din of war was late in touch-
Ing Abram's ears, how Lot was in the clutch
Of chains. The old man wasted zero time
And rallied up his men—those still in prime
And trained for special combat such as this,
Those chomping at the bit, those filled with piss
And vinegar. It was an army, crude
And vigorous. With these, old Abe pursued
The victor kings, and in a nighttime raid
He plundered all of them, their famished blades
To nurse on human blood. Who would believe
Old Abraham the meek could roll his sleeves
And conjure up an army at a whim?
This was not all his men; he got to skim
The better fighters off the top like cream—
The frothy stock and store with eyes agleam
For war, his mercenary men. But wait
A moment here with me, we might castrate
A bull before we're through. How does this jibe
When Abraham unto himself ascribes
A fear that he must life and limb protect
By lying twice about his wife? Object
If you now wish, but it to me seems clear.
If he was so concerned and had a fear
That he must lie to save his life, he could
Have formed his army at that time and stood

His ground should ever threat arise. I'm sure
There're some who, with a lengthy lecture, tour
The reasons why this wouldn't be the case.
But let us never overthink or chase
For details that aren't evident. We'll ask
The questions that present themselves and bask
In the assurance that we're true unto
Our text. We shouldn't jump through hoops or spew
Some logic why it all makes sense, each piece
To fit a cozy nook. We only grease
Our reason's palm by coaxing, all the while
Conflicting passages to reconcile.
But let me touch on inspiration here:
I pen my verse as hints my quirk, a queer
Profession, I admit. But where my urge
Decides to push—the lofty heights or dirge
Of boggy swamps—is thus determined by
My feeling at the moment, whether high
Or low. This feeling takes its shape or kind
(Whatever word preferred to it be twined)
From what has moved me at my very core.
Perhaps it is a woman, metaphor
Of all the ocean's rage, or something sim-
Ple as a piece of wood—by such my whim
Is moved with strings, an orchestra or tongues
Of multitudes. And it must sing! My lungs
Might burst were I to keep it in. We call
This inspiration; it's the wherewithal
Of any writer's bag. So thank the Muse
For blowing on my pen, but don't confuse
Who holds the thing. Though page had not been inked
Till I had seen her face, my pen still kinked
And bent to spurt some weak artistic juice
I still remain the author of, by Zeus!
And I won't blame the woman if my verse
Resembles rot, say of her face, "It's worse
For wear; the poor prosaic thing is sick
And needs cosmetic aid—yes, paint it thick!"
The buck stops here; I see my art is ruled,

By use and practice more than proper schooled.
You say, "Inspired is when our God has breathed,
The tongue Divine in human scribbles sheathed."
Well, inspiration many forms might take,
But writers move the pen—make no mistake.
So, there it is, my vital pulse no less—
And you quite bored to yawns (so I should guess)
And longing we return to Scripture's words
And toss this poet's alibi to birds.
Let's do just that and pick from off the sand
Our bloody blades stained with the kings unmanned
In their defeat. Old Abraham had gone
Into the north—a grueling walkathon
For any man near eighty years—to get
His nephew back. They went to Dan (forget
That city couldn't have that name) then made
The journey home with many sacks, each weighed
Upon the backs of camels with their coin.
But on his way, some kings rushed out to join
Old Abe's parade and give him their esteem,
And with these came the priest of Elohim.
Prepare to pay attention now—although
Your truant purse is penniless and shows
To only hold the slips of your arrears—
For this is paramount! And so, with cheers
Old Abe was met in Shaveh's gully by
The kings of men who clay thrones occupy.
With these, another—Salem's righteous king—
Had come, and he was good enough to bring
Some bread and wine to make a feast. They shared
The meal in honest thanks, for unimpaired
Was Abram's great campaign. But then, the priest
Melchizedek, who felt their joy increased
Upon the wine, had lifted up his head
Unto the skies in honest thanks and said,
"How bless'd are you, old Abram, son of dirt,
That God, Who has created all, would girt
You round the waist with favor? Bless'd be He,
For victor o'er your foes He makes you be."   (GENESIS 14:20)

From all the characters in Holy Writ,
This priest stands out—his constitution knit
Apart from human womb, no father's seed
Or mother's milk to infant hunger feed.
In fact, you'd be hard-pressed to ever find
Persona more with secrecies entwined.
Well, Enoch does come close—I'd take an oath!
Oh, it might be a tie between them both.
At any rate, this king of Salem keeps
A shroud around his character so peeps
And probing eyes that want to know are kept
Away. But let that go, and say he stepped
Into our world from who-knows-where, and so
Be done with questions that bring not the know.

The LORD still says unto my Lord, "Come sit   (PSALM 110)
At my right hand until Your foes are fit
To be a footstool for Your feet. I'll send
My scepter out from Zion's post; now bend
Your enemies unto Your rule. I see
Them stand before Your throne; they take a knee
In admiration more than fear; they're dressed
Up to the nines in woolen garments pressed
And sharp. The womb of morning, dawn, and dew
Will be Your youth. This I have sworn; no new
Advice will change My mind. As priest You're named,
In orders of Melchizedek ordained,
And at My altar You will serve your bread
And wine. From My right hand, in wrath You'll tread
Upon Your enemies; You'll break their backs
And shatter kings with judgment swift, the stacks
Of corpses high in every land. You'll crush
The chiefs to deference. The wren and thrush
Are heard as down You kneel to sip the brook
Of conquered lands—the lands You overtook."

Now back to Abram, who—when quite content
With belly full and wine of strange ferment
Still swirling to an altruistic mood—

Had motioned to his men, his food half-chewed,
For them to bring from off the camels' backs
A couple of the gem- and gold-filled sacks.
They brought the bags but struggled 'neath the load
While Abram with a bobbing finger showed
Them where to drop the clinking things—the fruits
Of first, or so it was, from all the loot
He had recouped in his campaign. They placed
Them near the priest and tried to slow the haste
Of gravity as best they could when down
The sacks were set to earth. From all the crowns
At dinner, then, this priest had foremost dibs
On what was handed out—that not in dribs
Or drabs but all at once. It was about
A tenth, so give or take. Now I don't doubt
The import of this gift, and let us make
A standard out of it. But thicker steak,
For those of you who have the teeth to chew,
Is what this Levite father paid—his due
Unto an order higher than his own.
The other kings looked on; they had no bone
To pick with Abram's acts. They said to keep
The gold; the only thing they wished to reap
From off that man's success was to obtain
Their people lost to war. "Let me be plain,"
Old Abram said, "and speak it clear so you
Will understand. When my ears heard the news
About the war, my main concern was just
To bring my nephew back. And on the dust-
Filled road, I swore to God Most High that if
He'd grant my victory, I wouldn't sniff
For gold that wasn't mine or so much take
A sandal string or flask or loaf of cake.
I don't want you to say your wealth's bereft,
That Abram was made richer by some theft."

CHAPTER 8

Cut a Deal

It seemed a long ride home once Abram had
Departed from his meal with kings. Nomad
He was, but life atop a camel's hump
Was harder with his age, and in a slump
His mind was bent. Who cared if wars he'd win
Or if his gold meant Need could never grin
His way? For still he had no heir, no boy
To carry on his name. He could employ
His wrinkled coat of skin a few more years
At best, for loyal bodies mutineers
Become in time, regardless of the pay
And benefits. You feed them well each day,
And yet they still abandon you; they quake
And shrivel up, complain of pains and aches
Until they quit. He more considered this—
How mortal life eventually must kiss
With death and how, upon approaching such

A tryst, he still remained within the clutch
Of childlessness. Whom would he leave things to?
He couldn't take it with him. No—he knew
That life achievements simply spoil and wear
A tarnish when bequeathing must forbear.
"It's all just vapid puffs of smoke," he thought;
"Myself and all I've done will be forgot
When I am gone." And all the journey home
His mind was tangled with concerns. No comb
Of hope could set them straight! Then sitting in
His tent that afternoon, his strength still thin
And feeble from the ride, he watched the dust
Blow through the canopies of camp. Each gust
Made flapping lips and canvas tongues of them.
They seemed to speak or laugh, perchance condemn.
He stared at them awhile; the tent mouths sneered
As more the wind kept blowing, more they jeered.
Now weary minds and bodies, you'll agree,
Give fertile ground for hazy auguries.
Old Abram needed not someone to tell
Him of the risks in omen cards, the spell
Pronounced by hungry bellies, or what's wrote
Upon the scrolls of Dehydration's throat.
He thought on this as down the sun still beat
With flogging strikes of summer-sapping heat.
Yet, when retreating Helios had gone
And with him tools of anvil pounding dawn,
The cool of eventide began its march
Into the camp, refreshing all the parch
Of scorching day. His lucid mind was calm
And sharp; he felt a beggar taking alms
Before great Wisdom's shrine. And then at once
It came, a noise, vibrating undulance
Across the night. He felt as much as heard
The voice that spoke out clear with weight, not slurred
Or mumbled mute—reverberating chords
That comforted like caring overlords.
"I am your shield and your sustaining hand,
And by My generosity you'll stand."

Those were the words that came (and they were gone
As quickly as they had arrived) and on
Old Abram stirred, then dizzy to detain
The voice a little longer. "Please remain!"
He said, "And tell me one more thing: What can
You give that lasts? I'm still a childless man,
And anything You give I must disperse
Unto my chief of staff—to Eli's purse."
The voice of God did not reply a peep
To this, the pitch of night just thick and deep.
Old Abe went on and tried to clarify:
"I mean, I have no heir, so when I die
My goods unto a colleague must be willed.
You see, then, why I'm not completely thrilled."
He waited, and the voice arrived once more.
It urged him from his seat and out the door
Into the night to see the stars. God said,
"This man you speak of, he won't get a shred
Of anything you have. Your son will get
It all. Just look into the sky. I bet
You couldn't count the stars were you to try."
Old Abram lifted up his head; his eyes
Were squinting at the stars above. He cleared
His throat, for such a challenge never feared,
And started counting them, first with the bright
Then moving to those of candescent light.
But somewhere in between, he lost his count
And thought to start again, at least remount
The horse. But God chimed in, some help to lend,
"The question was rhetorical, my friend.
I did not really want for you to count
But that you'd see how great your heirs amount.
I called you forth from Ur, this land to give.
In My inheritance your seed shall live."
Then Abram trusted God, though facts were grim,
And righteous by belief God reckoned him.
The next part of our text should not seem weird.
In fact, if we are honest, we have neared
The same request old Abram had; we've asked

For God to tell us more, or more unmask.
Imagine now: you've got the voice of God
Right there. What would you ask? This old nimrod
Just thought to probe about some proof. But what
Is truly strange is that God gives this scut
The thing he wants. Abe's putting out a fleece,
A question posed when faith decides to cease
In search of something tangible. We all
Have done the same when to our knees we fall
And say, "Dear God: oh, if You really want
Me to do this or that, then do not taunt
Me with the pain of guessing games. Just show
Me something I can see, and then I'll know
What path to choose." Such magic tricks, you fool,
From top hats would make God a rabbit pull!
A genie of the lamp or nickel flip
Sees faith constrained by senses' censorship.
Well, there it is—old Abram was no less
Or different from the rest of us, I guess.
He wanted God to give a small display,
Some evidence that things would end the way
He had described. Abe asked (when boldness grew)
"How can I know that what You say is true?"

A mountain lion will raid among the flocks
That roam the grassy hills. Its stealth will mock
The herdsmen who have never seen it with
Their eyes. Some joke and call the beast a myth
Or ghost until they take their spears to hunt
It down. Confronting it, they bear the brunt
Of all their disbelief. In fear they groan,
So palpable the terror in their bones.

So, Abraham would see it in the flesh,
The real and solid stuff, beyond the mesh
Of doubt, and certainty would be his song.
God spoke these words, "Bring me a heifer—strong
And numbered in its years of life but three.
A ram and nanny also bring, and see

There are a couple chirping birds to boot.
We'll cut a deal with these." Then, resolute,
Old Abram set to work; he felt a rush
And motivating spur. The citrus blush
Of dawn had just begun to light the tents
Of camp, and while the other people went
About their daily grind, in slower pace
The old man hustled round to find the place
He'd left his knife and gathered up the birds
And beasts he'd need as well. He pushed some curds
Into his tunic pouch and headed out
The door. But Sarah caught his arm, a stout
And sturdy woman since her youth, and sat
Him down. She didn't fuss or cavil that
He hadn't been in bed the night before.
Nor did she ask about the curds or bore
Him with her wants—just buttered up some toast
And said, "No husband mine will skip the most
Important meal of day!" With breakfast done,
Old Abram picked a spot, a site where none
Could silly questions ask or interfere
With work he had to do. The sun was near
Mid-morning when old Abram loosed the cow
From off the rope. He patted then her brow
And slit her throat while lifting at the chin.
And then the dirty work commenced: The skin
Around the belly Abram sliced with strokes
Precise to puncture till the casing broke
And spilled her bowels out to the dust. It warmed
The stones and dirt beneath as he malformed
The beast to something other than. The spine
He had to break to get apart—the twine
Of sinews tearing as he pulled the flanks
In two. The ram and goat looked on; a blank,
Dumbfounded shock was in their eyes to see
That novice with his knife in surgery.
Old Abram wiped the sweat from off his face
And left a bloody stain to take its place,
Then down he leaned to grip the severed half

That still retained the tail. He dragged the calf
Apart, but guts spilled out with this, and so
He tried his best to scoop them back—to show
A clean divide as best he could. He rose
And looked then at the ram, whose antsy pose
Was tugging at the tether in some hope
Of getting free. Unraveling the rope,
He led the ram's begrudging steps to walk
And stand the bloody spot—the butcher's block
Where he would breathe his last. The horns were held
And oddly aided rather than repelled
The shining steel. With neck in backward arch,
His throat was slit, and hot blood spilled to starch
And stiffen all the ground beneath. He dropped;
His buckled knees and weight abruptly stopped
Against the surface of the earth. Abe kneeled
Again. He found the heifer blood congealed
Between his fingers, and he had to flake
The clotted crust for them to move. The bake
Of day had charred the gore. His aged hand
Was not as sure as with the heifer, and
While making round the circuit of the gut,
He poked and tore intestine sleeves, the smut
Of scent to permeate the air. In truth,
While lacking all that nimbleness of youth,
He ripped more than he cut the tawny hide
With dulling knife down to the spine. He tried
And failed to get it through; annoyed for sure,
He propped his foot just at the curvature
Then jerked both horn and tail to snap the back—
An egg-to-pan with broken yolk, not slack
To show ingested meals. He grabbed the hooves,
Those on the bottom half, and pulled to move
It near the cow's, all tails with tails and heads
With heads while entrails smeared the void. Instead
Of starting with the nanny goat just yet,
He dipped his pouch and took the curds, then wet
With condensation juice. His hands still soiled,
Though many times against his tunic toiled

To wipe them clean. He may have only made
Them worse by such an act, for blood had sprayed
His tunic's whole, from knee to collarbone—
A splattered show Kandinsky might condone.
And wiping hands against that mess just mixed
A crimson meld. The sun was midday fixed
And beating hard while Abram stomached down
The tinted curds to keep his strength. No clown
Looked more the part than Abram did, to sit
Among the slaughtered beasts and sup a bit
On cheese made from the cream of victim-next.
That's when he saw the shadows come; they vexed
The ground like sweeping wraiths. He tilted back
His head, his hands to shield his eyes from smacks
Of sun that squinting still allowed. And there,
Between the earth and heaven's golden blare,
The birds of prey were floating—so at ease
To bathe in reek like pampered luxuries.
Old Abram finished off the last his curds
And rose to finish off the goat. No word
He spoke, but understanding nods were shared
Between the two. His waning knife then spared
The goat from any future breath with one
Hard press and pull. Of all that man would stun
With death, she was the easiest. Her hide
Was thin and parted as the old man plied
His blade around her girth. Her organs were
A dainty size but somehow heartier,
If that makes sense, and kept composure while
The savage broke her back. But all the bile
She held oozed out when that man set to drag
Her hind to meet the other ones. Her shag
Of fur worked like a mop and swabbed the gore
And dirt to streak across the desert floor.
Old Abram snapped the necks of both the birds—
Firm grip and spinning wrist. Then, afterwards,
He placed one with the heads and one with tails.
The old man sat; the wind had left his sails
And drowsiness was setting in. His knife,

Afflicted blunt from once a sharper life,
Was wiped upon his clothes and made to join
The leather sheath for bloody rest. *Why coin*
Your acts, O man, in brutal molds to make
A pact? Or do you really need to break
A beast in half to sign and seal? How nice.
Would not a simple handshake same suffice?
Well, Abram sat there in the sun, the stench
Of death still pungent and enough to wrench
The gut of any passerby. His eyes
Were getting heavier while in the sky
The birds of prey instinctively had flocked
In their unholy brotherhood, defrocked
Of decency and golden rule. They smelled
The ones the bells of death had cruelly knelled
That day. And as they soared above and kept
Their watch on piles of flesh, old Abram slept.

A man will feel his strength depart when day
Is halfway through. And though he sits or lays
Upon a bed, his eyes will feel the weight
Of sleep come on. He does not hesitate
To drift away, though sun be in the heights
And bright as gold. But then he wakes in fright
To find he's in a place he can't recall.

So Abram woke in dread and found a sprawl
Of flailing wings had brushed against his face.
The vultures had arrived, the sad disgrace
Of those who glide the heavens with their gift
Of flight. They made themselves at home, the thrift
Of meat discarded to enjoy, for waste-
Not-want-not was their attitude. They raced
Around the carrion in hasty squats
And pecked the pulpy flesh; the fur and clots
Of blood were dangling off their daring beaks.
Old Abram then arose like an antique
That needed oil. He grabbed his crook, and with
Ambitious aim, he struck,

As does the smith
When working at his forge attack the steel
When it is hot. The amber glow will feel
Each hammer blow severely dealt. The sparks
Burst out like tears to arch and light the dark.

Just so, each blow that Abram brought had sent
The feathers sailing through the air! He went   (GENESIS 15:11)
Right down the line and knocked each bird from off
Their plate, and each disputed with a scoff
In turn. Then, stammered flaps of wings gave boost
To awkward launch, suspending weight to roost
Some perch no man could see. The sky turned black
With clamor, a cacophony to thwack
The ears as off they flew and then were gone.
The sun was going down; the pitchy dawn
Of night was coming on, and Abram sat
Upon the ground. His face felt tight; a mat
Of blood had crusted from his ear to nose.
His thoughts then drifted to the lifeless pose
Of all the animals he'd killed that day.
All that to imitate Chaldean ways
Of swearing out an oath. Let's stop this train
A moment here so that I might explain
What's going on. It's no small thing to take
An oath, and, in that time, they'd often make
A promise with a rite. A beast was cut
In half, right down the middle through the gut,
And pulled apart. Then those involved would swear,
While walking in between the disrepair
Of slaughtered life, that they would keep their word
Or suffer fates the same. "It is absurd,
And so, I will believe," admitted sage
Tertullian. A slightly altered age
We live in now, where quick "I'm sorrys" wait
The wings and spare us disembowelment fates.
But in old Abram's time, before the heaps
Of legal papers twisted arms to keep
One's acts in check, dramatic rites could glue

Behavior down to stick. Imagine you
Were swearing oaths or vows by such a rit-
Ual and saying that you would be split
In half before you'd ever think to break
Your word. Now truly, that's undone. So, quake
Before you swear to death. No harder edge
Could Leonidas deal! They drank their pledge
With molten steel to chase it down. But let's
Return again unto our text and whet
Our brains a little more. So, Abram sat
There on the ground; the slaughtered beasts were at
His feet, and then he felt a darkness shroud
His mind. The sun was down, then disavowed
Of any right to shine. But what he felt
Was more than night, was more than just the pelt
Of darkness spread across his eyes. He knew
He was alone. That hollow feeling grew
Into a fear, as if he were in death.
But he was in a trance, where once the breath
Of life becomes the shades of Hades' realm,
Where darker visions take to steer the helm
Down stairwells of despairing thought. Then, all
Was still of sound; not even thoughts made call
Upon his mind, and he could hear it then:
The voice of God was in that place, amen.
God said, "Beyond the shadow of a doubt,
I'll have you know that I will carry out
My will. All paths, including yours, are planned,
And stranger you will be in a strange land.
And in that place your seed will come to serve
One hundred years by four, but I'll preserve
You in that place, and tyrant I will scold.
Then you'll come out with substance of their gold."
The voice was gone, and Abraham awoke
To some strange smell. A noxious scent of smoke
Had filled his nostrils deep with charcoal snuff,

The very scent a hearth, with dusty muff,
Will give when it is kindled in the morn.

The cold, cremated clay and ash adorn
The coals like sheets of snow. But this is swept
Aside, and breath is blown on that which slept
In death, renewed as might some smelling salts
Revive the senses back to dwell this vault
Of flesh.

Like so, old Abraham was stoked
To life by some pervasive stench. Half-choked
By it, he propped himself and coughed. "What could
That smell be coming from?" he mused and stood
To get a better look. And so he peered
Into the dark to try and see, unfeared
But cautious in his step, for he was blind
As any bat before that dark assigned
To watch the night. He didn't want to trip
On those he'd killed by bootlegged doctorship
That day. Nocturnal pitch was just like tar,
And starry lights above did not go far
To light that inky scene. Still, Abram caught
A glimpse of someone near; he almost thought
He could make out a profile on the night.
He squinted hard as if to extradite
That figure from the dark unseen, his eyes
Then working strict patrol to undisguise
That One who'd come. Old Abe had sensed no harm
In His intent, for apathetic charm
Was in that lofty gait. The silhouette
Was simply at a stroll. One odd thing met
The old man's gaze, and strange he had not marked
It there before: in His right hand was sparked
A flaming torch; a smoking lantern pot
Was in the left. "That must be what has brought
The smell," old Abram thought. He carried both,
That mystery half-seen, and swore His oath
While walking in between the slaughtered beasts.
He swung his censor pot, much like a priest
Might do at mass, and moved his torch about
To light His way. They looked to float, no doubt,

For both the glowing torch and smoking can
Were bouncing in the hands then of the Man
Who paced the night. The flambeau flame was hot
And seemed to cauterize, to even clot,
The open-wounded things upon the ground.
And so, the oath was spoken then. The sound
Of it was faint; still, Abram had attained
The proof he sought—by word and deed obtained.
"Though stranger in that land, you will sojourn;
In time, to Canaan's borders you'll return.
The twists of providence you can't unscrew,
So be assured that what I speak is true.
Since greater than Myself cannot be found,
I swear then by Myself, and so am bound."

CHAPTER 9
Two Mountains

I never want sententious tones to plague
My verse. That said, I neither want a vague
And sappy dribble from my pen. Too much
With either one of these will see us touch
The excess mark or point of no return.
Great Balance holds the scales, and this we learn
Is true of all things in this game of life.
Consider this: fresh water's good and rife
In its supply, and yet, if we would drink
A lake—our thirsty lips an open sink
To take it in—we'd bloat until we burst
From out our seams. No matter how our thirst
Might cry and whine, we are not fish, my friend.
And so, we can perceive when to an end
We bring the glass. We all know this; the rule
Of moderation's taught to any fool
Who sups upon the bread of earth. What would

They say if we had never learned what should
Be common knowledge to us all? They'd dub
Us antinomian or rashly snub
Us as a legalist. They'd bite their lip
Or classify, and ill-got stickers gyp
One out of worth or pass a credit where
There is no credit due. My ten gray hairs
And glossy pate have shown me that. Just stew
On what I'm sharing now; perhaps some new
And regal thought will come to roost. In time,
You may give birth to some fantastic rhyme
Yourself. Let's leave this off and get back to
My starting line and point, this avenue
Too much a scenic route. Although I don't
Now seek to moralize with you (I won't
And never will, my friend, so be at ease),
I can't deny there still are effigies
I will not totally deface. They stand
Apart from my appraise, already canned
For shelf and sale. Just tilt your heads and zip
Your lips, admiring the craftsmanship
That toiled the cloud. But greater work to strut
Is that of Man, that noble idiot
Who wears the garments of his God and shares
His image inasmuch as mirrors stare
Reflections back. Yes, Man's a piece of work!
He thinks his belly is his brain and shirks
His great capacity for thought as soon
As pipers pull their reeds and flute a tune.
How easy it becomes to dance away
To Rubaiyats of Epicure, to sway
Beneath the rhythms of your food and wine.
I don't demean these things; they are divine
And staples to my daily cup and fork.
Still, Balance calls and bids me, "Bottle cork."
So, stimulus—to bring this ship around
To where I steered off course again—is found
By those who simply plug their verbal throng.
You chatterboxes selling for a song

The capital of all your days and years,
Have you not learned that silent minds will hear
God's voice? An unavoidable amount
Of arrogance exists when e'er we mount
The horse of speech. In essence what we say
Is that our listener should put away
Their thoughts and give to ours the greater place.
To mutter just a peep in time and space
Is saying that our words deserve an ear.
So be a mute or monk, or commandeer
Your tongue for licking stamps. But you should know
To speak at all is one audacious show.
So, give it first some thought before your trap
Is drawn in two. Let fear and trembling wrap
Your words and dole them as a miser might
Upon the crowd. For they are pearls when right
And spoken true and savory as wine
Upon the tongue. Don't lay them out for swine
To gobble up or trample under cleft
As common mud. For what will you have left
With all your wisdom spent upon the mass?
No, over these let your discretion pass,
And save for those with ears to hear equipped.
And so, I trust the same you are—well gripped
With thirst for sacred things. With that, I'll start
This allegory, partial or in part
Of what the whole truth, in its glory, ought
To be. Sententious airs, be still—be not.

There are two sisters, twins, but they just share
A family name. For what they have to wear
And how they look are different, indeed.
The first of these two sisters, it's agreed,
Looks more to be a worker from the field.
Her skin is tan, for there's no shade to shield
Against the beating sun when tilling crops.
Both of her ears are pierced, and from the tops
There dangle rings, but more than beaten gold
Is there to mark her wretched trade: it's scrolled

Upon her skin with inky font that she
Is born to wait upon and serve the free.
The second sister has no callous palms
Or scars to show, nor melodrama psalms
To sing while at her providential toil.
In fact, the second doesn't plow the soil
But keeps the master's company within
The shelter of the house. That favored twin
Is sitting pretty at her rest and has
A place around the table there, whereas
The first must sup upon the scraps the kit-
Chen gives and eats where other servants sit.
For she, that sister first, was born to chains;
Yet o'er the second, only freedom reigns.
So now it is, these sisters, when they name
A child and give it suck, their station claims
That little tot as either free or bond.
All children from the servant girl are spawned
Into a life of servitude. But sons
And daughters born from free, these are the ones
Who never know of chains.

So, slave from slave
And free from free, the womb that crowns them gave
The rank. You see? Let's christen out some names
And call the first as Law (a cosmic shame
That I would dub a girl as such, but let
That go). The second sister, heavyset,
For she is at the Master's table day
And night, we'll call that woman—if I may
And might—we'll call her Promise. There: and now
It's done; my lame attempts to name the *fraus*
Was fun. Still, such comparisons are prone
To fail when closer up a light is shone
And blemishes or cracks upon the wall
Are brought to eye. How scrutiny makes fall
And peters out our glorious compares!
But let us push this more before we bear
It to the bin where it can feed the beaks

Of feathered scavengers and further reek
The heights and bounds of poor conjectured thought.
These women are two mountains, so it's taught
By Paul in his epistle long ago
When he desired that all Galatians know
How backward was belief that you could please
Our God with works, down on your hands and knees
And scrubbing floors of law. That's not the point
This story aims to make. And so, anoint
Your mind with contemplation oil. We'll dig
A little deeper past that pesky fig
Whose leaf keeps us from pushing further in.
(May all this serve as prologue.) Let's begin!
Now, Sarah, when again her husband had
Been told about the children God would add
Unto their family tree, had thought perhaps
They'd gone about it wrong. "Let time elapse
Till doomsday come," she said, "but change it can't
The fact that I'm a barren wife, and scant
Is any chance that I would bear a son
To you." The web her intuition spun
Would see a blunder caught. The old man looked
At her; he wondered what his wife had cooked
Behind those eyes. "I have—" his wife went on,
"I have this maid, this young Egyptian swan
Who's served me in all things. Well, almost all.
And she's been true, devoted in both small
And large affairs." Old Abram tugged the hairs
Around his beard. He still was unawares
To what his wife was driving at with such
A speech but thought he had at least the touch
If not the feel for his dear wife's intent.
"I'll give an ear," he thought, "but won't consent
To anything until I've had some prop-
Er time to think." He knew to window-shop
Around her needs while keeping both his lips
Well clamped and tight, on guard against those slips
Of tongue that see permission taking miles
Where inches should have been. And so, with smiles

He nodded at her, thinking, "Don't commit
To anything." His wife then said, "Come, sit
You down; you'll want a seat before you hear
The rest." And like a skillful puppeteer,
She lowered him upon a wooden stool
And thus began: "Now please don't ridicule
What I'm about to share. At first, it will
Sound odd, but if you give an ear and still
Your tongue until I've had a chance to get
It out, you'll see there's logic here; forget
That I'm a female for a tiny sec."
She cleared her throat and bellyached, "Gray decks
My flowing hair, and haggard wrinkles crease
My aging face. In truth, I'm not the niece
You made your wife in Ur so many moons
Ago. Now all my days and years lampoon
That youthful charm and fertile soil." The old
Man sized her up. She hadn't lost the gold
Of Nature's green (as Frost might say). As best
As he could tell, her body still possessed
The shape and zest of all her youth. Indeed,
She was as lush as May when farmers seed
The ground. "Bizarre she'd bring this up—" he mused,
"Want me to think she's past her prime." Confused,
He urged his wife then to continue on.
"In truth," she said, "my strength is all but gone.
I can't keep up with household chores, with meals,
With stitching clothes, because of age. It steals
The vigor from my blood. I've all but lost
The youth of Spring to Winter's stiffened frost;
It chokes my crop." She squeezed a tear just at
This point and snorted with her nose so that
It wouldn't leak. Her husband stopped her there,
His hand was raised. "Come now, my wife, despair
Will never change the facts. And what are they?
But that we have a body made from clay
And God's own breath within to make it act.
We're not spring chickens anymore, unpacked
Of shell and chirping for a worm." The girl

Drove in, "That's only part of it, the whirl
Of chores. There's one more thing affected by—"
Her husband cut her off: "Now by my thigh,
I think you keep up fine! The house is clean,
The meals taste good, and I care not a bean
How clothes are stitched." Since Abram saw that she
Had more to say and quite aggressively
Was ramping for round two, he thought it best
To spell it out for her and thus addressed
Sweet Sarah 'fore she spoke. "Just so I'm clear
On this, my gentle love, my wife, my dear-
Est pearl—to age is normal as the sun
Does set. But, wife, you still look great, and none
Beside you stand!" He felt he had done well
In how he'd handled that. The carousel
Of female thought required lots of tact.
In truth, he had a talent, sorting facts
From out façades like this. And he had no
Desire to see a blubberfest, a show
Designed to tug his sympathetic strings,
Coax his rheumatic joints to dance, and bring
Him fawning at her feet. He'd heard her say
Another time how, if she could, she'd pay
To have more help around the house. He'd put
An end to that; he was no tenderfoot
Fresh off the boat and knew that all this talk
Of age was just a ploy, a means to knock
Him off his well-attended guard. "There's more,"
Said that persistent wife, "to hear before
We end, my dear." "Oh, here it comes," he thought,
His cocksure pose upon the dunghill, taut
And ready for the crow. "It has to do
With how we haven't had a son. Who knew
When God had promised one we'd be beyond
The age?" She gathered wind. "Now don't respond
Until I've said it all," she warned with grace.
Her husband tripped more than he walked, his face
Had seemed to say. Sweet Sarah knew too well
How he would jump to false conclusions, spell

With letters she had given not his hand.
She'd speak it slow so he would understand.
"Now follow close: it is because of age
That now I cannot have a child, my stage
Of youth has curtains pulled. And not just chores
Have felt the strain, my dear. And so, therefore,
I think——" Old Abram couldn't hold his tongue
And had to cut her off before she'd sung
What he already knew she'd say. "I know
What's on your mind! You think a child will grow
To help around the house. I see this all
The time. Our friends have kids, and though they're small,
They still can handle chores and help. I know
You want a hand around the house and throw
Your age into my face because you think
It will persuade my pocketbook to clink
A coin and charter more to serve!" His bride
Just looked at him and thought, then mystified,
"He's missed all I have said. I see the gears
Are moving in his head, but still I fear
He's failed to grind the wheat." She held her tongue
As he joined in, "I know the days of young
Ability have all but slipped away
From you, but this is normal. Anyway,
The house looks fine, my dear. And so do you."
He kissed her then and wiped the residue
Of tears from off her moistened cheek. "I think,"
Sweet Sarah thought it better not to slink
Around the issue but be straight, "you should
Take my Egyptian maid! I think she could
Bear you the promised child. Take her to wive
A couple nights, and bed her down to swive.
Since God has thought it fit to seal my womb,
His promise may through slave be seen to bloom."

A mountain cave is dark. Though hammer-smacks
Of sun are golden in the noon, it's black
Within that cavity, and stepping out
Into the light will make one blind. No doubt

A hand is raised until the eyes adjust
Into the day.

So Abram's mind then must
Have felt adjusting to the words his wife
Had shared. Took by surprise, upon his life,
He never saw that coming, and what's more
Is that she meant it all. The calm décor
Across her face had not the slightest hint
That she was making jokes, nor was the glint
Within her eyes the kind that serves to tell
Of half-baked thoughts on paper plates to sell.
Abe thought it prudent, though, to tread with airs
Of caution, heedfulness, and ample care
Until her words were processed by his mind.
His wife in silence watched him then, quite kind
And patient, letting all that sink into
His thoughts. But in his gut, that old man knew
It wasn't right; the whole thing wore a stain
Of sullied aims. And yet, within his brain
He puzzled out, "God never said the child
Would come from Sarah's womb." Oh, meek and mild,
That wife of Abraham. How hard it all
Had been for her to bear. But protocols
Of womanhood see others' needs instead
Of self's with dinner and a snugging bed.
The more he thought on it, the more it took
To root. "The maid?" he said aloud and shook
His head to feign reluctance while a flash-
Ing spark was felt within his loins. That rash
Debate was quickly growing to a want.
The root was budding leaves and soon would flaunt
The fruit. "The maid?" he said again. "The maid,"
His wife returned then stealthily surveyed
Her husband's face. She'd caught a subtle whiff
Of some befouled desire. No hieroglyph
Needs tell how women will, by nature, hunt
What is perceived as weak, pick off the runt
From any pack

Just like a lioness
Will track a roe in midday heat, assess
Its movements hid behind a grassy patch;
She watches as the roe perks up to catch
The slightest noise upon the breeze. The stalks
Of grass are swaying as the soaring hawks
Command the heights. The feline lies quite still
Upon the ground and watches there until
It's time to strike. She waits and wets her jaws
As through the waving grass she squints, her claws
Sunk deep in caking earth.

So Sarah's gaze
Was leveled on that reoccurring phrase
As out it came again: "The maid." The root
Was now an oak and ready for some brute
To swing an axe and make a chair. "So that
We'll have a son!" growled Sarah, diplomat
And loving wife. Her blood was on the rise
The more they talked of it, for Abram's eyes
Revealed a little more than practical
Intent. There somewhere rattled in his skull
An impure thought. She wanted to extract
It with her teeth! But knowing how this lacked
Of what becomes a wife, she brought it down
A notch, composed her face, smoothed out her gown,
And said again, "So that we'll have a son.
That's why I brought it up—since we have none
To show for all your labor in my field.
Your plow beam's better days are done; it yields
No crop from out my dusty row. Perhaps
A greener field with fresher gingersnaps
Will do the trick for you." She made it clear
Enough. What more could she have done to steer
Her aging husband on the path to what
He wanted most, a son? So, Abram shut
His eyes to think. In truth, he'd had the same
Old types of thoughts himself, but to his shame,
He never had the guts to bring them up.

No, Sarah picked the fruit, and Abe would sup
His fill. If anything went wrong, he had
An out—it all had been her brainchild, sad
But true. What of the maid? Well, bittersweet
That part would be for that old man—a treat
For any man, if truth be told, regard-
Less of their age. And if that thought be hard
For you, dear reader, hard for you to grip
(So great your sensitivity), then slip
Your dull imagination in this dress.
Our hero, Abraham, no more or less,
Would not have firmed, arisen, or seen lift
To the occasion (if you get my drift)
Had not there been a craving in his heart.
The birds and bees, my friends, where all love starts.
The maid, you ask? Yes—duster, fishnet, and
The whole shebang. I say, these all made stand
That man and his religious long before
Viagra's vigor might assist. What's more
Is that the younger girl, that closely shaved
Egyptian warmth, is what the man had craved.
Now what am I suggesting at this spot?
Just that the man took pleasure here—was hot
To set aside his faith. He let it run
Amok because he wanted more, had spun
The promise on its head. His wants obeyed
And, consequently, a debacle made.
But hold on your imprecatory prayers
To see me hanged a moment more, for there
Is method here. Old Abe unclosed his eyes
And saw his wife in crouching pose, not shy
But ready for the pounce. *O graceful doe,*
O loving deer whose breasts would soon bring no
Or little satisfaction to your man.
That Sarah held his gaze while out the pan
He stepped to flame. She knew what he would say,
But on her life, she never thought the day
Would come when her own mouth pronounced and said
Her husband should another take to bed.

Abe didn't beat around the bush; he straight,
Like any pettifogger worth his weight,
Had told his wife that with her he agreed.
"I'll do this thing," he said, "but out of need,"
While all his shady wants, to not seem crude,
Were kept more to himself, quite well subdued
Behind phlegmatic stares. But then, he probed,
As if he were indifferent and robed
A saint of piety, "You think this course
Is best, my dear—coercive means to force
God's hand?" "Coercive means?" his wife returned,
Then not a little peeved! "He's all but turned
A deaf ear to our prayers! Yes, sure enough
He's there to make a promise and to stuff
Our ears with hope when suits His whim, but where
Is He when push meets shove? He doesn't care;
His promises are empty as my womb!
Now, either we go childless to the tomb
Or take the matter in our hands, my sire."
So Sarah spoke, accepting all the mire
And mud of sloppy thoughts her husband's mind
Would tread. She took one for the team, that kind-
Ly wife, and let great Reason, what makes sense
Unto the minds of Man, have rule. Suspense-
Ful faith would have to wait. They seized the day,
And Abraham with Sarah's handmaid lay.   (GENESIS 16:4)
Well, neither spoke of it, and after weeks
And months of Sarah hearing all the creaks
And moans that trickled out of Hagar's tent,
They saw the waist of that young maid ferment
With child. So, right or wrong, it had been done!
The elephant was in the room, and none
Would knock him off his little folding chair.
Each looker-on worked hard then not to stare
At that great mastodon as they went by.
But still, it swelled like some sore thumb whereby
Each person in the camp was in the know,
And gossip crooned like crickets in the glow
Of dusk. It just got worse when that young lass,

That ripe Egyptian bud, began to pass
Into her final term. No longer could
She wait on Sarah's needs; each time she stood
Or sat, a queasy sickness flipped her gut.
But Sarah simply thought the girl a slut,
A hussy, and a vamp, e'er since her man
Had bed her down! It may have been her plan
From that day one, but now it all had turned
To pasty ashes in her mouth. It burned
Her heated spleen to see her maid grow round
About the waist. Each day, more Sarah found
Her grace replaced with zero sympathy.
That slave was nothing special; why should she
Be on a pedestal above the rest
To act as if God's gift she were, possessed
Of golden crowns? When told to work, she'd cry,
And morning sickness was the alibi.

How easily glass splinters when it's broke,
And, just as easily, those pieces poke
And cut the skin to lodge beneath. They hide
Under the flowing blood, there fortified
Beside the bone. No matter how the cut
Is squeezed, it won't come out. Though oozing smut
And pus will drain the wound, that little piece
Of glass remains. In time, the pain will cease,
And forming skin will scar. But then the shard
Breaks loose and freely floats beneath the hard
And callous spot. It lives under the flesh.
So, each time it is touched, the pain is fresh
As when it first was cut. It bites like teeth
But cannot be removed.

Like so, beneath
The surface Sarah felt a splintered pain.
There was no help for it, and so in vain
She tried to wipe it from her mind. At last,
She thought to tell her husband, to lambast
That graybeard for his all-too-brilliant plot.

The trouble, after all, that man had brought.
"You are responsible for this," she said,
"And bear the bulk of blame! You are the head,
My patriarch." Like this, sweet Sarah spoke.
But when she saw her words did not provoke,
She ripped up one side, down the other tore.
"It's all your fault!" she yelled, and then she swore
That if he didn't act, God help them both,
He would regret it, and she gave her oath:
"I am the one who put her in your arms
And let you kiss her nether parts, her charms
For months on end to taste! Now she'd supplant
Your true and honest wife? By God, I can't
And will not stand for it!" She was incensed,
Poor thing, to say the least. The old man tensed
Under his wrinkled skin. His wife had put
Him on the spot and wanted him to foot
The bill on all this nonsense, likely in
Her head. Well, either way, he couldn't win,
No matter what response he gave. "Just deal
With it!" he said, annoyed, and tried to peel
The woman off his nerves. "She is your slave,
Not mine!" he griped. "I can't make her behave
As you would like. Why should I get between
Your female feud? I cannot intervene
While she is pregnant with my child. Just act
As you see fit, my wife. I'll trust the tact
Your kind discretion lends." Well, Sarah's kind
Discretion was on leave, and reassigned
To fill the void was brutal heartlessness.
By all accounts, she was a mean old cuss—
A total bitch unto the pregnant girl.
"Oh, what's the matter, clam who bears the pearl
My husband gave? You can't keep up? You need
Another break to rest? You only feed
Your laziness, you good-for-nothing stray!
Get up!" she'd yell and smack her on her way
To send her back to work. "Not on my watch,
You little skank. I want this place top-notch

Before we're through." And then she'd say things meant
To cut, to strike a deeper vein, torment
That girl, and stress her to the brink. "Perhaps,"
She thought, "she'll lose the child." So hatred traps
Our minds in wicked acts. "You know," she'd say,
"My husband mentioned, just the other day,
How disappointed he had been with you—
Said how he had expected more. Who knew
You couldn't satisfy a man?" She sighed
And whispered in her ear, "Well, on my pride,
A woman who can never please a man
Is not a woman in my eyes, nor can
She ever be." She sighed again. "I guess
You'll always be a slave who can't impress
A man in bed." And then she breathed in deep
And said, "Well, anyway, at least we'll keep
You here for chores. You better hope your child
Won't disappoint him like you have." She smiled
And walked away from her. So jealousy
Behaves, that counterfeited currency
That females mint to pass around between
Themselves, so distant from endearments seen
In men. Yes, jealousy they'd rather trade;
Forgive me if I call that spade a spade.
Well, Hagar had enough of that old bag
And couldn't stomach any more. The hag
Was out of line! For Sarah's mouth would fume
About the dumbest things, from how she'd broom
A floor to how she'd breathe when food was chewed.
It didn't matter what it was; she viewed
Poor Hagar's acts as never up to specs.
All symptoms proving jealousy infects.
Well, Hagar didn't need that woman's lip;
She'd strike out in the night, give her the slip,
And leave that battle-ax to scrub the floors
Herself. She'd rather go from door to door
And scratch a living begging bread than groan
Under the wings of that sadistic crone
A minute more. And so, she did. She packed

A carry-on, and so not to attract
Unwanted questions to her deed, she fled
Under the cloak of night, all else in bed
By Slumber's need. That Sarah wore a grin,
Stretched cheek to cheek, to taste the saccharine
Of victory, for in the morn she saw
The girl had gone. She wondered what the straw
Had been to break her handmaid's pregnant back
But didn't care that much. Her almanac
Predicted sunny skies just up ahead.
But her poor maid, as I have aforesaid,
Had left to strike out on her own, to wend
The desert's barren commonwealth, to fend
For meals and waterholes. By her own sweat
She'd make it work. She found a spring to wet
Her thirst and cool her brow. But while that maid
Was sitting there to rally strength, dismayed
About the way things hadn't gone, she heard
Someone approach. He didn't speak a word
But took to sit across from her. "How weird,"
Young Hagar thought, "that Someone just appeared
From who-knows-where and silently would sit
Across from me." He watched her for a bit
Then asked of her, "Where is it you call home,
And why on earth would now you seek to roam
About a place like this, poor slave and maid-
En girl of Sarah's house?" His voice had played
Upon the air like strings upon the harp.
Then Hagar answered Him; her words were sharp
And to the point, "I am her slave no more;
I've run away from her!" She knew the score
And consequences for her hasty acts.
She started then to cry, and dirty tracks
Of tears made march across her cheeks and carved
A zigzag path.

A dusty plain is starved
Of water till the storms arrive. The sky
Turns black with massing clouds, while birds that fly

And beasts that crawl both seek to congregate
Away from it. Then, heaven drops its weight,
A payload sent to drench the thirsty earth
With pouring rain. Those floods then stretch the girth
Of every stream and riverbed till out
They burst and cut their way through winding routes
That were unknown before.

Like so, the tears
Of Hagar cut her dusty cheeks like spears
That twist a ragged path through balmy flesh.
But when she finished up, she felt as fresh
As is the breeze when storms have had their say.
So Hagar, being done with tears—the spray
That both her eyes had mustered out—then dried
Her face and so composed herself and tried
To seem more welcoming. With that, the Man
Across from her then spoke and so began,
"I think you should return to what you feel
Is just a hopeless case. That whole ordeal
Is just a moment in the grander scheme.
You have to trust My plan, dear one; the theme
Of life is labor of a sort." So spoke
The Man, and then He moved in close and broke
The distance there had been before. He placed
His holy hands upon her pregnant waist
And smiled as He could feel the tiny kicks
Beneath. Just then He spoke a benedic-
Tion to them both and even prophesied
About her child. "You know," He said, "inside
Your womb there grows a son, a strapping lad.
I'm confident of that! You should be glad,
For you could not begin to even count
Or tally up the nations that amount
In you as I now speak. Know that I've heard
The tears you've cried and all the prayers your words
Have given breath. I've heard you all along,
Through all your misery and all the wrong
You've suffered at the hands of such a one

Who lets her actions by her hate be run.
But of the son you'll have, well, he'll be wild,
As stubborn as a mule—not reconciled
To any clan or tribe. He'll be at odds
With all, and everyone will raise their rods
To strike and take a swing at him. He's got
A rocky road ahead, for sure; I'm not
About to sugarcoat the facts." So spoke
The Man (or maybe God had thought to poke
Around in human flesh for just a while).
At any rate, He left then with a smile.
That meeting place, that spring in Shur, is named
"Our God has Seen." Yes, it's still there—well-framed
Between Kadesh and Bered's rocky ground.
And what then of the girl, you ask? She found
Her way to Abram's camp again and took
Her place within. She tried to overlook
The past; that all was water 'neath the bridge.
That house had been her steady patronage,
Her bread and butter, too. She wouldn't bite
That hand. She'd do her chores and not ignite
A confrontation with old Abram's wife.
She hadn't asked for any of the strife
Now on her plate in heavy portions heaped;
She hadn't asked to be third-party, steeped
Into their twisted little plan. And so,
Poor Hagar had consoled herself. She'd go
About her life and mind her own. Well, not
Long after she'd been back, her hips begot
The child, old Abram's son. Then all went still.

Consider, now, an arrow shot with skill
To strike a boar right where the hunter aims.
The wounded boar, in bloody rage, then maims
All in his path until he's burned his strength
Down to the last. His rampage slows, at length,
And death then clouds his eyes.

Like much the same,

Emotions slowed in Abram's camp. The flame
Of reckless words and childish acts was doused
With wet reality, and no more roused.
For tempers flourish, and in time, they're gone.
The sun still sets and rises with the dawn.
Admittedly, sweet Sarah's cheeks were flush
To see her maid with milk, that bosom lush
To nurse a child, while all that was engorged
On Sarah was the loathing, hotly forged
Beneath her wrinkled skin. She'd shut her trap
But not forget. In time, the earth made lap
Around the sun, by thirteen loops was yeared.
When all was resting fine—when all appeared
Content and so at ease with status quos
To stroll through afternoons and bungalows
Of stultified routine—this God decides
To show up on the scene and turn the tides
For Abram and his wife. And so God said,
"Before Me walk, and perfect be. I'll shed
My blessing unto you and those who come
From out your line, and countless will the sum
Of nations be that surely come from you.
And from your faithful stock I will issue
The perfect One to Whom you should aspire;
That all should trust in Him is My desire.
Redemption of the world this will install,
And, henceforth, *Abraham* your name I'll call.
For not by effort blessing comes to thee.
By promise Mine, redemption you will see.
And so you'll know My covenant is true,
Your barren wife shall give a son to you.
Though desolate, her garden's dusty row,
From Sarah's womb a son shall surely grow."
Old Abraham just laughed then at the thought
Of having kids. He was a hundred, not
A stud but more a gelding made by age.
"I think," old Abram said, "that at this stage
We should sort fact from fiction here. It's just
Not practical to think my rot and rust

Would give a son. I want it just as bad
As You, but facts of life are ironclad.
My withered loins have passed their premium.
Just make this simple: let Your blessing come
Now through the son that Sarah's bondmaid gave.   (GENESIS 17:18)
He'll fit the bill!" Like so he spoke. But grave
Was that Divine retort, and just as grim
God answered, "No!" And then He said to him,
"Perhaps I wasn't clear. So, listen up!
Within a year, My friend, you'll raise a cup
To toast the offspring out of Sarah's womb.
As for your other son, it is not doom
And gloom that I have planned. For sultan-might
Will flow throughout his veins, and by the height
Of heaven's throne, I'll swear by word and deed,
Twelve princes will be fathered from his seed.
But it is through the second son that I
Will keep My covenant; it is no lie!
You must believe and trust these words of Mine,
And so, by faith, will righteous be your line.
And one more thing, so that you have some skin
Here in the game: both you and all your kin
And even those you've bought over the years—
All males must cut their penis tip with shears
To take the flabby portion off." So said
The God of Abraham, without a shred
Of empathy. And then that LORD was gone,
Back to command the upper echelon
Of heaven's loft that overlooks the floor
Of earth and down on through the cellar door
Of Hades' realm. I'm sure you've heard the dead
Can travel fast, for who has never read
That eerie page whereon Bram Stoker wrote
That passage years ago? But now, devote
Some thought to how much faster could our Lord,
Unbound to flesh, have traveled to or toured
All that is seen and unseen at a glance.
But back to Abraham, his circumstance
More pressing with that plunge he was to take,

(Or rather snip). One hundred birthday cakes
He'd eaten up, one hundred candles blown.
And now his God was telling him a stone
Was needed, sharp upon the point, to keep
A covenant. Wake up! You dare not sleep
Here at this part and miss the finish line
I've labored hard to bring us to. Incline
That flagging mind a moment more; we're al-
Most there. Well, Abram found the wherewithal
To saddle up that horse like when you know
There can't be any turning back. And so,
With stone of flint, he kept the bloody pledge
And tithed his phallus-tip with sickle's edge.
And not just him, but all the males there, too—
Both born and bought were snipped alike. Who knew
That such an act would only serve in part,
That truest circumcision cuts the heart?

CHAPTER 10

Visitation

The passage we consider next is one
I call a fave. For which of you has none
You like far more than most in Holy Writ?
Of course, we all have favorites; to wit,
We make a reoccurring show upon
The doorsteps of these texts until their lawns
Are worn from truant tramps that would evade
The sidewalks off to school. We promenade
Those verses round the town because we think
We know the parts that mean the most, the links
That bind the whole of God's great chain. Persuade
Me this is not the case. Like you, I've played
That great reduction game whereby we shape
All complex things to self-help goals—escape
The irksome effort of a prolonged thought
With bullet points. Theology is not
So daunting when we shove it down (alas)

Between our carryout and yoga class.
All for the love of Cheerios and sit-
Com shows! Come, tell me—would it kill to fit
A little study in our day? I am,
Though, I suppose, not one to talk. I cram
My calendar as much as any mor-
On in this modern world, find books a bore
And rather fancy licking windowpanes
All afternoon. Such leisure is germane
For introspective thought, vocations spent
In one's own mind. Well, anyway, I vent
A little now but wanted to relate
How each of us have texts we gravitate
Toward. We leave off most to feed the birds
And gather dust, those poor, mistaken words.
I'm speaking here of that which we have named
As genealogies, for they are famed
For all the yawns they give—"then he begat,
And they begat"—and tell me, is not that
A turner of the page? Or what about
The books of law, that never-ending spout
Of somnolence, where pigeons, sheep, and goats
Atone for less-than-perfect acts, a moat
Of blood supplied around that meeting tent—
A system so complex that it has lent
To us some thirteen and six hundred laws.
Then, finally, before the prophets pause.
For prophets, on the whole, are bittersweet.
For we all know the minor ones complete
In one day's read, which really makes us feel
Like we are putting in the work. Conceal
The fact we understand a tenth of their
Original intent. But only stare
At that uncharted map of prophets who
Are known as major ones. My friend, both you
And I are lost in that expanse. We might
As well just lucky-dip all day and night
To gain some comprehensive views. Let's stick
To psalms and wisdom books, or let us pick

Our way through Paul's prolific opus penned—
The gospels, too, so that we comprehend
That moral goal, that great perfection set
For us to emulate, that silhouette
Of God and man combined, Emmanuel.
Oh, think on that! A sticky job to dwell
As God in human flesh. Think more: He would
Have been the perfect man, man as he should
Exist. Karl Barth explored this concept in
His work *God Here and Now.* He viewed the in-
Carnation as a thundering event.
Not just has God been clothed in skin; He's rent
That canvas known as Time, ripped it in two,
And stuck His foot between—a peekaboo
Of monumental scale. I, too, explore
The mystery of time a little more
In my amusing chapter on the death
Of Moses and his corpse. My poet breath
Expounds on how our God is not a slave
To Time—how Moses, though denied a grave,
Does not cheat Death's decay. You'll see that text
Yourself when it arrives in time. But next,
I've promised you that part I call a fave.
And let it come! I will no longer stave
You off with verbal flatulence, my bag
Of wind much like a prelude I am drag-
Ging round the dinner bell. Yet one more word
I'll beg before we sit to eat, absurd
That I should mention it at all. For who
Is not aware how much a tale can woo
One's curiosity—a fable or
An allegory, too? Perhaps these more.
Such are the lines I cherish most and glean
My bottles from, my vineyard mavourneen!
For tales are meant to teach! Yet are they not
Just simple narratives? Not just. We're taught
By stories of all kinds! I'd go so far
To say that, though the lengthy seminar
Is fitting in its way, the story told

Has more the bang for buck—sees buttonholed
The straying mind as much as those austere
To sniff a page. Was not our Lord's career,
At least in part, for telling parables?
And why? Because the story sits our skulls
To incubate a thought; sometimes it's hatched
A will to act, or maybe it's dispatched
A hive of hornets there, armed to the sting—
Not so much to the teeth, to let old king
Conviction have his say. Think of the tale
That Nathan told and how it did derail
A murderer from off his reckless path.
King David heard and, being filled with wrath—
Not knowing who that story was about—
Demanded his own judgment carry out.
I doubt a seminar could do the same.
A story is a prying bug whose aim
Is getting underneath the skin. Perhaps
That's why we might avoid the things, collapse
Into the arms of something less ambig-
Uous. We put our saws to work on twigs
And branches; anything with leaves we trim.
We take the forest down to stumps, then prim
The rest with Scotts' four steps. We want to keep
It simple as we can, and up we heap
Those piles of dogma high, the black and white
Like Tinker Toys, constructing little right-
And-wrong displays on spreadsheet charts for quick
And quoting needs. We toss the story, stick
To what we've memorized. We like the road
That's smooth to ride; we like what has been mowed.
We plant a flag like some explorer on
An Arctic trip or climbers when their brawn
Has seen them scale an Everest. They plant
A flag to say they've beat the thing. I'd grant
That's some achievement made, but hold the train
To say you've conquered it. We should refrain
From such remarks or find the mountain cuts
Our throats to spite the pompous boast that struts

Our face. Well, highlighters to sacred texts
Work much the same as flags. What once perplexed
Is neon stained. And this whole practice means
To turn our feral script to golf course greens.
It's foolishness to think we understand
Those things God never meant us to. We brand
And label, call out text by verse—"John three-
Sixteen and Proverbs thirty-one"—a sea
Of numbers where we all can seek to drown
The fact our competence is Shantytown.
No, not for me. I'll beat upon the door
Of someplace else and wander corridors
Of mystery. O Socrates, your ad-
Age still rings true, that any wisdom had
Is found when you admit to nothing know.
And Solomon, who rides the undertow
Of some philosopher, was said to say
That wisdom starts with fearing God, to weigh
Your understanding in the scales of how
You've come to know our God and if you bow
Before His throne, your face pressed into dirt.
I think they'd both agree when I assert
That wisdom is a humble thing—that it
Will not soon pride or arrogance admit.
And still, we want to know; we want to catch
A glimpse behind the curtain. And we scratch
That itch and tumble rabbit holes to find
What's buried there. Or maybe we're the kind
Of person quite content to make a meal
Of what the wordy commentators deal
Out to our gaping beaks in mangled forms.
They're giving us regurgitated worms.
Or maybe we can feel no itch at all,
Our skin too calloused, varicosed, and dull
To have sensations of that fleeting kind.
Whatever your case be, how you're defined
Within and so content, work out your own
Salvation, then. For my part, I won't moan
About the path I have; I'll make the most

Of it. I'll sip my wine and even toast
This opaque glass I'm looking through. But now
I'll speak about my favored text and plow
Ahead upon this field that reaches to
My death. (Oh, God—I'm so dramatic, through
And through.) But listen to me now, my friend,
Though well I know the longer way I tend
To take in such affairs. You've asked my goal
In all of this? It is so that the soul
Of our pursuit is mystery, to seek
That thing we'll never find, to hold mystique
Above our need to know, to not demand
An answer all the time. Yes, with me stand
For mystery and suck the lollipop
Of childlike faith a little more. We'll stop
Our questions when our God sees fit to close
His holy mouth. For now, we will repose
Together in that country of the mind
And take our leave for afternoons, inclined
For nothing more than simple wonder at
The way a cloud looks like a biscuit, flat
Against the skillet of the sky. You know,
Since I was young—before the vertigo
Would haunt my awkward bends, before the spurs
Had paralyzed my heels, made loiterers
Of both my feet—yes, when the throes of youth
Were still my vital pulse, I loved, in truth,
Those stories where the Bible gave to me
A view of some Divine encounter, be
It either God or angel in the guise
Of flesh. A preincarnate glimpse that eyes
Could tangibly perceive. The author of
The Hebrews made a point to say, above
All else, we should be kind to strangers and
To entertain each guest who comes to stand
Upon our step, to give each one our hos-
Pitality. Moreover, to emboss
Our acts with charity of will. For we
Don't know when such an opportunity

Presents itself to us. Compared to men,
The angels look the same. Consider then
Those times you might have intersected with
An angel dressed as man. Let go the myth
Of wings, my novel friend; they are but bells
And whistles for the Seraphim who dwell
The throne. But what a tantalizing thought
It is; it speaks more than a polyglot,
If you ask me, that in our daily grind
You may have seen or spoken to or dined
With someone who in heaven lays their head.
At least, that's what the Hebrews' author said.
Now, if that author's words are taken true,
You couldn't know when such a rendezvous
Had thus occurred—and that's the point. And so,
When at my start—my *in principio*
To Christian faith, there toying with the build-
Ing blocks of patriarchs—I ever filled
My mind with such the same. My favorite,
If you've not guessed (or guessed how to acquit
Me from this introduction yet), is that
Of Abraham when those three angels sat
With him on Mamre's plain. Yes, this part speaks
To me above the weighty rest, unique
As any Studebaker freshly waxed
And glimmering on freeways overtaxed
With Teslas, Subarus, and Cherokees.
Oh, maybe it's just George C. Scott who sees
That part played out so well. I don't know why
That story stands up high and typifies
The pinnacle of humble faith. But some-
Thing's in all tales that tell of angels com-
Ing down to men. There's also something in
The way our hero makes his case and wins
His way with God when these three go to leave.
I simply like the scene and make-believe
I'm there with them. Imagine it with me:
We're there with Abraham and see these three
Approach. "But wait," you warn, "the text says they

Were simply there when he looked up." That may
Well be the case, but have semantics put
Away for now. An absolutist foot
Will pass up dollars for a dime to grab,
And may our God see fit to keep such drab
And dribble practice far from me. We're there
And sitting underneath the oaks that bear
The brunt of all that midday heat. The leaves
Are tossing with each gust of wind and heave
Their undersides upturned as to divulge
A secret green. They rustle and indulge
Themselves, confessing as they paint in shades,
A flowing brush stroke with each branch that's swayed.
We look out from our trees and brave the glare
Of sun, relentless in its blinding stare
Of bludgeoned white. We squint and do our best
To recognize those figures cloaked or dressed
In who-knows-what an angel wears. At last,
They're close enough for us to see, roughcast
In all the flotsam of a desert trek.
Our hero stands and runs to meet their beck
And call—tells them to rest, that he'll prepare
A meal for them and water bowls to spare
Their feet from dusty aches of journeys long.
And Sarah, Abram's wife, then tags along
By filching looks behind the canvas tent
And filling bowls of wine. With these she sent
The bread prepared and roasted lamb, as well.
But let's get to the story now and tell
It as our text describes. And so, these three
Were served a meal and ate it languidly
Beneath the oaks of Mamre's plain. And when
They had their fill of food and drink, these men
Or angels (one of them, at least) had asked,
"Where is your wife, my friend, the one now tasked
With dishes for the meal we all enjoyed?"
Then Abraham, a little paranoid
That they would ask about his wife, replied,
"She's in the tent, my Lord, and occupied

As you suggest." The Stranger who had posed
That question eyed the tent and seemed disposed
To speak a little more about the girl.
He dipped some wine and gave His cup a swirl.
The sloshing red resembled waves that mass
And beat the shore—an ocean in His glass,
It seemed to Abraham, at least, so great
His fist and grip. With motions firm as fate,
He moved that glass then underneath His nose
And sniffed. His manner was of one who knows
How to enjoy the luxuries of taste
And smell. He drank it off, and then He placed
The cup back on the fine upholstered rug
Whereon they sat. Now Sarah was quite snug
Behind the canvas door, there dropping eaves
And listening to all that fabric sleeve
Would lend her ear. It served to filter out
The wind and swell each whispered word to shouts.
She heard that Stranger, God concealed, as He
Then said, "It's so enjoyable for Me
To kick My feet up and to share this meal
You have prepared. Such things have an appeal
For all who toil beneath the heavens' sun.
Who doesn't feel the urge, when they are done
With all their sweaty labor, to recline
And feast on what has been produced—the wine
And bread, the curds and cream? It has been sown
Into our very blood and marrowbone
That we should reap those things we put to seed."
Old Abram gave a nod, said he agreed
With all the Stranger spoke. And then that One,
That holy One, that Stranger and that Son
Of mystery, did breathe in deep and said,
"I do not want to go; in fact, I dread
What we intend to do. But still, I must.
Yet I will leave you with some hope and trust
It is enough to get you through. This time
Next year I will be back; the autumn clime
Will be about the same." (Now, don't forget

That barren Sarah was all ears to get
Each word fresh off the press as God spoke on.)
"Yes, right about this time next year, when dawns
Are coming later in the day, we'll share
A meal again. By then your wife will bear
A son to you. Indeed, she'll bear him by
The time that I return." Just then, a cry
Was heard: a blurted, bouncing, muffled laugh!
It sounded like a jackal panting, half
In scoff and half amused. The strangers turned
Their heads to hear the noise, for each discerned
The laugh that came from out the canvas tent.
Old Abram swallowed hard; he would have rent
His clothes for all the shame to come. Although,
His wife was unaware to what a show
She'd given them. She didn't think those guests
Had heard her tiny laugh. Indeed, with jest
Still growing bold upon her heart, she said,
More to herself than anyone instead,
"Shall I, with cycle fluids long run cold,
Find youthful pleasure with my lord, so old?"   (GENESIS 18:12)
Both Abram and his wife would eat a slice
Of humble pie before the end. Suffice
It then to say that Sarah laughed, and those
In earshot heard it all. Now, I suppose
The ears of angels are much more adept
Than those of men, for mortal ears have crept
Or rather have been crept upon by age.
I mean, the old are deaf! I'll grant they're sage
In all that gray—but also deaf. I trip
Here on myself and fumble penmanship.
My point is that an angel hears much bet-
Ter than a man who swings the bassinet
Of years. And Abraham, if anything,
Was old. Perhaps he hadn't heard the thing
At all (the laugh, that is), for without doubt
Our text says she laughed to herself; no shout
Or grand display but quite discreet behind
A twitching curtain was that laugh confined.

But that's what makes it great! The sound of it
Was like a thunderbolt that came to sit
Upon the ears of those three guests. And she,
That wife, did not believe her secrecy
Was compromised. She didn't have a clue
About the ears of angels as do you
And I. That said, when all the echo died
Away from Sarah's laugh, the lively stride
That conversation kept was made to cease.

Think on a forest now, how it's at peace,
When night has come to weigh the eyes of all
That move. The rays of moon then gently fall
Between the branches, still in windlessness,
And light the trunks of ancient elms, no less
Than stoic in their posts assigned to guard
The hours of vacancy beneath the starred
And lonely skies that shine above in maps
No man can read.

Like so did all collapse
Into a silent still. You could have heard
A pin then drop upon the sand. No bird
Gave call; the wind left off unseen campaigns
Of blustering. The very earth, inane
In that one mindless job, forgot to turn.
Yes, all went very still with a concern
To hear what would come next and occupied
The edge of its own seat, ears open wide
In hopes to catch the sovereign LORD's reply.
Our God was calm; He didn't vilify
The girl for such a smack across His sa-
Cred face; He didn't throw a fit and say
He'd take His marbles and go home. Oh, no—
He leaned against the tree as if to show
Disinterest, and then He took to clean
His fingernails of any grit then seen
Beneath. And when some time had so been passed,
He slowly raised His holy eyes and cast

A glare at Abraham. And thus, He gave
A question to the man. "Why does your brave
And saucy wife now laugh? Why does she joke
That she would have a son or have a poke
When she is old?" Poor Abram sat there speech-
Less on the rug and let that question reach
The crushing depth within his lower bowel.
It bounced against that floor, and then a foul
Taste beached itself within his mouth. The old
Man felt just like a fish there flopping cold
And gasping for a breath, like he had just
Been clubbed about the skull by some robust
And weighty priest. Let's stop our tale a mo-
Ment here and talk. Now I am all gung-ho
To have this laugh so loud it's heard by all
Beneath the clouds above. Still, by Saint Paul,
I cannot bring myself to think of it
As being louder than a whispered whit
Of noise. That means old Abram didn't hear
The thing. So, when God probed that musketeer
About the laugh, old Abram sat there sword-
Less on the rug and quite the overlord
Of Ignorance. That man was lost, a deer
With headlights shining off its eyes—sincere
But caught off guard. That said, it wasn't long
To get it squared; it was the same old song
He'd sung himself—the laugh, that is. And so,
When God said Sarah laughed, put on a show
For Him and both His friends, the old man took
Those words for truth, no questions asked. He shook
His head in shame. How did he then respond
To such embarrassment? Was anger spawned
From out his blush, or did that mild and meek
Of men pull out his rule of thumb and seek
To teach a thing or two? It's safe to say
That's not how things turned out. Oh, no—old Gray
Was just a modest chap and not the sort
To give machismo any kind of sport.
He wouldn't drag his wife from out the tent

To answer such a charge, nor could his bent
And feeble frame have done such things. So, leave
Those narrow-minded thoughts to misconceive
All by their lonesome selves. Those shoes are way
Too small and give us hammertoes when play-
Ing little piggy has to market went.
His wife was not so simple nor so pent
Within our male-constructed walls. But hark,
Let's get back to our dazed old patriarch,
Old Gray, whom we have left upon the rug
To quake within his sandal-boots and shrug
His shoulders up and down quite aimlessly.
Now, Sarah heard that question capably
Behind the tent. It made her hot and rash;
Her cheeks went flush from all the balderdash
That welled within. She found her acts informed
By some deficient thoughts, and out she stormed
From her great hiding place to vindicate
Herself and plead her case before that great,
That Lordly potentate of heaven veiled.
"No, I did not!" Indignantly she wailed,
And wiped the bangs from off her forehead sweat,
That matriarch, that childless suffragette.
She steadied up the bus and clarified,
"I didn't laugh. How could you think that I'd
Make light of all You said, of all You shared?
I'd never laugh at that," the girl declared.
But truth, my friend, from God is never hid.
"I beg to differ, ma'am," God said. "You did.   (Genesis 18:15)
We heard it plain as day, both I and these."
He pointed to His friends then took His ease
Against the tree. He didn't seem upset,
And this disarmed the girl. There was no threat,
And she calmed down. But then she asked and said,
In honest airs and without any dread,
"You really think I'll have a son, my Sage,
Now that I'm old and dried up in my age?"
The LORD replied, His bearing never jarred,
"Am I some mortal that this would be hard?"

The visitors then laughed! Their tone was no-
Thing to be feared and not the least draco-
Nian at all. They dipped their glasses in
The bowel of wine and asked the girl to pin
Herself upon the rug with them. God bid
Sweet Sarah also raise a glass. Amid
The heat of afternoon they'd have a toast.
God spoke then to the girl more than the host.
"Rejoice, thou barren, you who labor not;
For childless tears your God has not forgot.
And 'fore that final day and eventide,
You'll have more kids than Youth itself provides."
All drank the flaming, potent ferment down
Till it was gone. That wine then worked to drown
Their disbelief and fill the void with some-
Thing else. Yes, something worked like opium
Upon their minds, allowing just a peek
At possibility, enough to tweak
A cynic into faith. Imagine this—
Or you might even fondly reminisce,
If your experience informs; indulge
Me if that be the case—I'll kneed a bulge
Of yeast into another's dough. What if
Those three had come to visit you, the cliff
Of life decisions at your feet? I mean,
If you were pondering your path unseen
Ahead or at the crossroads where a choice
Had need be made. You thought you'd heard the voice
Of God within your head, His will pronounced
Or just a promise that had been announced
To you. Yes, you might trust it, but how much
Would it convince you if you'd felt the touch
Of God, a finger grazed when passing food
Or cups of wine? I mean the real, the nude,
Ungloved, and meaty hand of God Most High
Has brushed against your thumb. Now, don't deny
That He has ever taken human form,
That God is spirit and does not conform
To arms and legs, to hair and teeth. No doubt

You think the earth an evil thing and route
All that has shape and form to discard bins
Up stacked for judgment day. Oh, yang and yin,
Where are you now? Alas, I am not of
That strict, ascetic camp and work to shove
My gob in ways that feed my plump physique.
Did not God say all things were good that bleak
And dreary day the earth was made? Well, let
Me ask you this; your strawman statuette
Will have his pants pulled down: How do you come
To terms, then, with our text, that bothersome
Collection of remarks, when it makes claim
And calls the Leader of the three by name?
The moniker of God, grand as the dawn,
None other than the tetragrammaton.
Now that is one ten-dollar word. The ver-
Y name the Hebrews tie in knots and wear
Around beneath their shirts and to this day
Refuse to speak all out of fear they'll say
It wrong. An issue with the vowels, you see?
Now you cannot deny and must agree
The writer of our ancient text believed
Our God was there in flesh. That writer weaved
A tale where He (our God, that is) then ate
A meal. He had to chew, to salivate
And taste. Who knows the ins and outs of el-
Ements comprising Him, and who could tell
How such things really work? It matters not
And is a pointless web. So, don't get caught
In it. Remember what I wrote before
About the mystery? Let us explore
The text with wonder, not with grids exact.
He ate and He was there—take it as fact.
The pure and unadulterated form
Of inquiry should always be the norm.
Thank Occam for his razor since we find
With it our answers on those paths defined
By least resistance to the ends—which means
The simple answer blows to smithereens

Complexities that keep us from the true.
But let's get back into the text; corkscrew
Another bottle if you must. Now when
The three were done with all the meal and then
Had shouldered up their haversacks to leave,
Our God then said unto Himself, believe
It so or not, "How could I ever hide
What I intend to do, this heavy chide
To come on Sodom's soil? How could I hold
This from the mind of Abraham, My old
And faithful friend? I have to tell the man
What I intend to do, tell him My plan.
I will not keep such things away from him."
Like so the God of men and cherubim
Had said unto Himself. He motioned then
To Abraham while both the other men
Went on ahead. "Come walk with me," God said.
"And let us talk as friend to friend. We'll tread
A slower pace, for there's a matter that
I'd like to speak about. A little chat
Will help, will ease the load from off My chest."
Like so, God spoke and hoped to decongest
His cluttered thoughts cathartically. "You know,"
The God of all that is began, "we go
To see the land of Sodom now. It's come
To My attention that all heathendom
Is rampant there. Indeed, I've heard a cry
Against that place, and I can't wink my eye
Pretending it's okay. I need to see
And test out Sodom's hospitality;
I hear it's all but shot. On top of this,
I've heard their ways deny and would dismiss
The fruitful mandate I have set in place.
I want some concrete evidence to base
My judgments on." Like so, the One who fits
All souls to mortal shells and neatly knits
Them there within made done with speech. Old Gray
Just looked at Him, not knowing what to say
Or how God might respond. Abe knew that Lot

Now lived in Sodom's town, some big hotshot
With city life. The old man felt a tinge
Of guilt for that. It almost made him cringe,
For he had given Lot the choice to pick
Between the Jordan plain, with hardships thick
As thieves, or he could head to Sodom's soil
Where money grew on trees and didn't spoil.
Old Abraham made sure of all his words
Before he spoke. He didn't want them slurred
Or hashed up in the least; he'd need both tact
And subtlety of speech. He would, in fact,
Advise the Lord on high. And so, the old
Man jumped right in, deciding to be bold.
He spoke these words: "I see that more and more
You have Your work cut out for You, to tour
That place and see if things are as You've heard."
Now Abram was aware that Sodom blurred
All sense of hospitality, would take
Their guests and make them squeal, for pity's sake.
Those Sodom-men were highwaymen who'd rob
The rear of its virginity, all throb
And ache for uninvited thrills. The old
Man knew what they were like; the centerfolds
Of Sodom were no secret to be kept.
All lines to sand that town had overstepped.
But still, his nephew lived among that crew,
And how much Lot was like the same, who knew?
So, Abram asked of God, as if he'd weep,
"Will You, the righteous with the wicked, sweep?
I'm sure You'd never do a thing like that,
To make the righteous suffer tit for tat
What wicked people buttered to their bread.
That's so beneath You, Lord. I know instead
You'll do whatever's right. I have no doubt
That God on High will justice carry out."
Old Abram took a breath, looked at his God
And spoke, but more it seemed he hemmed and hawed
Around in afterthoughts, "Let's say You find
Some fifty righteous, would You be inclined

To spare the city for the sake of these?"
Then God, so reticent in balconies
Of secrecy, had said, "Yes, I would spare
It for the sake of fifty righteous there."
"Boy, that was quick," old Abram thought. "I should
Have asked for less." His confidence then stood
Up higher than before. He cracked the knuck-
Les of his mind and flexed. With any luck,
He'd dicker down that price from what he thought
Might be a number hard to reach and not
So feasible. "I'm just a little bit
Concerned, is all," said Abraham. "Permit
Another question, then. You know, it's just
That fifty might be hard to find. I trust
If You could locate only forty-five
You'd feel the same, that You would keep alive
That city for just forty-five." And God
Then didn't hesitate but gave a nod
That He agreed. He said, "Yes, if there were
But five of fifty lacked, I'd still deter
My wrath and see it backed away." But well
Before those words had left God's mouth, the swell
Of syllables still on His holy tongue,
Old Abe was chiming in again. He'd sung
A lower price. He was an auctioneer,
But oddly so enough, he had his gear
Stuck in reverse. For if the truth be told,
The lower number was the better sold.
"What if You find but forty there?" Old Gray
Could bargain hard and keep the pace all day.
Momentum manifold, Abe's every sail
Then bellied out with that propelling gale
Of wind. But God did never miss a beat
In His reply, and swift as any feet
Familiar with their dance did say these words:
"For forty's sake, I'd see My wrath deterred."
Still, Abram couldn't let it rest. He knew
Enough of Sodom's brood to know that few
And far between were of a righteous bent,

And fearing what just might be consequent
If God did fail to find the quota set,
He pushed a lower number—hedged his bets,
As some might say. "I know I'm only ash
And dust," old Abe began. "My words are brash
And more uncouth than I would have them be.
Yet still I'll speak to You as any free
Man might. I hope You are not angry when
I ask this thing. It's just that forty men
Might be a number that is hard to count."
Abe's pertinacity was tantamount
To that of Sisyphus who pushes on
A boulder day and night, who never yawns
Or takes a break in hopes he might succeed.
Like so did Abraham then intercede
For Sodom's sake. "Suppose you only find
But thirty there. Will You see their fate signed
The same or have them share the same dessert
That wicked people eat? I'm only dirt
And mud; You understand. I'm sure God knows
What is the proper path and how to show
His justice to them both." So Abram spoke,
And God, when He considered this, then broke
The silence with these words. "If thirty right-
Eous people I can find, I will not smite
That place with Judgment's hand nor see them dined
Upon the same cuisine." Like so, the kind-
Ly God of heaven made reply. "I hope,"
Old Abe pulled hard against that same old rope
And said, "I hope You are not angry, but
I still just need to ask" (so obstinate
For nephew's sake). "I have to ask this thing.
I know I'm only dust and ash and bring
My petty troubles to Your ears. But still,
I have to speak. It sounds like overkill,
I know. It must. But what, my Lord—what if
You only twenty find? Will You be stiff
And rigid in Your mood, and will You lump
Them all into the same old pot to dump

Them out, the baby and the sullied bath?"
God answered Abraham and said, "My wrath
Will be on hold if I find twenty there."
With that the LORD was gone, and it is fair
To say that His departure was the same
As was the manner in which He first came.
That means that it was cloaked in mystery.
And for the ones just tuning in, you see,
We need not wonder, "Did He disappear,
Or vanish, or just walk away?" It's clear
He left; let's leave it there so much as are
The facts concerned. The story, though bizarre,
Will tell us more. He left when golden Sun
Was easing off his axe to grind and done
With blatant exhibitions of his strength.
Then Abram ambled back to camp; at length,
His thoughts were still consumed with all the talk
That he and God had done. He knew the clock
Was ticking down. He wondered, though, just had
He done enough for Sodom's land, to pad
It from the Lord's almighty hand? All these
And other thoughts and even homilies
Of simple living and the simple life
Were mixed upon that old man's mind, and strife
Was in there, too. And then old Abram did
A thing that he did not expect: he slid
Some words across his lips, more quiet than
A whisper told by butterflies. Words ran
Across his tongue, feet light as air, and said
"My Lord, what if there're only ten?" So pled
The dust and ash of Abram's mouth in tones
The speaker couldn't even hear. Well, stones
Have voices, do they not? What heavy words
Do those cold burdens speak? Well, God had heard
Old Abraham and answered in a voice
Like wind, "I'll save that place for ten." The choice
Of God was made and written down and sealed.
Well, later on that day, when Abram kneeled
Upon the rug—the same rug he had used

That day at lunch to serve the guests—he mused
About the day. The whole thing wore him out.
He felt a weariness come on; no doubt
He'd go down hard when heavy sleep arrived.
Yet one thing kept the man awake, deprived
Him of his rest. One simple thought still kicked
Around his mind, and he could not evict
That thought, try as he might. It pitched a tent
And had a bonfire going then, prevent-
Ing him from needed sleep. It was a thought
And only was a thought, for it had not
The breath of life. "I should have asked for four."
But answer from his God was heard no more.

CHAPTER 11

In the Know

What does it mean to be a righteous man?
Put off the urge to jump the caravan
To Answer Town, and think about it for
A sec. What comes into your mind before
Those ready definitions crystallize
To meet the cause? What better testifies
Before the bias shows its claws? What makes
A righteous man, I ask? Without mistake,
It's when one does the things they know are right.
How's that for pithy answer, erudite
And to the point? To do those things we know
Are right does make a righteous man. Ergo,
The word explains itself. And yet it begs
Another sip to polish off those dregs
That float down by the stem. For I said *what*
We know is right. I will be obstinate
About this point, that what we know is linked

Somehow to right and wrong. The two are synced,
Joined at the hip, and one can't even stand
Without the other there to hold its hand.
You need to have some knowledge of a thing
Before you can reject it or can bring
Your actions out of line (or into check)
With it. It's by the spine we straight the neck.
Likewise, if you don't know what you should do,
Then how, in turn, could guilt be charged to you
When you have failed to do the thing required?
All wrong is just intent! Now, was it sired
From out rebellious loins or those that would
Deny the will? Rough Schopenhauer had stood
Up to proclaim this most his life with all
His crazy hair—that man's own will, his gall,
Does make the choice; on this the rest depends!
We hear the rule, our mind will apprehend,
And then we choose the way in which we'll act.
How easily we then deduce this fact
That there is not a sinful thing just in
And of itself. Intent becomes the pin
That locks it all in place. Consider James,
The brother of our Lord, whose other name
Was James the Just, the Righteous one. That man
Had served as head of God's own church and ran
It well before old Petros took the reins.
In his epistle, that same man explains
<u>That those who know to do a thing that's good,</u>   (JAMES 4:17)
<u>And then to do it not, it's understood,</u>
<u>That thing for them undone becomes a sin.</u>
Let all philosophers renounce their grins
As we proceed with caution and with care,
For such endeavors may do well to share
An ounce of grace with academic chug.
It's rather nice when cream tops off the mug.
Let's hear the text again. <u>For those who know</u>
<u>To do a thing that's good, for them to blow</u>
<u>It off as meaningless—that's when they miss</u>
<u>The mark.</u> To Miss the Mark: To candy kiss

With euphemistic phrase when one embarks
To parse a wrong. Just say we missed the mark
And have your bite defanged. I know my speech
May sound and look as if I mean to preach,
But be assured, my fellow sinner, that
A Hedonistic echo ever chats
The walls that buttress up my mind. Take no
Offense. I'd have you waving cheerio
To guilty conscience cares in no time flat.
For God is God, and man is man, and that
Is that. Let's argue not against the things
He's sown into the world, the furnishings
Our souls will sit upon in comfort or
In agitated angst. Our very core
Can never change; the acorn will become
The oak; the Greeks will conquer Ilium.
I'm saying that I feel no deep-set urge
To swap with definitions or to purge
Vernacular from edges unrefined.
I still, by Jove, will ever be inclined
To call a spade a spade and even hope
Those words of Wilde have not the broadened scope
To cover me. Remember when he penned
That those who call a spade a spade should spend
Their days in using one? Perhaps you don't.
It matters not. I never want and won't
Go kick against the goads. I say take hold
Of all that shakes, and ride that coaster rolled
Until it breaks. You will not change a mite
With any fluff of words to overwrite
Those things engraved with adamantine chis-
El strikes on God's own palms. It takes no whiz
To gather things are just the way they are!
How's that for waxing deep? My seminar
Is almost through, so stay with me! Let's get
Back to our text—and since I quite forget
Where we left off a bit ago, we'll hear
It one more time, just so we both are clear.
<u>For those who know the right thing they should do</u>

<u>And fail in turn to do the thing they knew</u>
<u>Was right—that person sins.</u> Now this here speaks
Of when omission plagues our acts, critiques
How we rejoin the call. Now, there are two
And just two types of sins: I'll follow through
With naming them as sins committed and
Omitted. Now, whenever we have planned
Divergence from a standard set in place,
Committed sin is done—to our disgrace.
And that's when rules inform, so that we know
What we should do. Think of Pinocchio
And when Geppetto said to go to school.
He didn't listen and, much like a fool,
Had hitched a ride for Pleasure Island's shores.
I love that scene, that clever metaphor
Of life! How much our choices make an ass
Of us and have us munch the vast morass
Of baser thoughts. Still, there are things the rules
Will fail to touch upon, and now comes cruel
Old moral code with conscience as his guide.
I think there is a cricket, teary-eyed
And tapping at my windowpane. We hear
A voice inside our spacious heads and steer
Our acts to match with it. It is our choice
To either follow or reject the voice.
But just remember this: that, if we snore
At opportunity—choose to ignore
That we had ever seen the thing—well, that
Is when inaction causes crime. We've sat
Upon our hands, and an omitted sin
Is done. Or think of Luther, Augustin-
ian monk, when called to stand before the board
(The Diet formed), he had addressed the horde
Without equivocation—nothing wry
Or off the point. He said it cut and dry:
"To speak against my conscience is not right
Or safe." Where is the day when such a might,
What's more, conviction held its sway to rule
Our lives? We're too much in the vestibule

Of luxury; our modern world grows numb
While sucking at the dangling tits of scum
And scabby Apathy. Well, not for me!
I'll latch my lips on nipples that will see
Me drinking deep on what the great ones passed
Our way. I'll tune in to the telecast
That lifts our race up higher than it was
Before. So great our heritage because
There were those ones who put their thoughts to page.
Oh, thank the maker, Gutenberg, that sage
Of ink! Or thank the ones who memorized
By word of mouth. How much they must have prized
Their wisdom gained and spent both night and day
Verbatim to repeat, verbatim say.
We toss off this inheritance, for shame—
And right in turn, we've nothing great to claim.
I think I've finished with this diatribe
Against the modern push to superscribe
The history of thought as frivolous.
Back to our text, what conscience speaks to us
Is what we should and need to do. But right
Or wrong can conscience be, and still, in spite
Of that, we have to act in line with it.
If not, omitted sin we will commit.
So, if that cricket in my ear said I
Should give my toasty ham and swiss on rye
To some repugnant beggar on the street,
And then I fail to heed the call, retreat
Into a corner where I stuff my maw
In peace—well, that is when I break the law.
The law my conscience made, that is my own
Internal code. So, just as Hamlet moans
That "Conscience does make cowards of us all,"
We also groan at how our conscience calls
On us to act. It is the voice that tells
Us what is right and with conviction spells
It out for us. It's how we know. But do
It not, that knowing makes us sin. Virtue
Depends on what we know and on intent.

It stands to reason, then, that time we've spent
In learning has been time that's gone amiss.
Moreover, yes—that ignorance is bliss!
Let's go a little further with this chain
Of thought: the ones who know, the fluffy mane
Of education's head, these ones must be
The greatest sinners of the lot. We see
That Paul, apostle to the total globe
Save Palestine, put on himself the robe
Called Chief-of-All-Who-Sin. No doubt that some
Of Paul's self-loathing sprang from out the slum
Of his own past, his reckless zeal to slay
The early Christians, People of the Way.
Yet if I might just speculate a touch,
He also thought of this: that insomuch
As knowledge he was given from on high,
A greater standard he was held to by.
Who could dispute that Paul was anything
Besides the first and foremost man to sing,
In pristine tones, the doctrines of the church?
That man was in the know and sat the perch
Of lofty citadels all livelong day
And picked there at the mind of God. I'd say
He knew a lot and, subsequently then,
Was held to higher rules. Remember when
That dullard Peter talked of Paul and said
He's hard to understand? That hammerhead
Was better casting nets and chopping ears
Than understanding deeper things—sincere,
I have no doubt. Well, anyway, once Saul
Was quite the nerd compared, and later Paul
Was even worse than what he'd been before
In knowing things he shouldn't do. The more
He knew, the more he sinned. So, when he says
Of all the sinners, he's the chief, he lays
It out as fact and not as some charade
Of modesty. So much for accolades
Of great enlightenment. But let us press
A little more: what if we teach no less

Than what we think we know? We tell someone
That something's right or something's wrong and stun
Them with our grasp of weighty things, pretend
We've got the scoop on what God wants. My friend,
Go crack your brain before you make a claim
On what you think you know. Again, from James
We read that it is no small thing to teach.
What is the text? Oh, yes—he said that each   (JAMES 3:1)
Should think both long and hard before they take
To teach the flock. For these play patty-cake
With Judgment's hands and may well run the risk
Of leading sheep astray. Take heed and frisk
Impulsion's pants; you may find contraband
In pockets hid. At last, my pen has spanned
The burly neck of that ferocious beast
I sought to tame back at the start. At least
I think I've done some justice to the weight
This odd conundrum makes us contemplate.
Yet now I'm confident we sit secure
Upon the ledge of understanding. Sure,
It was a bumpy road for us, no doubt,
And "Bedlam bound" I even thought to shout
A time or two. I trust you feel the same,
And Straitjacket might have my keeper's name.
Regardless, I have labored at this point
And to this end—that knowledge is the joint
Between an act and that called sin, that what
We know ties us to wrong and right. But cut
The fat until our blade has hit the bone.
What if we didn't know, the baritones
Of law had never sounded in our ears,
Didactic standards never made premiere
Upon our stage? What if we never knew
The law of God? You must admit, it's true
That without law there'd be no law that's broke—
No laws we learn or laws our conscience spoke
To us. If laws did not exist, my friend,
Then by the thunder clouds above, we end
This talk of breaking rules. There would be none

To break. We'd bear our guilt to Stygian.
I may not have my hands around the whole,
But I have something here. It was my goal
In all of this to ask one simple thing:
What did the peers of Abraham then cling
Unto as laws of God? Remember now,
There were no tablets carved that might endow
The people with God's will, no Moses yet
To write the rules, no Levites there to fret
About in bloody robes, no preacher on
A soapbox shouting down the street. The dawn
Of law was still asleep. Oh, let me be
As modest as a Mennonite, for we
Have hit the sticky parts. I'm saying that
There was no formal, written law whereat
Those people knew the will of God. Remove
Yourself away from all concerns till you've
Achieved an abstract view. You'll find you just
Might think I'm right. Let go compliant trust
That will accept for poor acceptance' sake.
That charity will see a tyrant make.
We deal to Justice not the crummy hand
That unsuspicious clergymen have panned
From out their streams of ignorance. No, quite
The contrary—to think and test is right
And safe, as Diocletian proved the chest
Of Saint Sebastian, finding then, assessed
With arrows launched, a robust saint who would
Hold up beneath those shafts of bronze. He stood
The test as cushions stand against all pins
And needles pressed. We likewise test and win
Assurance when we prove our text was not
Coerced. But if we find it leaks a lot
And doesn't water hold, then toss it out.
An empty pail is better at the spout
Than one that's filled with crud. It still remains
There was a time before God's laws became
The system that we know today; the great
Judeo-Christian codes that dominate

The West were not forever on the throne.
So how, in times before, were people shown
The things to do? How did these people know
What's right? Well, grab your shovel and your hoe;
We'll dig a little, possibly unearth
A text to speak to this—one that is worth
Its weight in gold considering the top-
Ic now discussed. We go not far and stop
Right where we find that wondrous fool, that one
As Noah named. To him and to his sons
God gave some rules. Right there in chapter nine
We find the only laws our text assigns
To male and femme alike—new verdant plumes
Of garden greens, for circumstance presumes
Another Eden, as it were. For they—
That is, for Noah and his spawn—could say
They had survived the flood. That means they were,
Or would have been, if I am to defer
To Logic's rules, the only humans then
Alive. This all assumes, of course, that men
And women both, or most of them, were killed
In one great tidal wave that once had spilled
The heavens' brim. But let that go. We will
For sake of argument assume a spill
Like that occurred. Well, afterward, some laws
Were given out to them. Hold your applause,
For I have counted them to number four.
Well, three or four, so give or take. What's more
Is that there are some admonitions, too.
But let me summarize the laws for you.
It all comes down to this—that humans are
The stewards of the earth; and (insofar
As we are able) have a bunch of kids;
And don't be cannibals; and God forbid
We kill someone. How's that for short and sweet?
Those were the rules they had. Seems incomplete,
I know. At best they are but sorely vague.
Medieval medics guessing at the plague
Might better fare in their endeavors launched

Than we might with our hermeneutics, staunched
By time, by culture, and self-interest.
I think all four could even be compressed
Down into one. Reflecting on it now,
I think that might be true. Well, anyhow,
The first of four commands is given twice,
And repetition is a grand device
To make one's point! Yes, one of those commands
Our God repeats. It is a law that stands
Attention in my mind, both sharp and straight!
Be fruitful. There it is! Don't hesitate
To read between the lines; connect the dots.
A loose translation might just run *have lots
Of sex, and make a bunch of kids*. What more
Could one conclude, but that the Promisor
Of all our hope tells us the most essen-
Tial thing for us to do is for all men
And women, too—that both should labor hard
To spend their days by fur and lumberyard?
Be fruitful was the first command; like so,
It then assumes the highest role, although
It's such a simple thing. I'll note one fact
About this first—this simple thing, compact
And to the point. Remember at the start
When God had promised then He would impart
Redemption to mankind? It was to come
From out the woman's seed. Oh, now we plumb
Some cryptic creeds. Do you recall I wrote
That part, that crafty little anecdote,
In marching feet? And such remains my verse—
Verbose, of course, and not the least bit terse
When making points. Well, it was in the Seed
That they would set their hope. In turn, the need
Demanded kids be had. You know, this might
Shed light on why the Catholics ignite
Their torches, gird their loins with boot and strap,
And battle cry against the Trojan wrap.
Do they not know the seed has since been had?
I'm all for straining gnats; I'm even glad

That to this day there are those ones who'd choke
A camel down. Who doesn't love the folks
Who need the black and white? They think this world
Was only tailored in those two, not purled
With gray at every stitch. Those mules of wit
Might better go on fours and suck the tits
Of Senselessness than be allowed to make
A judgment call. Their simple jaws might break
When there's a tougher cud for them to chew.
No, let's apply a little dental glue,
For wisdom is like dentures on the gums
And helps to grind those larger bits to crumbs.
We'll leave what blenders have pureed to paste
And little crackers, cleverly encased
In shapes of animals and carried round
In circus boxes, sealed and neatly bound.
Such snacks are for those destitute of teeth;
A baby eats such food. What lies beneath
My rant is that the main command—the big
Kahuna, as it were—was that each wig
And proletariat alike should be
Producing kids. At last, I feel that we
Have hit the summit with this talk of guilt
And how our knowing laws can either jilt
Or wed this thing we're calling sin. I say
We've hit the summit height, yet on the way
I noticed just a few were nodding off—
The Prodigal of sleep still at the trough
Of wayward thoughts. Revive yourself with me,
Still ever wary of that French ennui
That gives to Boredom more than income earned.
We're almost to the end. You look concerned;
Indeed, I swear that much is true! *Forgive*
Me, Lord, for I have unclean lips and live
Among those who are even worse. My case
Is sound, so don't for other answers chase.
This is my great conclusion then: if one
Who keeps the law is known, all said and done,
To be a righteous man (for doing what

Is right does righteous make), and when we glut
Ourselves on reading into what the law
Demands——the fundamental point, the raw
Command for kids——it stands to reason, then,
That being fruitful makes for righteous men.
So, let's go hit the sack, shout *holy here*
We come! But first, I'll pass a souvenir,
A little token for your pains endured
Upon this road we've marched. Well, be assured
This prize I give has greater worth concealed
Than any box of Cracker Jacks might yield.
The souvenir I'm handing out is like
A pearl, a precious thing; no look-alike
Exists, as far as I can tell. And still,
There will be those who toss it off, such thrills
Regarded only dull enough for drawers
Of pocket change and lighters growing sore
With mingled clang. Yet still, I'd pray this prize
Was something greater in your passive eyes.
With that, and with no further feigned ado,
I'll give the trophy as it is——a clue,
An insight to our tale where it does touch
On irony. That when and insomuch
Our text calls Abraham a righteous man,
It's done before he has a kid. Go scan
The text yourself and see——I'd love to wait
Until you've made review——or navigate
With Strong's to save on time, or simply trust
My words. But if you are like me, a "must"
Would be to check it for yourself. I hold
No feelings either way; I am consoled
By rustling pages in a silent room.
"Not found," you say? My patience wanes. Let tomb
And shroud and euphemistic eulogies
Be knelled upon your doubts. It's there! Now please,
If we might shift the business back in gear.
There's too much time in neutral lost, I fear.
The righteous people were the ones with kids.
It's basic——yes, and not some message hid

And only found by those who jury-rig
The records so they turn reverse, a big
Concern with Zeppelin years ago. I say
You duct tape devils when you forward play!
My point is that they had the rule, and it
Was pretty clear. And even though the writ
Of law was not on page, our buddy Paul
In Romans tells us that the earth and all
Creation makes it evident for us.
We know our God and what He wants, and thus
The way to act, because of what we've seen.
Yes, Nature is our teacher now! We glean
From out her school what conscience needs, for what
We see, the visible, is adequate
To make us know our God for who He is.
You ever hate someone? I hate old Mis-
Ter Perfecthair who works the bistro down
The street. Why does he get the plumy crown
When my pate looks like Mister Clean? Still, I
Admit his affogatos are worth dy-
Ing for, and, yes, I have been known to spend
Time writing in his shop, but condescend-
Ing looks I cannot stand! I called the man's
Gelato "ice cream" once. Since then, he scans
Our meetings with a deprecating glare.
Of course, I hate the man, young Perfecthair.
Oh, maybe I dislike him more than hate,
But neither does much good. I must placate
My ego by another means or poke
My eyes like Oedipus till bloody soak
Has drowned offended sight. So many things
Could pass me by in peace. But now I'll bring
Us back into the text; I'm done with craft-
Y commentary, wholesale paragraphed
So well above. My point's been made. Now, where
Did we leave off before? Like Robespierre,
I've lost my head (or more so lost my place),
Apparently; there's tell-tale on my face
Since Perfecthair just shot a look this way.

Well, mind your own! Reach in that little tray
To pull gelato out in stingy scoops.
You try about as much as Betty Boop
Has tried to hide her thighs in bawdy tights.
I feel for you, unworthy parasites
Who swallow all your sugar mixed with cream.
Poor man, that must be hard. What's this, the steam
Your dimples lend your charm is almost spent?
Perhaps you're only built for looks. *Content
Yourself with aging gracefully.* You'll trade
That raven plume for what will soon be grayed
And held in place by spray. I'm not sure how
I ended here; but let that go. For now,
Let's wrap this up and see how all I've shared
Plays out upon what's next. Hope you're prepared.

CHAPTER 12

Grand Schlemiel

At last, we've come to you. How does it feel
To be the laughingstock, the grand schlemiel
Of characters I'll write? You must be proud
Right now; I'm sure you'd like to give the crowd
A couple words or rattle off some half-
Remembered gratitude to friends and staff.
Oh, don't forget to thank your God—where would
You be without your faith? It's also good
To say it's for your kids. What were their names?
Don't act as if I'm off the mark or claim
Absurdities. It was unanimous,
You know. Each judge agreed. But there's a plus
That comes with such a prize. You get to feast
On infamy, forever robed and fleeced
As one we should avoid. At least, that's when
It comes to your example set for men.
The perverts have to register; they made

A law. They also take your accolades
Away and ban you from the kiddie pools.
"But hold your wagging tongue," you say. "You'll fuel
A poor opinion of the man. He's not
As bad as that!" You think I have forgot-
Ten halls of faith and genealogies?
You say he's of the same old pedigree
As Abraham, and that's a godly line.
What else but piety should then define
The man I mock? "Why, even Peter called
Him righteous, don't you know?" Who's not enthralled
With intellects like yours? I just might ask
You to expound or even to unmask
The mysteries of transubstantia-
Tion and why wafer-hosts upon the tray
Are better ones than bread. Let that be next;
Put our debates to rest. We've been perplexed
For two millennia. *That's by my count.*
Such flattery would gag an ox! Dismount
Your horse and stand in line. We'll see you shaved
As hairless as a eunuch, those enslaved
To serve without a bulge between their thighs.
Sam Mullet and his kin are standing by
To have your beard removed. You don't deserve
To wear the thing. He comes at night, *the nerve,*
And finds you doing who-knows-what. A snip
And tuck is all it takes. Such craftsmanship
Is hard to come by now, to shave a beard
At two a.m. A single razor steered
By candlelight. *That's Amish hazing, dear.*
Now, once your chin has lost its boutonniere
And so been lightened of its load, we'll need
To paint your face with eggs. It's remedied
By such a mask—the skin, that is. Your pores
Need tightening, and all the yolk restores
The moisture, friend. *Pass me the cucumber.*
Oh, we're fresh out? Well, be that as it were,
Just use a butter squash. When all these eggs
Have set to cake, you'll need new clothes. This begs

That one of taste be given charge, a mind
That's governed by creative bents, defined
By flourish and a heavy hand. Let him
Select the apropos attire, the trim
And stitch that sees your character complete—
A modest fashion that will not deplete
The bank, what five-and-dimes or Goodwill thrift
Could yield. Such clothes will suit our needs. Just sift
Around to find the tights. They should be flash
And make a statement—something with panache
That rivets public eye, commands the stage
Like any jester able to assuage
The king and court. Oh, one more tiny thing—
There should be bells around your hat that ring
And jingle as you walk. "You know, the priests—
When tending to the sacrifice and feasts
Prepared—had pomegranates mixed with bells
Around the bottom of their robes, expel-
Ling one congruent clink as they would shake
While year's atonement they would yearly make.
They tied a rope around the priestly girth
To tug them out the holy place if worth
Was wanting from that sacrifice. I swear!
See, no one but high priests could enter there."
Again, the scholar has arrived! What might
We do without your constant need to cite
Obscure and long-forgotten bits of fact?
Oh, reach inside your endless well and act
As if you've got the scoop; pretend your stale,
Insipid certainties would sit the scales
Great Wisdom holds. Oh, please. Go memorize
For Bible quiz or try to Christianize
Some pop and culture tune. We do not need
Your Band-Aid-soft attempts, nor will we plead
For seats that bleed the nose. At last, we've dressed
You to the part, O Lot! Might I suggest
We take a little stroll down Memory Lane?
It's such a lovely day, by father Cain,
And I would hear your greatest hits. What were

You doing on that day? Why would you stir
And run to meet those two as they approached?
I'm sure no guilty conscience could have coached
Your legs to speed. You must have just been sit-
Ting there and looking to the east, legit
And uncorrupted, even justified
To sit upon the wall. What should you hide,
O pious Lot? You were not casting dice
Or at the swindle of some merchandise
The travelers had brought. "The elders used
To sit there in the gates, and they diffused
The civil arguments with sage advice."
I'm sure that's what it was. Let it suffice
To say that you were there when they arrived.
I like how you entreated them and strived
To keep their presence hid, how you had urged
Them both to stay within your home, diverged
Them from their plan to sleep there in the square.
Who sleeps within a strange town's thoroughfare
When someone offers them a bed? Perhaps
It was your breath or that cologne you slap
Upon your cheek. It's odious! You had
To press them hard about it all, forbad
A "No" from out their lips. *What terrible*
Suspense. I hope it lasts. You dutiful-
Ly led them home, a cozy little scene
Around the table there, a quarantine
Of holy people sharing one big feast.
I thought they ate with Abraham? No yeast,
For it was matza bread, with curds and cream.
Oh, pass the bitter herbs this way; it seems
I missed the plate when it went by. You'd done
So well in Sodom's commonwealth, and none
Would have denied it then. You sucked the fat
Like any leech, a chubby plutocrat
To lounge the luxuries their cash had bought.
And Mrs. Lot, the wife, had only thought
She finally had whipped the house in shape,
The stainless-steel appliances, the drapes

And carpet complementing walls. In fact,
She had a dinner party planned and racked
Her brain to think of how she'd cancel it.
She stood beside her brand-new stove and grit
Her teeth when those two said, "You have to leave,"
Evicting her from garden life, the Eve
Of Sodom's land. "Again," she thought, "I'll reek
Of livestock dung." She didn't want to speak
Of it. She was more cosmopolitan
And needed city vibes. She'd long been done
With life in tents and knew the nomad way
Was not her thing. She almost thought to say
She wouldn't leave—she'd stay in Sodom's land
And make a home there for herself, command
Her own damn way. Why not? But would her kids
Then understand if she just bid good rid-
Dance to her life with Lot and all those pains,
No longer bound to husband's whims and chains?
Who knew? With any luck, she could and might
Just come to make a happy home despite
It all. She'd even shack up with that cuck-
Old maker she just met, the one she snuck
Around with twice a week. That stud could flex
Her ways she'd not thought possible. Their sex
Was something rigorous; she'd even shed
A couple pounds because of it. "The bed
Can be refreshing in so many ways,"
She thought. Reluctantly, she'd kiss those days
Goodbye. She had her kids to think about
And husband, too—let's not forget that lout
And undertaker of a dunce, the man
She'd stay with till the grave. *Well, there's a plan
To be short-lived.* She'd let the lover go.
Her kids would never understand, and so
She'd give it up. Her days could be a bore
Again. That's when you all had heard the door
Begin to shake insistently with knocks.
You knew why they had come; it was no shock
To hear them there. The prepubescent looks

Of your two guests had caught their eye. Those crooks
Would steal their innocence. *What do you mean?*
I'm sure it's fine. It's simply good routine
To introduce oneself to guests. What more
Could these men want? I think they're looking for
Some strange to tap. The rapists were aroused
And wanted more to know the men you'd housed
There for the night. *Well, isn't that so nice?*
They want to take us on a date. The spice
Of life is good relationships, you know.
What do you think? I think they are not go-
Ing for consensual; that's not the band
They're marching to. Now, be a dear and hand
Me all the soap upon a rope. We'll need
It soon enough. Oh, Lot—you refereed
The whole event when you were in the street.
You reasoned with that mob, somewhat discreet,
But pushed the envelope when you said they
Had wicked acts in mind. *You're in my way!*
Here, step aside so I can see. That's bet-
Ter, dear. Now, tell me what he said to set
Them straight! Why don't we watch for now? You had
Your daughters in the house, two undergrads
With hymens still intact, and in a stroke
Of innovative foolishness, you spoke
And offered these to take the place of your
Two guests, some swift exchange that might detour
Their lust away. *They call it bait and switch,*
My dear. You see, the salesman makes a pitch
For products over here. But they had none
Of it. Then answering, they spoke as one
And said, "This joker wants to be our judge!   (GENESIS 19:9)
He came to visit; now he wants to nudge
Us to the side and rule our roost!" "That's not
The tune he sang to me last night." But Lot,
You simply felt like any poet might
And viewed reforms with that same appetite
That sees indulgence also fed. They pressed
In hard to trample you; they'd take your guests

By force. And then they barked, "You should have let
Us in before, but now you're gonna get
It worse!" No lack of invitation would
Have stopped them then, and all there was that stood
Between the mob and both those guests was air.

A rocky mountaintop sits solitaire
Among the heights. In time, the peak will swell
With falling snow as winter winds propel
A freezing blanket down. It covers all
With whitened silence there. But spring still calls,
And underneath that ice, the mountain shrugs.
The sheet of snow comes loose. It tries to hug
The stony cliffs but finds no grip, and down
It goes to crush what sits beneath. The town
Below has no defense against that weight.

Like so, your house, O Lot, would suffocate
Beneath that wave of rapist men had not
Your guests took matters in their hands. You ought
To show some thankfulness; they saved your rear
A flogging in the first. I'll engineer
A better word than flog that might define
That male religious train of valentines
That surely had your name all over it—
Some weeks or months at least before you'd sit
With any comfort in a chair. But this
Will wait for now. So, let us reminisce
About what happened next, both strange and kind,
Confounding all the mob by striking blind.
Now, are these suppliants or sycophants
Who grope about your house—these ones who want
Their sight restored, who feel about the streets
Now moistened with the urine of some bleat-
Ing goats? *I heard the prodigal was in*
A state much like this, dear. He wiped his chin
Of piggy scraps when he had felt the pinch
Of poverty. He wasted every inch
And ounce of what his father gave, reduced

To eat with pigs. That's when the lad deduced
He'd go back home. I think you've got it wrong.
The text says that he looked, that he did long
To have the scraps the pigs were gnawing at.
It doesn't say he ate from out that vat
Of slop. But still, that's called rock-bottom, dear,
When those who snort the slop become our peers.
That was a sight to see, to watch the mob
Reduced to trepid steps, to see them swab
About the mud to find their way. You knew
The caliber of those you housed, the two
You put up for the night as guests. This act
Had made it clear. And how did you react
To them, these ones who held such dominance
Upon the mob? You gave no utterance
Of words, but all your affectations hit
The stage. Now, if I might, let me admit
A little something of myself: I'm all
About libations poured, from alcohol
To coffee in the morn. I'll tip my glass
And spill my offerings. And if, alas,
I happen to forget, too much has thirst
A grip around my mouth; it is dispersed
Against a wall when I must take a piss.
But when I do remember not to miss
The chance to spill my drink before I take
A sip, I spill the right amount to slake
Both God and dirt. I have no bone with share
And share alike, but let us not so dare
To pay out more our dues with pious shows
That merely wet the earth. This goes to throw
Our drink away and makes for itchy throats.
Is not a tithe a tenth? Still, someone wrote
That David dumped his cup of water, wet,
The drink his men had risked their lives to get—
Yes, dumped it out completely on the ground.
I'm sure that budding king no sooner found
This action ticked them off! But here's the point—
That you, O Lot, determined to anoint

The ground with too much piety. You laid
It on too thick!

Think when the sky has paid
His debt of steady drips. The ground will soak
And nurse at it. But when the clouds are broke
Apart, a burst of water all at once
Will hit the earth with force! The sustenance
Is lost because the ground has not the time
To suck it up. It runs away to prime
Some stream or riverbed, then further on
To seas, forgotten underneath the yawns
Of sleepy waves.

Like so, your grandiose
Reforms that night were surely right, but close
Without cigars. They proved a minute late
And dollar short. What louder spoke were traits
And habits practiced day by day. And these
Were steady drips that soaked by slow degrees
Into the eyes and minds of those you knew.
My case in point, consider when these two
Had urged and said to gather up the ones
You'd save—you know, like daughters and like sons,
And don't forget that strudel of a wife.
Yes, these you'd save, for cranky Afterlife
Was calling in the loan. Those two had told
You then to get them out; your town was sold
Into the hands of angry Deities.
I'll take a little moment, if you please,
And make a footnote at this part. The wrongs
Of Sodom emanate and more belong
In failing to be fruitful—that and there,
The only law they had to keep! Beware
The urge that would project too much the blood
This culture bleeds upon that period.
It's entry level hermeneutics when
We must determine first who held the pen,
The speaker, and their audience—tell what,

With poorly educated guesstimates,
Were their concerns. What did they understand?
Once that is known, then guess how, secondhand,
It all applies to you. Let's put to bed
That myth that says the Bible should be read
As if each word—yes, every little word—
Were just for me, *God's lettered love.* Absurd!
To bed, I say again; another tale
You will tomorrow have! So much for stale
And crusty notes that loiter in the bor-
Ders of our page. At any rate, you swore
You'd only be a sec and made your way
To see your future sons, that is to say,
The ones betrothed to marry your two girls—
Your sweet and supple lollipops, the pearls
You tried to feed the mob not half an hour
Before. *There're better ways to lose one's flower,*
My dear. Perhaps he doesn't know you should-
N't cast your pearls to swine. And so, you stood
Before those would-be sons and told them how
They'd have to leave with you. You gave your vow
It was the truth, said Sodom's days were set
To end. And then, incredulous, they met
Your gaze and laughed! They thought a monkeyshine
Was in your eyes and undertones of wine
Were on your garlic breath. *They might have heard*
Of what he tried to do; a little bird
Has told them how he offered up their brides
To feed a mob. But they would not divide
Themselves from disbelief! The first of these
Two men (I do not know his name, so please
Don't ask), a docile little monk who spends
His days in lifting rocks—a caveman trend
To haul a boulder six or seven feet.
That's atavistic throwback. He'll compete
In growing fingernails or snapping sticks
This afternoon. The second man restricts
His time to butcher shops, a man who looks
To be a side of beef himself. He cooks

In his spare time and also makes an ap-
Petizing sausage, truth be told. He'll wrap
It in the entrails of a beast or fowl.
He's ever eager then to disembowel
For casing where he might deposit meat.
O future sons-in-law, how we must greet
With grace and grains of salt. In spite of these
Redeeming traits, they wouldn't give your pleas
The time of day. They really thought you meant
To put them on, and they would not consent
To leave with you. Oh, Lot—their blood is on
Your hands. You left to sing some woebegone,
Some melodrama tune, the best you could
With that falsetto voice—like brotherhoods
That chant in minor chords—as down the streets
You strolled and tried your best then not to meet
The blind men on their knees. It's difficult
To think you walked with urgency. Consult
The record for yourself and tell me that
I'm wrong. Your footsteps lack that pit-a-pat
I would expect from someone on the brink
Of doom. Or did it cross your mind to think
You'd save as many as you could? *The chil-
Dren and the women first. Come on, let's fill
The rafts!* You'll tell me next your hope was just
To play, in any form, revivalist—
To pass out tracts and preach your flaming brim-
Stone down, to sound old Sodom's walls with hymns
That see the altar wet with tears. But no,
That's not the truth. Your speed had gone to show
The great regret you hauled around, the ball
And chain of malcontent, and this you'd haul
Till heaven's harp. You made it home, of course,
And started loitering. They had to force
Your hand to pack a bag, and there you were—
Just begging for the cattle prod to spur
You off the couch. You had to liquidate
Your bank accounts; the stocks and market rate
Would plummet with destruction in the morn.

Investments must be moved, and any born
Of heaven wouldn't ever understand.
You have the safe box, too! Oh, yes—you'd land
Upon your feet; you had security.
Again, they urged you all to run, to flee
The doom to come, but still, you would not lis-
Ten to the call! You thought you would dismiss
Their great alarm. You idiot! Believe
Those angels well enough to rashly heave
Your daughters to the sewer rats, to serve
As vestals for the dirty-fingered pervs.
But asked to leave your home? Well, that expense
Was just too much to bear. Makes perfect sense.
You're making Agamemnon look the saint!
That despot mollified the great complaint
Of Artemis and cut his daughter's throat,
All that for wind to launch a thousand boats
For Troy. But you, you'd sacrifice your girls
Before you'd ditch a hut. Pedantic churl,
You major in the minors, and the mi-
Nors fund your doctorate. Why should I try
To understand your ways? *Ignore thyself,*
Excuse thyself, the maxims on the shelf
Within your mind. But have you ever heard
Of *know thyself*? The teachers have conferred
And feel this proverb is a vital part
To any wisdom gained. It seems Descartes
Was on to something when he proved that man
Could nothing know until he makes the span
Of his own mind. All other thoughts depend
On his own knowledge of himself. But spend
No further time on this, for we alread-
Y know you are an imbecile. Instead,
Let's get back to the part when you were made—
Yes, made—to leave your home. You would have stayed
If they had said you could; that's obvious!
I'm sure you begged and pleaded, made a fuss
And told them all the many reasons why
You couldn't go. You tried to classify

Reluctance as a medical concern
And said the gout was flaring up. *He'll earn*
That title, Grand Schlemiel, before the end.
I think he may already have. Go rend
The shirts in your donation piles or pray
With beads that tell you which comes next. I say
That tepid drinks will make God puke! Your bluff
Was called; those angels knew and had enough
Of it. They grabbed your hands and led you like
A child, and that was one reluctant hike,
A trudge where you had dropped your mental crumbs
Like Hansel with his clever stratagems,
As—so it says to us by Brothers Grimm—
So much the homeward path had puzzled him
(And sister Gretel, too), he dropped his bread
To lead his steps back home. The birds had fed
On foolish Hansel's trail of crumbs. Consid-
Er this a moment, if you will, and rid
Your mind of thoughts so anchored down with dirt
And logic blocks. I mean here to assert
A little gadfly, as it were. What if
By feeding birds we then avoid the cliff
Of fate? Stay with me now; this will move quick,
And thinking caps work well to warm the thick-
Ness of a skull. Before recorded time,
Our uncles and our aunts, still in their prime,
Would look up to the sky and note the birds.
If danger came that way, the birdies stirred
From lofty roofs because the ones who fly
Can see beyond what grounded, biped eyes
Perceive. It's normal, then, to figure out
Why omens would be read from this. The stout
And sturdy men of old would mark the flight
Of birds and see it as a sign that might
Explain things good or bad. They soon became
The pets of oracles who sought to tame
Those lightweight and spasmodic feathered priests
Since ready consultations with a beast
Of air explain what still is unforeseen.

But let's get back to my first point. I mean
To keep this tirade on the track. You see,
The birds have thus evolved: What once were tree-
Abiding citizens, the simple brutes
Who startled at a whim, pulled parachute,
And landed as a prophet on the ground.
They saw an opportunity and crowned
Themselves the Delphic mediums, the ones
Who'd tend the rock that Kronos belched. There're tons
Of stories I could twist to make my point.
But let it stand as truth! The birds anoint
Our omens either good or ill. And now
That we've established this, by sweaty brow
And my inflated pen, I think we would
Do well to firstly ask if even could
And second how we might so grease that palm,
That claw. I'd rather be direct and calm
These metaphors, but tell me how to grease
The claw of feathered priests. My expertise
Is irony, but if I had to guess,
I'd say that one should do no more or less
Than feed the birds to get the omen mak-
Ers on your side. It worked for Hansel. Take
A look and see there for yourself: he fed,
Though inadvertently, the birds his bread,
His little manna path. Like so, in turn,
The lad escaped the oven where the burn
Of flame was stoking hot. He got to eat
A candy house instead. The short and sweet
Of it is this—that we should buy our bag
Of seed and hang our suet like a flag
Upon the pole, yell "Better futures here
We come!" But let this go. We'll persevere
Upon the tale we left some time ago.
Our Grand Schlemiel is there, about to throw
Another fist of crumbs. Sad news, old boy:
They're closing Sodom down for good. The joys
It gave are at an end, and any bread
You're dropping in your mind is only spread

To feed the birds. It leads to nowhere, son.
Let sleeping dogs alone, and so be done
With Sodom's moneybags. Don't worry, friend;
I see your candy cottage round the bend.
You'll feast on marzipan and caramel,
The tasty tales a pedophile could tell.
He means the part where Lot plays sugar dad-
Dy with his girls. We'll get to that. But pad
Your eagerness with some solicitude
Since first we need your wife to die. *How shrewd!*
I know—still, first things first, though it might hurt.
Have meat and your potatoes, then dessert.
The angels led you out of Sodom's gates.
But tell me this: how did you transmigrate
So quickly, friend? Was it some vanish and
Appearing act? It says they grabbed your hand
And you were out in no time flat. The text
Then says they set you down. Now I'm perplexed.
So, tell me, were you flying out, or did
They carry you like two-year-olds, like kids
In tantrums, ones who would refuse to leave
Their sandbox for the day? I half believe
This was the case. It seems to fit and feel
With your own person's selfish commonweal.
I think they left the bags you packed behind.
At least you'll travel light. With prayers declined,
Your prayers to stay in Sodom's land, I mean,
You had no choice but go. Your drama queen
Performance was for naught. The angels said
To hit the hills before the sun had shed
Its light upon the plain, said not to drag
Your feet. I'm sure they thought you'd lollygag
Around. They also told you not to look
That way again. Let's hear it from the book:
"But second thoughts let not your gaze allow;   (GENESIS 19:17)
Unworthy servants turn back from the plow."
The angels then had wasted half their breath
Thanks to that pastry of a wife; her death
Was not far off. That strumpet didn't heed

The warning given her and mutinied
Away from better sense, to say the least.
She held to passion like some failed artiste,
For when she heard the brimstone start to dance
On Sodom's streets, she thought to throw a glance
That way and watch. She didn't want to think
She'd ever have to leave, nor could she shrink
So easily away from what had proved
To be the lover of her life. Then moved
To sad regrets, she thought to leave a kiss,
A final act for him whom she would miss
The rest her lonely days—her seconds, more
In truth, for what was coming next was sure
To happen swift. She pursed her lips and blew
A kiss. Such things had always felt like dew
Within her mouth, to wet her lips and give
A luscious kiss, but that provocative
And loving gesture then was more like grit
Upon her tongue, as if her moistened spit
Were only dried-up sand, not sweet and damp
But salty as it left her mouth. The lamp
Of day was glaring hard, and as she watched
The city then in morning sun, debauched
With flame, she noticed something stranger still:
Her legs and feet no longer moved, their skill
Forgotten in a passing moment's time.
They felt like heavy roots that work to climb
Not up but further underneath the ground.
She pulled with all her might, but they were bound
To earth and wouldn't budge. She thought to cry
For help; she needed you to come and pry
Her feet from *terra firma*, that sweet wife
Of yours, your mate in any sickness, life,
And death. She really thought you'd be there in
Her time of need. But when she went to spin
Her nimble body round and call for aid,
She found the motion of her hips was spayed
Of potency. She couldn't move or twist!
All parts below the chest were stiff. She'd missed

Her chance to turn away from Sodom then.
Her feet, her legs, her hips, her abdomen
Would never move again by will or chance.
And there, in what would be her final stance,
Your wife was forced to see the city burned.
She'd had to watch it then, although she yearned
To run—and if she could, she would have run
The way one sometimes runs in dreams, been done
With all the charms and the extremes of life
In Sodom's realm. *Oh, sweet and loving wife*
Of our Schlemiel, that's not within your cards.
The Matin's sounding, dear. Just pray, pray hard!
Your wife did not pray hard, for who in times
Like those would think to rid their souls of grime?
Not she—oh, no. She'd rather yell your name
Instead, a last-ditch effort to exclaim
A need for help. But you weren't there. You went
Ahead with your two girls, gave your consent
To let your wife say one or two goodbyes.
How could she know you'd left when both her eyes
Were firmly stitched and riveted with thread
Upon the very place you all had fled?
She'd face that one alone. Just then, was it,
She noticed how her arms and hands had quit
Their operations, too. They all were glued
And stuck in air and looked as if they hewed
At bugs and held their swat like sticks that had
Been caught mid-swing. That's when a helpless sad-
Ness came. She gathered her last breath and tried
To call for you, but words had calcified
Within her throat. She stood there, fighting thirst,
As veins from normal functions were reversed.
A Galatea, but returned to stone—
Not soft beneath the fingers but like bone
To touch. And there, *Forgotten* was her name,
A figurine of salt the girl became.
One single briny tear made bold to streak
The wrinkle of her eye, then down her cheek
To dangle off that blanching mound. It hung

A moment only to reflect the tongues
Of flame that licked at Sodom's walls and dried
To nothingness. Well done, old boy! She died
And was returned to dust, *returned to salt.*
Who'll wash your dishes now? *It's not his fault.*
He's taking this one hard. You know, I think
His serotonin's low. You need a drink!
At least you all remembered that; you brought
The bag of booze. Just leave your wife to squat
The plain, or haul her round so we can dip
Our Margarita cups. Her Ladyship
Will serve our ends. But cover up her eyes
For this next part, the nasty enterprise
Of what would be your finest work. It strikes
My fancy so! It looks as if it's like
A Sabine rape, but on its head it stands
And shows men carried off in female hands.
Don't worry, friend—your secret's safe with me.
But don't assume I'll buy the heresy
You sell the mob; naivety is not
My thing. Still, that's a daring lie you've taught!
You ought to peddle potions next, dispense
Them in the streets. All costs are on expense
Accounts; your daughters have to pay it back.
I'd go so far to say you have a knack
For duping all the pillared cloud of saints,
From Peter down to who-knows-whom—acquaint
Your clueless self, and then get back with me.
At any rate, you've fooled a lot. I see
So many taking your defense in hand
When what they ought to do is reprimand
Your sordid show. "Oh, don't you know? They gave
Poor Lot some wine to drink there in the cave.
They made him drunk and had their way with him."
Apparently, they've never had their limb
Run limp from too much wine consumed. I'm speak-
Ing for the men, of course. You know how weak
And feeble those erections stand when drunk,
So little shove and even less the spunk.

But more than this, you really think I would
Believe two virgin girls of sisterhood
Could then devise and execute designs
That see their father drunk on too much wine?
And, if that's not enough, push further still
To have them bed you down against your will?
And still, you'd give me more this locoweed—
Say both girls in two nights did take your seed
And by some miracle conceive. I just
Don't buy it, friend. Now, give it all the thrust
Of many nights, your jug of wine a sack
That knows no end, so that they can attack
Your wits with drunkenness till ovula-
Tion comes around. That seems to hold more sway
Upon my mind; the sound of it is sweet-
Er to my ears. I'll dress you in a pleat-
Ed smoking robe, Hugh Hefner to explore
The fleeting charms a younger girl will whore
From out their vast commodity of youth.
But no—you swear, you're telling us the truth!
They held you down with cinder blocks and plucked
The lengthy hairs from nostril aqueducts
Then painted all your toenails taffy pink.
I see how this could push you to the brink.
Your kicks and screams were pouring out, I'm sure.
No doubt you're chaste as any Epicure
I ever met. *Perhaps he hasn't heard*
You shouldn't bounce your daughter's bed. The word
Within eugenic circles states it makes
For kids with eyes of varied shapes and breaks
Immunities beyond repair. Let's say,
For sake of argument, it went the way
Our text describes. What did you think when both
Your girls began to show maternal growth
About the waist? I'm sure you would have thought
It odd; perhaps your uncle's God had brought
The thing to pass. But still, no matter how
It came about, the milk, not from the cow,
Was spilled. No crying then, but moving on—
You named the bastards Moab and Ammon.

CHAPTER 13

Stolen Flower

The prince was young but not so gullible
To think none lied to him—improbable,
Perhaps, but not unthinkable. But that
A holy man, an Ur aristocrat,
Would have the nerve to bold-faced lie to his
Quite royal and attractive face—well, this
Was not a thing he ever would expect.
He never guessed his path would intersect
With such a fibber as it did. The tale
Ran like the other told. They had a sale
On grain, and Abraham—that herdsman who
Had goat, had nanny-kid, had lamb and ewe—
Had come to buy the food they sold to feed
His herds of sheep then bleating belly needs.
He said his sister rode with him, a card
He'd played before with poker face and hard-
Boiled stare, for Sarah was a pleasant fare

Commanding each man's head be turned, each glare
Be held beyond a simple look. It worked
To Abram's gain before when he had shirked
The tight constraints of telling all the truth.
It had been easy money, for the youth-
Ful charms of Sarah were enough to bait
That king to love. Perhaps it was the weight
Of fear on Abram's mind that caused him first
To lie about his wife back then. The worst
He got was just a slap upon the wrist.
But what could be his reasons now? We twist
The truth when we excuse or wink at this
And browbeat our own reason down, dismiss
Clear thought for wives' tales told. Such words are spelled
With letters of a superstition held.
Let's let our admiration dwell among
The frailties of these characters when sung.
It happened thus: the prince invited him—
That Abraham—by some impromptu whim,
To come and share a meal. That prince had spread
A lavish feast—the best in fowl, in bread,
And wine. And so, it happened on that night
That Abram's wife, sweet Sarah, with delight,
Prepared to dine. She even did her hair
In pretty curls; she still was unaware
That Abraham was cooking up a lie
Upon his shepherd tongue. His alibi
Could be it was half-truth, himself he told
While combing out his beard, somehow consoled
Therein by splitting hairs upon the blade.
He would be found correct, though fool be made—
For it was true, yet only that in part.
For wife became, but did as sister start.   (GENESIS 20:12)
Well, both prepared and round each other danced
Till both were preened, then hand-in-hand they pranced
Across the lane to where the castle sat.
They rang the bell, and on the carpet mat
They polished off their feet. Yet while they stood
There waiting, Abram thought it was as good

A time as any to come clean, at least,
With wife. "You know, my dear," he launched, "this feast
Is special for us both." His wife looked up
From smoothing out her dress. "And though we sup
With kings of men, my mind's on you." The man
Went on with suavity, "And I could scan
This whole wide world, but still I wouldn't find
A lady half as lovely, half as kind."
He stopped to cough and clear his throat; the next
Words would need ample room to fit. He flexed
His cheekbones high and clenched his teeth to get
Them out. But then his wife cut in, "I bet
You are upset about the way things went
Before." Her man just looked at her. "You sent,"
His wife went on, "me to that other king
And said I was your sis, or some such thing?
I've got it all behind us now. In fact,
Tonight, I think we finally have backed
Away from all that nonsense you had put
Us through before. You really had your foot
Inside your mouth on that one, dear!" Abe gawked
At her, a blank, dumbfounded look, that mocked
No one but him who wore the thing. He squeezed
The words, "You know I love you, right?" It eased
His mind somehow to mention this. "I feel
The same," his wife returned. "But I can't deal
With it when you are acting in such ways.
I am your wife, you know, and I won't play
Those silly games again." Just then, the door
Was swung upon its hinge, and there before
Them stood a husky man of beastly size.
His chest bulged out to button's-brink, his eyes
Were fixed in some cold-sober gaze, and on
His head was neatly wrapped a turban, drawn
And tied with two silk-braided ropes, dyed red.
He looked at them and mumbled more than said,
"My master has been waiting for you, sir."
And then he asked, though somewhat clumsier,
"And who might be this lady here with you?"

Old Abraham then spoke and lied straight through
His prophet teeth: "My sister, sir. I thought
I'd bring her here with me. I hope it's not
A problem that I did." Then Abram rolled
His eyes around to catch the bitter cold,
The death-and-dagger stare his wife had aimed
His way. She didn't speak, just too ashamed
Or filled with anger at that point to pinch
A word. The doorman looked at her; no flinch
Of hesitation as he took to leer
At her quite openly. A jolt of fear
Shot straight up Sarah's back. She turned away,
And off he led the couple (or, we'll say,
The siblings) to the meal they'd come to share.
And that the prince might have a chance to stare
At Abram's sister while they ate, he sat
Her right across from him so they could chat
And so he might her single charms inspect.
The prince had seen the lovely girl direct
Her eyes his way throughout the meal. He knew
This meant her interest, a rendezvous
Was surely on her mind. For what else could
It mean? And he was not a prince who would
Let such a chance for love be left to waste.
He watched her as she ate; her eyes were laced
With such seductive lash. His appetite
Was growing as he saw her place each bite
Between her rosy lips. He had the itch.
And he was quick to undo every stitch
Of clothes within his mind. He wouldn't stop!
It was his task, the kingdom stud, to drop
His princely seed in each maid up for grabs—
A challenge that he willingly would stab
At day by day and night by night. But of
The man—the brother—well, he seemed to shove
A lot of food into his mouth from each
Tray passing by. And so much so, his speech
Was very limited because his maw
Was always full. The sweets and baklava

He liked the most and looked to make a game
Of tossing each into his mouth. He'd aim
Quite carefully each time and hit. He did
Not miss a one. Nor did the prince forbid
This little show, but seemed amused and took
To counting each he landed in that nook.
At last, when they had munched their fill of food,
The prince pronounced the close, and then he glued
His eyes again on Sarah's frame. He waved
His man to take the girl away; he craved
To see her later in his chamber suite
For what was sure to be a sweeter treat.
No other word was said, and Sarah stood,
Wiped off her mouth, and did the best she could
Then not to cry. Her husband looked her way;
He gave a glare that, wordless, seemed to say,
"Be faithful now, my wife." Then out of sight
She went. That old man knew it wasn't right
For him to put his welfare just above
The safety of his wife. What kind of love
Would see just self-preserve without the twin
Of sacrifice? Well, Abram saved his skin,
And thinking it then best he should withdraw,
Placed one concluding piece of baklava
Into his mouth and took his leave. That night
He'd sleep by lies, not little and not white.
But at the very moment when he laid
His head to rest, his wife—yes, I'm afraid
To say, his wife—was getting into bed
With that young prince, that hunk and thoroughbred
Of man. And they were right across the street.
Now let me tell the next in both discreet
And candid airs—I'll speak it as I dare,
Or rather how I wish. For what I share
Is neither bound by inhibition nor
A wicked need to vulgarize. My chore
Is but a simple one: to scribe the words
Our text omits but what I have inferred
From it. With that, I'll start again. Now where

Did I leave off? Oh, yes—poor Sarah's there
Up in the bedroom of that potentate.
If truth be told, the place was quite ornate!
There in the center stood a bed, a firm
And bulky thing, where maidens served their term
At night. It had nice sheets, the thread count high;
He wanted to impress each damselfly
Who'd come to rest his ledge. The bed was lit
With lamps of oil, the canopy befit
With purple silk that draped in many pleats
Upon the sides; the folds then reached the sheets
In sloping curves. There was a honey scent
Upon the silk, and Sarah mutely went
And sat upon the pillowed plush. She tried
To calm her restless breathing, and she sighed.
Her man would get it when she saw him next!
She thought, "He's safe at home, but I am vexed
And wait the what-and-where of this man's whim."
The what she could have guessed: dessert for him—
For that right potent magistrate, that beast
With appetites voracious and unpoliced.
His manly reputation was displayed
On females all, from queen to chambermaid.
Sweet Sarah knew that she was next upon
His list. She scanned the room. A long divan
Was near a dormer space, and there beside
A table sat with crystal ware supplied.
A slender-necked decanter stood there, too,
And it was filled with wine, the rosy hue
Of pomegranates when in June are lush.
Meek Sarah crossed the room; her cheeks were flush.
She braced her will, dug deep to find the brass,
Then picked up the decanter and a glass;
With both she fumbled, trying not to spill,
And poured herself a spot. Perhaps a swill
Of wine would calm her nerves. Just when she got
It down, when tears had rushed her eyes, she thought
She heard a knocking at that door. Then in
He walked, that prince, with open robe, foreskin

And all to show the world. Again, for wine
She reached; she needed more before that swine
Would see her lily breached. "Come here, my rose,"
He said with tacky words that smacked of prose.
She drank her wine and poured another glass.
He urged again, "Come, come, my lemongrass."
He took her arm, leaned in to smell her hair,
Then kissed her neck and said more debonair,
"I couldn't help but notice how you kept
On watching me throughout the meal." He stepped
A little closer then. "Who, me?" the rue
Replied, a touch perplexed. The prince then threw
His arms around her waist. "Come, don't be shy,
A thing like that would not escape my eye."
"I think you are mistaken," Sarah said
And twisted from his grip, "and overfed
On too much self." A smirk then grazed his face;
He liked the catch but much preferred the chase.
"Come here, my daffodil—let me be kissed!"
He leaned in for the kill. She moved. He missed.
"I need another drink before all that,"
The girl exclaimed, and then she went and sat
On the divan and poured what still remained
Of wine to glass. In one quick gulp, she drained
The cup, and feeling light as air and not
So stiff, she roamed the room and quite forgot
Why she was there at all. The prince remarked,
On seeing how her eyes glistened and sparked,
"I see you have a taste for wine as much
As does your brother for the sweets and such."
Then Sarah looked at him. "My brother? Who?"
And then she laughed and blurted, impromptu,
"Oh, yes—my brother! Yes, he likes the sweets."
The prince moved to her side and said, "I meet
So many ladies day to day, but it
Is rare I find a hyacinth with grit
Beneath her charms." Then Sarah smiled, a faint
And fleeting smirk. The walls of her restraint
Were wearing thin; her thoughts were in a swirl.

She said, "You know, I did my hair in curls."
It was too much to take, and add the charm
Of that young prince, his chest and bulky arms.
They caught each other's eyes, and they were locked.
Then Sarah stumbled forward, and she knocked
Her head against his nose. She gazed at him;
The wine was working hard upon her limbs.
The prince helped her to sit, then asked, "Are you
Okay?" She gave a smile and laughed anew.
"You know, that brother, mine, you need to watch,"
Sweet Sarah said. "Why's that, my butterscotch?"
The prince returned. But Sarah only winked
And passed out on the bed. Then indistinct,
She mumbled something else, then nothing more,
Till all her open mouth produced were snores.
The prince still thought it early in the night,
But tucked her in; perhaps he could ignite
The flames of love in morn. He'd need his rest;
He lay down with his hands upon his chest.
With nose still throbbing from poor Sarah's fall,
He tasted sleep—sweet sleep that covers all.
But then he woke! His robe was covered with
A sappy sweat, as if he were a smith
At work upon the forge. He sat up then
In bed and tried to slow his breathing. When
The prince was calm, aware it was a dream,
He pondered on its meaning more, the theme
Of which he couldn't rid from out his mind.
He knew, for sure, his death had been assigned
As punishment for acts he hadn't done.
He racked his brain there in the morning sun,
Remembering each scene as it occurred
Within his dream. The first thing was he heard
The wind, a howling thing in both his ears.
It was so loud, he even had a fear
That it would wake him from his sleep. He was
Upon a field, a verdant plain because
Of all the leafy green. There on that field
He saw, caught in the grass, a crown. He kneeled

To pick it up. But then he saw around
The crown were floret vines with blossoms wound
And looped about the band. And so, he tried
To pull them off. Each strand and shoot he pried
From off the crown. But what came next was odd,
As odd things go within a dream's façade:
From out the ground there sprung, around his feet,
A multitude of flower buds to meet
Him as he walked. He thought to pick a few,
The pretty budding stems, and these he threw
Into his rucksack as he went. The day
Was spent in strolling on that grassy way
And picking flowers as he walked. But what
The prince saw next had stopped him in his strut
And picking spree. He saw upon the ground
A royal bud, a flower like none found
Before that point—a rare, enchanting gem—
But it was long since severed from the stem.
It lay upon the grass, a priceless shoot,
And so, the prince, to gather for his loot,
Kneeled down to take that flower from the grass.
Just then the sky, with charcoal clouds amass,
Was gearing up in some dark, stormy tone;
Below that roaring force the prince was thrown.
A voice, like thunder, then commenced to speak,
And at that voice the prince would dare not peek.
"I am the One who dictates life and death;
The wind of animation is My breath.
Now for your destitution I'm resigned,
For with another's flower you have dined.
So try these words to get your head around:
To servant whom I favor she is bound."
The prince then pled his case before the wind,
His knees a shaking mess, his nerve unpinned
From all courageous acts. "It's not my fault!"
The mortal cried to innocence exalt.
"The man said she was sister, not his wife!
That said, do You still want to take my life?
For me and mine are guiltless of this act.

Go on and probe my will; it is intact."
Then God responded, "You are not to blame,
But still your fruitful orchard is now lame.
You must return the flower where it lay,
And ask the prophet, for your kingdom, pray."

A climber scales the rocks of mountain sides
With cautious grip, for it alone provides
His tether to this life. One misplaced hand
Could mean a fall and plummet to demand-
Ing earth below.

Like so, the prince had backed
His hand away from Sarah then, retract-
Ing all the flirts he'd given her. He would
Not touch the married girl! He only stood
A moment watching her, asleep and in
The morning sun. She looked quite young; her skin
Was caramel in shade, and raven curls
Fell from her head and rested, as if pearls,
Around her eyes and on her slender cheek.
She looked as though she were a bud, all sleek
With dew, about to blossom in the spring.
But at that moment, love was not the thing
He had in mind. He wanted justice, swift!
He'd bring the lying prophet then; a shrift
Was to be made. He left the sleeping lass
Upon the bed and called the man, the ass
Who'd lied to him. When Abraham arrived,
The prince could only stare. He had deprived
Abe of a reason for the call, and now
He thought to let him sweat and guess, to cow
Him with his disapproving eyes. He probed;
His glare was all interrogation robed.
"I want you to be straight with me; don't spoon
Me lies," He said. "The girl who has been strewn
Across my bed, the one you say is just
Your sis—is she your wife?" Then Abram fussed
About. He wondered if his wife had talked,

Had spilled the beans. But still, he acted shocked;
He would pretend it all was news to him.
"My wife?" he said—before he'd drown, he'd swim.
"What makes you think that girl would be my wife?"
And then the prince, who watched the old man fife
His way through words, thought better they should come
Right down to it. "Be plain with me; don't drum
That lie again." Then Abraham, who knew
The jig was up, confessed, "Well, yes, it's true.
If we are splitting hairs upon the knife,
She started as my sister, now she's wife."
And then the prince, refreshed that he had pried
The truth from Abram's aged jaw, replied,
"It's good to hear." He said, "I thought my mind
Was gone, considering the dream divined
Last night. I'm sure I heard your God speak loud
And clear, right through a charcoal thunder cloud.
He threatened my own life because of you."
The prince was serious, and Abram knew
He'd gone too far. "My God, you say?" His talk
Was more the meek and even filled with shock,
Now that his God was there. He wondered, though,
Why God unto this godless whelp would show
Himself. Abe said, "You're sure it was my God?"
He had to ask. The prince gave him a nod.
Then Abraham, ashamed and quite sincere:
"I did not know the fear of God was here."
And then the prince, who thought the whole thing strange—
That lies for Sarah's beauty would exchange—
Made bold to ask, "Why should that matter, fool?
If God be God, your honesty should rule
If I had feared the same or not." And then
He pushed it more: "But tell me this: as men—
Or man to man, whichever you prefer—
What causes someone like yourself to blur
The truth about their wife while knowing well
I might have bed her down? What profit, tell,
Or scheme was in your mind?" And Abraham,
His head hung low, the pieces of his sham

Across the floor. "You see——" he stammered out,
"You see, there was this promise spoke about
My wife and I, that we would children bear.
A daunting task, considering my flair
Is all but dried up by my age. You see,
I thought, perhaps, you'd do this thing for me."
The prince then stopped him short—oh, what a sight,
A heathen more than prophet knowing right.
"I think it's time you leave," was all he said.
He got someone to fetch the wife from bed
Then sent the couple on their way with gifts
Of every sort, a ransom paid to lift
The curse from off his house. And all this served
To highlight how the promise was preserved—
That not through action, right or wrong coerced,
But trusting God would see God's will dispersed.

CHAPTER 14

Promise Fulfilled

In His good time, when time was fullness stuffed,
The LORD saw fit to keep His word—not bluffed,
But told in earnest to them both. They saw
The waist of Sarah grow—a common law
Well learned by every boy and lass but not
By elderly who've long since youth forgot.
To Sarah, then, while brittle in her bones,
A buoyant boy was born. The painful groans
Of labor were quite easily dismissed
As off she cleaned the brine and forehead kissed.
They called him laughter—Isaac was the name.
For when they'd heard the promise, to their shame,
They both let belt a hardy, deep guffaw.
And who could blame them? Anybody's jaw
Would drop with news like that. Their laughs were jeers
At first, but then their chuckles came from cheer.
"Who thought that at this age," Sarah expressed,

"I'd give a newborn suck against my breast."   (GENESIS 21:7)
As soon as Isaac felt the blade, a stamp
And snip as witnessed by all those in camp,
A feast had been announced. The fattened calf
(If calf they had for feast) was cut in half
And portioned out on spits. They set to wrap
Those flanks with strips of fat. The meat would lap
The dripping, fatty juices that would glaze
A tasty char upon the crust. The blaze
Would roast beneath the spits for most the day
As on they turned till golden brown. Then, trays
Were brought to catch the meat that fell right off
The white-hot metal pikes. Let vegans scoff
At those who eat this way, but I won't lie—
It is a primal urge I can't deny.
But when the meat was turning still, when hands
Were cleansed and faces washed, they shook the sand
From out their shoes and pressed their finest dress
To wear. They poured the wine in bowls no less
Than full and mixed in honey spice and herbs
To fit their taste. They tried their best to curb
Their appetites with potent wine so sweet
As round them floated scents of roasted meat.
The carpet had been rolled; no red compared,
For not a single one expense was spared
By Abraham for his late-coming son.
And all were glad with him! Yes, all but one—
For Abram's son from Hagar felt a sting
Within his chest. There was no feast to sing
His birth, no celebration made, no mirth
Within the camp when his poor mother's girth
Had labored him. And now he had been told
Those first in line would second places hold.
He'd had about enough of that! His ma
Had tried to cheer him up, had said a Shah
He'd be, that princes and that kings would come
To follow him. But these were only crumbs
In Ishmael's mind. The juice, for him, was in
A father's favor, pure and genuine.

For years and years he'd held the honored place,
Been told he was a son to them, that grace
Had brought him to the man of age. But now
He had to step aside! The why and how
Seemed insignificant. His days were done!
Old Abram wore a glow for this new son,
And Ishmael had to come to terms with it.
But what about his mom, the one whose grit
Had suffered underneath the dirty looks
And churlish tones of Sarah, who partook
In disrespectful words for years? What had
She ever done? *Poor, songless bird—unclad*
Of joy, you suffered under jealous hands
For doing what you had been told—to stand
And let your body so be used beneath
The wrong intents of man, a paltry sheath
For Abram's seed. All knew it wasn't right
That she was used that way. Who else would fight
For her if not her son? So, Ishmael nursed
His silent judgments of contempt and cursed
Beneath his breath the child of promise born!
But Sarah wasn't blind; she saw the scorn
The son of Hagar held and knew what brewed
Inside. That night, the feast was had—not lewd
Or near debauched, but good, clean fun (amen).
For truly wine makes glad the hearts of men!
Yet when the darkness fell—when all had had
Their fill of meat and wine, exhaustion (add
That also to the mix)—then someone heard,
Or thought they saw, a sneer; perhaps a word
Or mock was whispered in among the crowd.
"It came from Hagar or her son," one vowed
That was the case. It may have been a threat,
But something said devoid of etiquette.

A mother bear will let her cub explore
A field of bracken fern. He wanders more
Ahead to where the grass is thick and hides
Behind the waving stalks of green. His stride

Is confident and courage-fed as on
He goes from sight. He watches waking Dawn
Then reach into his hefty bag of seed
And cast the morning's golden rays; they bead
Above the mountain peaks and gently land
As freckled light upon the waving strands
Of dewy grass. But then he stumbles on
A clearing trampled down. He sees a fawn
Is mangled on the ground, and there's a beast
Who's tearing at that carcass of a feast.
His snout is smeared with blood and gore, the guts
And entrails of that shapeless mass. He gluts
Himself upon the warm and tender parts.
But then he notices the cub; he starts
At him and growls. He thinks he's come to steal
The flesh and bone that constitute his meal.
The cub cries out in fear and turns to run
Away. The mother bear then hears her son
And rages at the threat, to counsel blind,
Prepared to maul whatever she might find.

So Sarah raged when she caught wind her son
Might in some harm's way be! She would have none
Of it! And right or wrong, her biased tongue
Determined Ishmael's future be unsung.
"Cast out Egyptian child; he'll be no heir,
Nor with my child of promise will he share
In any blessings that we give!" So spoke
The pious mother of the faith. It broke
The heart of Abraham in two. It was
His fault; he never should have put his paws
On Hagar's curves nor listened to his wife's
So-wise advice to bed her down. Now strife
Was born from his own lack of faith, which acts
Would see a guilty conscience now exact
The payment for. He didn't make the choice
To cast her out so easily. His voice
Was shaky in his age, but moral code
Was strong. To tell that girl to hit the road

Without a thing to show for all her sweat
And tears would be a thing he would regret.
But if he let her stay, that mix would brew
Into a harpy fight between the two,
His wife on one side with a wit so sharp
To animate her mouth in constant carp
Till dead horse died again—and servant maid
On other side, compelled without a shade
Of attitude or greed and strung with ropes
Of shallow promises and empty hopes
Of grandeur for her son. With vows like pearls,
Abe whispered on that ear—*poor trusting girl.*
But pillow-promises were on recall,
For things had changed. The writing on the wall
Told something else. Old Abram's God came through
And kept His word then, in the end. Who knew?
But Hagar was the casualty, deceived,
Expendable when Sarah had conceived.
But that was that! His wife was wife and she
Was not! Now Abram was too old to see
His household torn apart if he allowed
The girl to stay, and good intents were cowed
To cold neglect! And what else could he say?
He promised he would alimony pay
And see the boy on weekends, too. And such
Is life, when all those weighty matters touch
Upon Discernment's knee for sound advice.
We find our actions wanting at the price
Of wrongs we've done. So, Abraham then turned
To God for consolation, for he yearned
To know he had the lesser evil chose.
God said, "The boy will be just fine; he goes
To make a mighty kingdom, which will call
One-third the earth to number in its wall.
The choice you made, though hard, was still the best.
Take Sarah's word—the bond with free won't rest!"
Then Abram watched as Hagar and her son
Departed from the camp. It had been done,
And he had sent them on their way. And yet,

If we have clever minds and don't forget
The ending of this tale, we'd surely know
That Hagar and her son did not then go
So far from out the camp that never they
Were seen again by Abraham. Let's say
They occupied a weekend place, a house
Just on the fringe of camp where partial spouse
Was safe. But if on truth you can't decide,
Remember who was there when Abram died.

CHAPTER 15

Pass the Test

Some tales are better allegory spun,
This more than most. That said, it had begun
With tactful lies, and that, without a doubt.
No wife lets husband kill her child, devout
Or not. And if that little part is true,
Then there's no way in Hades Sarah knew
What Abram planned. His purpose had been hid-
Den! For, if she had known, she would forbid
Him from departing out the camp. It's safe
To say that Abe, before his wife could chafe
His masterplan, had packed his bags and left
At break of dawn. She never saw the theft
Of their own son take place. All heard the rant
She brewed at breakfast meal! She was no aunt,
But mother, and she had a right to know
Where he would take their son. She thought to go
And track him down, to give a hefty piece

From off her mind. She'd see to his decease
If Isaac came to harm. Her womb, she knew,
Had grown the lad, and from her breasts he drew
The very milk her body made like sap.
At night, his tears would calm as he would lap
Each droplet off that heaving reservoir.
It was not just the husband whom God swore
The promise to. It was more hers than his!
Think now; he had a child with that young miss
And slave; they knew his plumbing still could fit
The bill. Indeed, it proved quite adequate
And worked just fine! In truth, the promise was
For barren wife to have the son. Because
Of this, she had at least an equal share
In how the boy was raised. It was her prayer
God answered, too. But Abraham assumed
A lot and took the boy to be consumed
Upon a sacrificial pyre of wood.
What pagan courtship in the flirt! How could
He honestly consider it? I'm not
Inclined to give this man a prize or swat
Him on the back for his continued marks
Of faith. I'll say this much—that patriarchs
Do not require our credulous advance.
Their actions right or wrong came not by chance
But ever in their own ambitions done.
They're dirty as the rest and haven't won
Our admiration by their excellence.
Indeed, it's fitting that irreverence
And something critical should ever be
The spectacles through which these men we see.
And please don't ever fail in your recall
That grace abounds when short of standards fall.
We do God's mercy some injustice when
We sugarcoat the acts of girls and men.
But let that go. "This tale is not the same,"
You say. "In fact, our God Himself makes claim
That Abram, through his exploits here, was shown
To fear his God and that his fear was known

To God because of them. And when so much
His actions were complete did angels touch
The man and say to put his knife aside."
But step from out that box wherein you hide
And ask the inescapable: would not
The God of heaven know before He got
To see it all played out that Abram feared
His God? Or think of this—that God, unteared,
Would ask then of His friend (for Abram was
A friend to God) to kill his son because
God had to know that Abraham was scared
Of Him. *Oh, don't you know respect is paired*
With fear? That's what it really means. I think
I've said enough on this and at the sink
Will wash my hands of it. Believe that which
You will. For me, I'll shovel fact to ditch;
I'll praise the allegory ever for
Its meaning and its purpose and, what's more,
Its making sense of stories ludicrous.
But back to Abraham, for him (not us)
Our text would more explain. That man then must
Have questioned his own feeble mind. Unjust
It all would seem, absurd to say the least,
To kill the son of promise like a beast
Upon a pile of stones. Or maybe he
Was only hearing things. *Senility's*
A common flaw of age. But what of God's
Great promise for the stars? Was He a fraud
To guarantee the ends and kill the means?
Or view it from pragmatic heights: who gleans
A profit when they kill their son? Let all
That go, and only think upon the gall
Of such a God in that inane command,
Dictating out an act that He had banned
Not long before. After the flood, God said,
"If by a man another's blood is shed,
Then by another's hand that one shall die."
And if that be the way of it, then why
Stop there? Let's bring another who might kill

The justice doer in their deed. But will
We let that one escape his punishment
In turn? Oh, not upon my watch! Consent
To stand in line like dominos and wait
Sequential turns as we officiate
The deaths of those in front and then receive
Our own from those who stand behind. But leave
This logic off to rest. We'll need a brake
Applied or all the earth a ghost town make.
Our story says that Abraham had heard
God's voice and, like some minuteman, had stirred
To meet the call when it had come. Debate
It all you like—Abe would propitiate
His God and His preposterous command.
A weighty chore, but Abram's palsied hand
Would see the job complete, and it was in
The grayer hues of dawn—that stretching grin
Of coming day that stops the snoring mouth
Of night—he packed his bags and headed south.

A man will take a journey far into
The barren desert sands, a trip that few
Would ever dare to take. He plans to fast
And seek his purpose there, try to outlast
His body's need for food. He presses on
For many days alone; each rising dawn
Foretells the scorching heat that stands ahead.
His mouth is dry, and footsteps where he's tread—
The ones that mark his path for home—fill up
With sand. He sips the final drops his cup
Has left and stumbles on against the wind,
A blinding, dusty heat. He can't rescind
His choice and feels his tongue begin to swell
Within his cracking mouth. His spirit tells
Him more than will his body in those times.
It's more alert as more his body chimes
The bells of death. His mind plays tricks, and he
Believes he's found a water hole. He sees
It with is eyes but cannot bring his mind

To trust it's there. Yet still he is inclined
To seek it out; his thirst tells him he must.
His footsteps then are not in sense but trust.

So Abraham, uneasy in his gait,
Pushed on. His troubled mind saw that debate
That comes when doubt takes hold of it. And yet
He would persist; belief in him was set

As is an anchor dropped from hollow ships
When storms rush in across the sea. They tip
The wooden bulk from side to side and lift
It on each crashing wave. The ship will drift
By shores and jutting rocks with such a squall
Till oars are stilled and men within the hull
Sit mutely on their benches soaked with spray.
They hear the heavy steel plunge down; away
It dives, the clanking chain like rattled teeth,
Until it's lodged the bedrock underneath.

So Abraham was tossed within his thoughts.
They jockeyed in his mind for what he ought
To do. And this was not some rapid trip
Of half an hour or so. No, scholarship
Would have us so assured—it took three days
To reach the spot where Abraham would slay
His promised son. He had the time to turn
His mind, his caravan, around—to spurn
The whole endeavor as a farce. But still,
He bullied on regardless of the chills
He felt when Isaac smiled at him. Or say
The man was growing numb, and more each day
That torment of a trip went on. When they
Arrived, had made their camp so they could stay
Awhile, old Abram looked then at the mount,
Preparing for what would be tantamount
To murder in the first. And then, with speed,
He crammed his bag with all the things he'd need
And tossed it on his shoulder blades whereon

He'd carry it. Then, like some Myrmidon
Who gives no second thought before he storms
The fields of war, old Abe abandoned norms
Of parenthood and loaded on the back
Of Isaac all the wood and tinder stack.
Abe turned and to the servants said, "Stay here.
I'll take the boy to worship. Watch the gear,
And in a couple days we'll both be back."   (GENESIS 22:5)
Then Abraham and Isaac hit the track
That led unto Moriah's distant crest.
Before too long, the old man needed rest
And stumbled for a seat. He was too old
For mountain hikes, and pain was manifold
Within his aching joints as down he sat
To rest. The boy was patient, though, at that—
And even helped his father sit and stand.
The lad reached out and took that wrinkled hand,
Then tepid with its hampered flow of blood.
He pulled his father to his feet, the bud
Of youth then lending aid to rusty shears
That then had planned and soon would engineer
A harvest cut too soon. The day was spent
In walking and in resting as they went
Up slopes and crags to summit tops. And there,
In the formation of the rock, was hair
In tufts of grass on what looked like a skull.
It had the teeth, the mouth; its eyes were dull
With vacant shade, and for its bony nose,
A tree half-bent and in that posture froze.
They put their bags where dimples, cute as beans,
Had been, and then they piled the stones. The scene
Was set; the pyre was stacked with brittle wood.
Then Isaac went up to his dad. He stood
There for a while and in no way unkind
(The boy thought it had slipped his father's mind)
Asked in a sheepish voice of Abraham,
"We've wood and fire, but where now stands the lamb?"
With timid words, old Abraham replied,
"My son, our God will sacrifice provide."

The old man stood in silence, waiting there
To see if God would speak and somehow spare
Him from that moment, hard in truth. He heard
No voice, no wind or rustled shrub, no bird
Above. He didn't hear the slightest sound!
Reluctantly, then, tiny hands were bound,
And up the lad was placed upon the sticks
And stones. Then Abram said, his heart quite sick
With grief, "I've heard but do not understand.
Our God has bid I strike you with my hand."
Then through their tears, both dad and son obeyed.
The son lay still; the dad unsheathed the blade.
But Abraham just couldn't lift his hand
To strike the lad and kill him as he planned.
Then Isaac said, "My father, turn away,
Look not on son of promise whom you slay."
Old Abram thought that good advice and closed
His eyes. No other thing then stood opposed.
While leaving stroke to fall, Abe made his choice.
Then came the sound of knife-arresting voice,
"Lay not your faithful hand against the boy!
I see the pure intents that you employ
And know—yes, now I know—that you fear God.
Your faith, My friend, is something to applaud."
Then Abram heard a noise (at least, he thought)
And turned to see a ram that had been caught
By both its horns. The old man smiled and pulled
Some rope from out the bag he'd brought. So tooled,
He looped an end and fed it round the neck.
He then untwined the thicket that bedecked
The ram around his gnarled and spiral horns.
The whole appeared to be a crown of thorns
Wrapped round that jerking head. When he was free,
The old man led him over, peacefully,
To where the altar was already made.
Up Isaac rose, and down the ram was laid.
Then sacrifice was made in Isaac's stead,
The very place a future Lamb would tread.
So Abraham, his actions thought unflawed,
Had served to represent, by type, his God.

CHAPTER 16

Bride

Mortality should come in daily dose.
That doesn't mean we should run comatose
Through life with melancholy needles in
Our arms nor push extremes of wearing grins
From dawn to dusk as if that somehow wards
Away the jaws of death. Our room and board
Upon this earth will neither shrink nor stretch
The span of days our God saw fit to etch
Before our birth. My friend, that time is fixed!
And even if you disagree, by Styx
And Stygian, you still are logic bound
And must admit that to the chilly ground
You will be laid one day. Here is my point—
That death will touch us all; it is the joint
That sees us linked. But why the daily dose?
Well, Spurgeon, prince of preachers, more verbose
In pulpit brim, said something of this sort.

In quoting him, or more by loose report,
He said, "It isn't hard to die, per se,
When one dies more to self the more each day."
And take it from the guy who writes beside
The granite graveyard stones (a dignified
Profession and a sexton, in a sense)
To see the rocks of death each day, to cense
Them with my wordless breath—does well remind
Me of the looming fact, more true than kind,
That life is not a given thing, that years
Are short, and soon that crabby gondolier
Will take my obols, not just one but two.
But let me ask a question now of you:
Will you do more, when after you have died,
Than choke the worms upon formaldehyde?
Or tell me, will you just give name and date
To weighty telamons we situate
Atop our bones in hopes they might just hold
Our memory up or see our exploits told?
Or will you leave behind some legacy
To speak when body shows a vacancy?
This thought was drilled into my mind when I
Was young and in my zeal, when thirst and cry
Were ever for my purpose on this earth.
I had to know and even judged my worth
In how I knew myself—or insomuch
Why I was born. This thought would not declutch
Until I knew, and then, in finding out
In middle years of life, dismissing doubt,
I set myself to work. Perhaps you've guessed
The thing I've settled on—it is confessed
The more you read my angry sermons here.
But as for you, be glib or be sincere—
But be yourself and what you're meant to be.
But let's get in the text, for there we see
A man called Abraham, when he was full
Of years, had started more to feel the rule
Of death upon his life. What would he leave
Behind? That man of faith would ever cleave

To hope that in some way his children would
Be like the stars. That's what he understood!
But flex your Latin now upon this phrase:
That *Per aspera ad astra* in ways
Comes close to what he was about. He reached
For something that he couldn't see and leeched
Himself to hope. The more he grew in age,
The more he trusted then his God. Marriage
Had ended when sweet Sarah, tender wife
And love since youth, was laid to rest. That knife
Cut deep, and more and more he sensed the need
To find a wife for Isaac's future seed.
With frail and dying words, the old man spake,
"My son will not a wife from Canaan take."
Then to his trusted servant gave the chore
Of finding him a bride. "Go and explore
The land of Ur; it's there where you will find
A woman for my son of promise—kind
And gentle, tactful, sage, of good report.
The ones in Canaan's land are not the sort
I want for him." Old Abe thought they would taint
His son's pure heart away from God, acquaint
Him with some stranger worship. So, to Ur
The servant made his way to find a "Her"
Who might his master's grave request fulfill.
His journey stopped at Nahor's gates. The frill
And pomp of wealth was lavishly displayed
Outside those walls, his camels well arrayed
With heavy bags of jewels and gold. He set
His camp beside a well, and there he'd vet
The maidens of that town. He'd surely find
A girl who could be Isaac's wife, refined
And simply better than the rest. She'd be
A girl with many virtues held; beauty
And looks were only part of it. She had
To be immaculate as Galahad,
As reticent as are the ocean hues,
And resolute as any goddess, true
To wisdom more than passion's changing flame.

Yes, that's the kind he would select and claim
To be his wife. The same that man would choose
For Isaac, too, not by some trick or ruse
But by an irreproachable intent.
He'd speak it plain, tell her why he was sent
And what the expectation was. Yet still,
There was the chance he'd get it wrong. His skill
Was only human, after all. He'd need
Divine direction if he would succeed.
And so, that man had thought to place a fleece
Before the Lord, the whole time hoping peace
Would come unto his master, Abraham.
"By this I'll know You favor my exam,"
He prayed, "Let she who comes to water draw
Give tumbler of refreshment to my jaw,
And then, in turn, the camels here with me.
And this will serve as proof." So was his plea.
And with those words still dangling from his tongue,
A maiden ventured near; her pitcher slung
Around her shoulders, delicate and fair.
He could not get his eyes to break their stare!
So, mutely that man watched the virgin dame
For water come. Her beauty made him lame
Within his bones; his heart began to race!
Enchanting were the features of her face!
She filled her pitcher, turning then to leave,
He blurted out, "Won't you, my thirst relieve?"
She turned and smiled with what could well assuage
The angry storming of a Mars's rage.
Rebekah, gift of God, then gave him drink,
Poured also for his herd to earthen sink.
"Well, that was fast," he thought. His mission crowned,
And quickly round her neck some jewels were bound.
He told her all about his quest and how
He made a distant journey there, his vow
Sworn to his dying master that he'd find
A woman for his son so they'd be twined
And take some wedded vows. Such was his task.
"What is your name?" that servant thought to ask.

She told him she was born a relative
Of Abraham, then off she ran to give
The house a good once-over clean and sweep—
Not every day they had a guest to keep.
And then her brother Laban sniffed the gold
A mile away. He greased his hair and strolled,
With all the swag his limbs could muster up,
On out to meet this one who'd come to sup.
Still flustered, though, from side to side he swayed,
To see one ostentatiously displayed.
He urged the servant, "Stay!" Eyes greener glowed
And ogled all the camels' heavy load.
There was some back and forth upon the price
For such a bride, and Laban had his dice
In weighted skew. Hard bargains then were shoved
Around the tent, rapacious and ungloved,
For Laban knew the servant's mind was set
To take Rebekah home. He knew he'd get
His asking price. But down the question came
To what the girl would do. She wasn't lame
To make the choice; she would decide the course
Her feet would tread! No brother's hand could force
Her way ahead. But then that graceful doe,
Without compulsion, said that she would go
And make a life with him she'd never met.
And there were tears, of course, for don't forget
Rebekah had her sisters there with her.
The Kleenex box was put to use as were
The sweet goodbyes. But then her sisters said,
Or more pronounced, their hands on Bekah's head,
"Dear sister, may our blessing go with thee;   (GENESIS 24:60)
May you endure, a mighty mother be!
This God who calls you now will surely bless
Your line, and they'll increase and will possess
What their opposers hold. Go dwell that land,
And to a thousand-thousands you'll expand."
When all was said and done on that account,
When Isaac saw his bride-to-be dismount,
It was as if she held the morning dew.

And in that moment, Isaac's heart she slew.
The girl became his wife, and at her breast
He found some peace since Sarah went to rest.

CHAPTER 17

All for Stew

The belly is a beast to be obeyed.
Great Homer thought it so and even made
A point to call it such one time of note
Within the *Odyssey*. He said, I quote,
"It is a shameless dog not soon ignored."
Well, I agree. The stomach is a horde
Of angry peasants who have come to beat
On our Versailles of diet plans. They greet
With pitchforks and a torch. "Enough with grass!"
They shout, "Give us the cake!" The wars of class
Might easily be settled with a din-
Ner card—your wine and cheese, your violin
To lullaby the mongrels back to sleep.
The stomach grumbles constantly and keeps
Us waiting hand and foot—from morning crack
Through lunch and dinner bells to midnight snacks.
It seems an ever-willing candidate

To make its voice be heard, to demonstrate
The great coercive means at its dispose.
And all who breathe in life have felt the throes
Of that thing's whim. It is the voice all in-
Fants hear before their mother's milk comes in.
It's only when our death makes its descent
That appetite will die, a life well spent
In making mighty men of earth succumb.
So, futile it would seem to try and drum
This dog in check—this shameless beast who sends
Our will and power packing, even mends
Our wagon for the road. Why fight a mutt
Like this? We may but only turn to glut
Ourselves on all the food we were denied
On roads of self-restraint. Ascetics chide
The weak who say they cannot miss a meal,
Those Puritans who'd rather set their heels
To wilderness patrols or fasts of for-
Ty days while sucking breath mints down and pour-
Ing Listerine in caps. They'd have us starve
So that we somehow chisel, somehow carve
A spirit with a sixpack and a tan.
I really think the *Übermensch* or superman
They're going for will suffer anorex-
Ic fits. But let the Gnostic pontifex
Proclaim *ad nauseam*, as if God has-
N't made the body with the soul more as
Companion, not a simple shell to store
Eternal things. I'll take this one step more
Than Dorian; I say we only know
The soul by what the senses tell. Ergo,
Deny the teacher and the student fails
The class. But who am I? Pull out your pail
Of water and your bar of soap; go scrub
The sackcloth down against your lack of chub,
The washboard of your chest. *I see the ribs*
Are pushing through. You think God doles in dribs
And drabs and has a penny-pinching mind?
Your soul is not far off! I'm more inclined

To think of balance in such times as these,
To keep the dog but rid him of the fleas
And his persistent need to smell a crotch.
We'll loosen up our belts and add a notch
When girth sees fit. We'll taste and even feast
Here at the table of the earth. Our beast
Of hunger will be proper shaved and clipped
With meals enjoyed and not with ones we've skipped.
Why, even Buddha gave it up at length—
The skipping meals, I mean. He found more strength
In tasting and in teaching humble ways.
As for myself, when in my younger days
And wanting zeal of something more devout,
I'd try to fast a day, at least, hold out
As long as adolescence could delay
A need to eat. I'd meditate and pray
But found my mind distracted and much more
Than usual. I thought I could ignore
The shameless dog, the moaning mutt, put down
My need until I'd reached some peak, some crown-
Ing point for my accomplishments. I'd leave
That race with cheap concessions made, retrieve
A steak that Mom had frozen, see it thawed
Against a pan, then plated up and jawed
In haste. That prize for my short trial of pain
Worked wonders on an empty gut, sustain-
Ing though it was. But when I look back now
Upon those times—when I consider how
My lone devotions were distracted by
A hungry beast and how much calmer I
Could give my time to God when shameless dogs
Were fed and on a rug—my epilogue
Most surely makes the case that meals should not
Be ever missed. Now, furthermore, it's taught
That God has made the soul (the body and
The soul) and given these into our hands
To teach mankind some stewardship. Now tell
Me how a steward ever could dispel
A hungry tenant in their care, ignore

The basic needs for them to live? What's more,
How could they starve that one and think it will
Please God? Oh, sick and twisted ways to drill
Some mock obedience. Just flowerpot
Your common-sense, then go and pick a spot
Upon the sill where it gets lots of sun.
We'll look at it from time to time and run
Our fingers on the leaves; we'll even kiss
Them like phylacteries, some benefice
Of God that sits unused. Why bring this up?
Why go to such extents to state that sup-
Per should be recognized, that daily bread
Might have a double meaning but is spread
To both with equal care? Oh, it's because
Of this: that Esau, though that heathen was
A brute, a hairy Philistine—he still
Was just a man, a hungry man who'd fill
His belly like each one of us. Who knows
How famished he had been, what vertigo
Or dizzy spells had worked upon his mind
When meatless he returned from hunting hind?
Such hungry moments make for cannibals!
We shouldn't judge the brutal Hannibals
Among our ranks; we'll need these Sons of Mars
When seasons turn to war. But chances are,
Poor Esau left the field by some Divine—
Indeed, some prohibition or design
Of God to make him hungry all the more!
Or maybe you forgot Almighty swore
To have the older brother bowing down?
You must remember it. He said the crown
Would sit the younger brother's head. Therefore,
He'd tip the scales and auspice underscore.
I simply mean to emphasize that God
Had kept that hairy nincompoop and clod
From killing any food that fateful day.
Or maybe I would go so far to say
That many days had Esau gone without
A morsel crossing underneath his snout.

His hunger must have been immense! Let go
Your judgments, friend. Our daily dealings show
The paths God sets our feet to wend. Perhaps
The story slips your idle mind, some lapse
Now brought about by who-knows-what. But set
Yourself at ease. Unlock your cellaret
And put your screws to use. But I would urge
To only have a glass or two. Submerge
Those woes enough to get them soaked, but care-
Ful not to drown the things. And, if I'm fair,
I'll tell you that I am a man who's filled
Recycle bins with empty bottles, killed
In decadence, a graveyard set to curb
Too many times. But still, it is superb
When we consume no more or sip no less
Than just enough. That is the goal, I guess.
At any rate, we'll have this story told,
Or rather have my mind to verse unrolled.
Well, after Isaac got his bride and went
And married her—the needed compliment
For many men—he found (or rather they
Discovered) how her womb was dry as clay.
You see, Rebekah was a barren wife.
It's crazy when you think of it, the strife
That Isaac's mother felt would be the same
His bride would feel. It also proved a shame
To her, that she would fail to have a child
For Isaac's line. Their way of life was styled
On this contingency, to have a son—
The only thing they had to do, the ton
Of bricks they carried round. The blessing had
Been spoke to Abraham; God said he'd add
A bunch of kids unto their line. "Like sand,"
Their God had said. Well, Isaac hadn't planned
On struggling this way, and so he prayed
About it all—about the troubles weighed
Upon his mind. The answer had come quick,
Considering the many years—the thick,
Slow-moving years—his father spent with that

Great pedagogue called Time. Old Abe grew fat
On patience pie. But Isaac got to sing
Another tune. He didn't have to wring
His hands or sit the edge of seats, or bite
His nails while waiting out the dial. One might
Just say the answer came too quick, for words
Had hardly left his mouth before he heard
His wife was found with child. In spite of this,
Of quick replies to their requests, the bliss
That Bekah felt would prove but sweet and short.
For she had twins inside her womb, the sort
Of twins that just don't get along. She felt
Them fight around the clock as each one dealt
A blow against his brother's frame. She could-
N't get a break, nor had she understood
The ruckus in her uterus, the spat
That kicked the ribs and on her bladder sat.
She prayed to God for what had seemed her bane;
The very thing that should be joy was pain.
She said, "Oh, God—there must be something wrong!
This fight within runs morn to evensong."
Then in a dream she heard what would ensue:
God said, "Inside you, nations number two.
In rustic fields the first will hunt the stag
And find his camp on Edom's mountain crag.
The second will a humble life suffice,
Persistent for the pearl of greatest price.
Yet, I have chosen favor fall on he;
That second should be first is My decree."
And just as God had said, when labor crowned,
The first one out with hairy flanks was gowned.
As furry as a rug he was, and red—
From heel up to the top his shaggy head.
The second, wanting former place to steal,
Had clung and dangled off his brother's heel.
He held it tight; the midwife had to pry
The fingers off! The first one gave a cry,
For he had lost some hair unto the sec-
Ond's fist. Then, like some speedy turtleneck,

The arm was pulled back in. The midwife screamed!
She never had imagined or had dreamed
She'd see a sight like that. But it was seen.
Then out he came, the twin, bald as a bean
And crying like he just had lost a race,
The shame of second place still on his face.
In time, on other paths the lads had grown
To men, and love from different parents known.
The father loved the first because he filled
His belly with the meat that Esau killed.
The younger, Jacob, mother thought more dear
And whispered hopeful dreams within his ear.
But Esau held the sole and final claim
Upon his father's blessing hand. The name
Of elder always got the lion's share
Of the inheritance, and it was rare
The younger would have much to show when all
The deathly-divvy had been done. The brawl
Between the Siblings ever rages on.
But mother was a cunning cat! Her spawn,
The younger of the twins, was proper fed
With words how he would lead. She filled his head
With visions and a hope that would preserve
His creed, that elder would the younger serve.
Her bedtime stories drove a wedge betwixt
The two till, finally, young Jacob fixed
His eyes upon the blessing (birthright, too)
While Esau cared for neither one, it's true.
Each worked their trades as younger men, the art
Innate ability had taught. Apart
They grew, with Esau in the field, his bow
Thought well the only friend he needed know,
While Jacob learned to make a tasty soup—
He learned this brewing for the time he'd scoop
The birthright from his brother's grubby paws.
How constant will a jealous urge so gnaw
The mind? One day, when Jacob had outdone
Himself, that pot of stew was next to none
That he had made up till that point—the spice

And flavor, perfect mixed. Upon a slice
Of bread that soup could win a prize! The scent
Was in the air and moved around his tent;
With this he'd catch his prey, the one who'd been
On hunt for most the day. A hearty grin
Hit Jacob's face when he saw Esau leave
The field. That older brother seemed to grieve
An unrewarding hunt. Jake stirred his pot
And watched Esau approach, sad and distraught.
"What is the Esau-ailment of the day?"
Asked Jacob. "Why the vigor spent this way?
For you, my brother, seem to be quite sapped
Of strength. Exhaustion's cloak looks tightly wrapped
Around your neck and back." "Why do you care
So much?" asked Esau, cautious of a snare
That might be laid in Jake's beguiling words.
"You rarely conversation make." Jake stirred
The pot and said, "Come, brother, take a seat.
But tell me, where's your kill, the one you'll eat
Tonight from your great hunt? Don't tell me you
Left with an empty hand." Jake sighed. "The stew
I make does not compare with those choice cuts
Of meat you always get. Our father gluts
Himself upon those juicy steaks." "My hunt
Bagged nothing, and my hunger bears the brunt
Of it," carped Esau, sniffing Jacob's stew.
Jake saw and ladled out a scoop, then blew
On it to cool and taste. Esau went on,
"That's pungent porridge you have made; upon
My life, it smells so good!" "What, this?" asked Jake,
A bit too modestly. "It is not steak,
But still it warms the ribs on such a night
As this." Then Esau felt his appetite
Complain, his stomach let a rumble go,
And then he said, without much thought, "You know,
That is a lot of soup you've made. I'd pay
For some." Then Jacob said, a coy display
Of some regret, "I have already swore
To give some to the staff and such. Those poor

Things are already underpaid. I'm bound."
Keen Esau's mouth was dripping like a hound
Upon the scented trail. His stomach was
A master to obey—his fingers, claws
That bored into the dirt beneath. Jake stirred
The pot. And Esau, with his reason blurred,
Pronounced these words, not even thinking twice:
"Then sell me your own share; just name the price."
Jacob was calm, though all his innards smiled
To think of his advantage gained. The child
Was in the candy shop to pick a prize.
Jake gave a final stir to tantalize
His brother who was drooling like a mutt.
"There's one thing you have that I'm wanting, but
I don't think that you'd part with it." "Just tell
Me what it is," snipped Esau, "and I'll sell
It for some soup." Then Jacob coolly said
(So many times rehearsed it in his head),
"Sell me the birthright you, as elder, hold.
By this, and this alone, my soup is sold."
Then Esau, quick his choice to justify,
"What use are birthrights if I starve and die?"   (GENESIS 25:32)
He chose to live the moment, and he threw
A great inheritance away for stew.
A healthy helping Jacob ladled out
On bread and placed it under Esau's snout.
Then with his burly appetite he ate
Till it was gone. And with the bread, his plate
Was swabbed quite clean. It surely seemed a waste
To Jake; his brother didn't even taste
The meal he slaved upon, the reprobate.
He dipped the scoop, and on his brother's plate
He ladled one more helping of the stew.
Jake thought this was the least that he could do.

CHAPTER 18

Digging Holes

There was another famine in the land,
And Isaac, son of Abraham, had planned
To lean on extra crops Abimelech
Provided from his store. There was no speck
Of trouble in that help; the younger king
Had simply offered aid without a string.
Still, God unto the son of Abram said,
"On Egypt's soil, your sandals shouldn't tread.
Just walk before Me as your father did
In former days. And though you dwell amid
Your enemies, still I'll see fit to pour
My favor out; I'll keep the oath I swore."
So Isaac, in the green of Gerar, made
A home for quite some time. He also played
The fool, like father Abraham before.
I mean he lied about his wife and swore
She was no more than just his little sis:

"I travel not with Missus but with Miss."
Some lies die hard! Old Abraham had told
His truths half false, and lies half true he sold.
But Isaac didn't have the luxuries
His father had when giving guarantees
About his wife, that she was sister born.
That wasn't even close to true! He'd sworn
It was and round about that man had went
Parading falsities, he quite content
To live a lie. But Bekah, don't forget,
Was tasty treat to see, and on gazettes
And by the word of mouth, the news then spread
Of her availability. Misled
By falsehoods told, the budding bachelors—
Those Philistines then feeling all the spur
Of virile youth—had cast their famished eyes
Upon that verdant maid, which then gave rise
To each their implements of interest.
Each one who looked on her was quite impressed
By Bekah's sweet appeal, not just in form
But also in the sage and crafty storm
That brewed behind her eyes. She was complete
In all her female mysteries, a treat
To all who happened on a lucky peek.
And so, within the course of days and weeks
And even years, the mystery had grown
With suitors who desired to be known
To such a woman on the market free—
Abimelech the most of all! To see
That lovely maid, he'd set a lookout post
Beside his windowsill. He was engrossed
For many afternoons, the tomming peep,
To catch whatever glimpse, however cheap!
On such a day, when in the sky there hung
The noonday sun, so ever neatly slung
Between the morning and the dusk that glows
Its rosy hues, he noticed, in the throes
Of midday love, that one called Isaac there—
And he was chasing round his sister, bare

As ever one could be in birthday suits.
Abimelech then screamed, "Oh, what a brute!
What kind of man would act this way? What sort
Of kinky brother gives their sister sport?"   (GENESIS 26:8)
But Isaac didn't hear and took the maid
Into the shadows of his tent, the shade
That hides such deeds a man and lawful wife
Commit. Oh, then Abimelech was rife
With rage! Not just the object of his lust
Turned out to be a wife, but the disgust
Of seeing Isaac in the nude was more
Than he could bear. He'd heard some tales before,
How Abraham had thought that he could skim
The truth with some deceptive little hymn
About his wife, that only sister was.
And Abram said it was all just because
He thought his life was surely on the line.
The prince then thought he'd bring Isaac to dine
With him and have a little chat. He'd trap
That fraud within his fibbing words and clap
The shackles of the truth upon his tongue.
So, Isaac came; he didn't smell the dung
About to hit the fan when in he stepped.
He only smelled the food, which had been prepped
In proper hospitality. "Here, sit,"
The prince did say. "I'll get right down to it.
That girl you travel with, is she your wife?"
"Oh, her?" Isaac replied. "No, on my life
She's just my sister, but why do you ask?"
Abimelech went on, "Tell me those tasks
Your sister does perform around your tent."
Though Isaac thought the question strange, he went
Then on to list the chores. "She milks the goats,
Does dishes, too. She makes sure all my coats
Are pressed." The prince, a better question framed,
"Does she give sport?" "Give sport!" Isaac exclaimed.
"What do you mean?" "Come on, man—don't be dull!
I saw you from the window down that hall
The other day, as naked as the noon."

But Isaac still persisted, the buffoon.
"I don't know what you mean. Is this a jape?"
"Look, man—if she is not your wife, then rape
Is what I must have seen!" Then Isaac still
Would not give in. (How strong is errant will?)
The prince then said, "Leave off your false report.
I saw you, man! I saw you giving sport
To that fine maid you call your sis. And now
You sit there with that look upon your brow
And say I shouldn't trust my very eyes?
You think I can't perceive a lie? It cries
Of treason, reeks to heaven rank! What if
A passerby or countryman were stiff
Enough within their purpose, her to wed?
Or what if I, Abimelech, had bed
Her down? Oh, what a curse upon my crown
You would have brought." At last, the squirming clown
Came clean and said, "Forgive my lies; they were
Told out of fear. I never meant to stir
Up mischief in your kingdom, lord. This lie
Provided comforts that I'm living by.
My wife has beauty, easy to seduce.
I know how all this sounds; it's no excuse."
The prince was oddly pleased with Isaac's plea,
And over all the land, that man was free
To pitch his tent and roam. The prince still gave
A warning to the men around to stave
Off any upstarts who might give advance.
"Pass not on this man's wife your lusty glance."
So blessings came to both and spilled the brim,
But Philistines began to envy him—
One prospered like that man, the most untold,
But still so much the land could hardly hold
A one like him. His flocks ate grass like moths
Of plague, and on their lips ran salty froth.
But wells that Abraham before had drilled,
With dusty earth the Philistines had filled.
To dig the wells again was Isaac's chore!
And this became his life's great work—restore

And quarry out the wells of their supply.
But locals, in some feigned abuse, made cry
About the first he dug, said rightful claim
Was theirs and theirs alone. He gave the name
Of Discord to that well. And so, he found
Another well that he might dig. But round
The locals came again; their elbows thrust
Into the sides of Isaac's men. They fussed
How such a water source could not admit
Both Isaac's flocks and theirs. They wouldn't fit!
So, Isaac gave that well the name No Room
And swept it from his mind, as with a broom.
At last, that Isaac, blessed with many herds
From God on High, was not the least deterred
And thought to dig a final well—the last
He'd dig. And round those muddy walls were cast
The stones his labor pulled up from the earth.
That well he named Provision at its birth.
Then Isaac saw some proper tribute paid
To God above, for that man had been made
To prosper from God's hand. Well, God appeared
And spoke these words: "Let not thou be afeard.
Your father's God, I Am—and also yours.
My favor pledged proceeds and ever pours
Upon your seed forever, without end!
I'll be your God and also be your friend.
And like your father, too, I'll give rewards
When faithfully you walk with Me as Lord."
So Isaac spent his life on humbleness,
And those who blessed him God saw fit to bless.
As for Abimelech, this much is fact:
His friendship with our Isaac stayed intact.

CHAPTER 19

That's Not My Hair

Old Isaac had gone blind! And even death
Was creeping up on him; his final breath
Of life was coming soon. Because of this,
It was high time for that man to dismiss
Most, if not all, things on his bucket list.
He had to bless his son before he missed
The chance—it was the blessing Abram passed
To him some years before. It'd be his last
And final act; he didn't want to hash
It up. And so he called his wife, that sash
Of beauty worn around his wedded chest,
And said these words: "Rebekah, dear, I'm pressed
For time since death is knocking at my door.
I need to bless our elder son before
I give the ghost away. Please call him here
So I can say the words I must, my dear."
So Isaac spoke, that songless patriarch

Of no renown, unto the matriarch
Who wears the crown of crafty women. All
Who follow in her steps can't loose the shawl
From off her neck for lack of worthiness.
That was old Isaac's wife, the sweet Countess
Of Aptitude. Don't ever fail to note
Her role in this, our tale. She underwrote
The ins and outs and orchestrated it
Until complete. One wonders at the bit
Old Isaac played and how that laissez-faire
Of men the sidelines sat without a care
For how things went. So, it was Bekah's ear
That God then spoke a promise in.

Severe
Are gusts of wind in early spring. They shake
The leafless trees with turbulence and quake
The earth with moaning howls. Those gusts upset
All things then set in place. But something whets
Our minds with courage, stepping from our doors
Into the breeze. Wind shakes our frames while floors
Of earth remain quite stiff in winter's chill.
That unseen blow disrupts the status still
And moves our stiffened world. We suck that breeze
In deep, the warmer air that oddly sees
Forgotten hopes to thaw.

So Bekah felt
Hope's animating breeze upon her svelte
And nimble frame. Old Isaac's words had warmed
A thought she'd set aside, a thought malformed
By icy pondering. She turned and left
Her husband then, and with a pace both deft
And quick, she marched to Esau's tent. A smile
Enriched her face when she arrived, all guile
Then hidden out of sight, and so she knocked
On Esau's door. That elder son just gawked
At her as in she stepped. The whole tent stunk
Like muddy sheep or like a rancid skunk

Was rotting there, and Bekah left the door
Ajar to air it out. "Good Lord!" she swore
And waved her hand around. "It wouldn't hurt
To have a bath, you know?" Her voice was curt
But half polite. "And you should sanitize
This place, as well." He looked at her. His eyes
Were hardly seen, for much his hair did drown.
His beard curled up and unibrow curled down.
"Your father wants to see you," Bekah said.
"And what about?" her son asked from his bed,
Still half asleep and combing at his beard
With fingers tined. "A blessing," Bekah sneered
And turned to leave. That woman then, too steep
In craft, determined that her younger reap
The blessing from her husband now. For Age
Was done with gifting years and soon would stage
A coup to take his throne. She couldn't leave
Who got the blessing up to chance. Deceive
She would if need demand! She hid behind
The folds of Isaac's tent, herself enshrined
In secrecy, and passed some time that way
Until her elder son arrived—bouquet
Of stink escorting him. She smelled him long
Before she heard these words. "Is that my strong
And strapping progeny I heard come in?"
Old Isaac asked and raised himself to pin
That posture with a pillow. Isaac glowed
In doting hues as Esau buffaloed
His way inside and said, "It is your son!"
His deep, resounding voice was like a ton
Of bricks. Then Isaac said, "Come here and sit
By me. My ears and eyes, I must admit,
Aren't what they used to be." Now Bekah leaned
In hard against the folds of tent and gleaned
A vantage view. (Remember her intent:
The younger would the older circumvent.)
She listened from the shadowed corners where
She could be out of sight. The sputtered flare
Of bonfire light did not betray her spot

To human eyes, and from that perch she got
To hear as Isaac then went on to say,
"My manly son, I want for you to slay
The food I love." See, Isaac's clinking jaw
Still loved to eat of venison cooked raw.
What's more, his son—the elder son—would cut
Him steaks from off the flanks and off the butts
Of all the animals that he would kill
In his great hunts. It was old Isaac's thrill
To fill his belly with the tender meat
His son prepared. He said then, short and sweet,
"My son, I want you now to go and hunt!
Go kill an animal—not just a runt,
But some great beast revered. By this, you'll save
My stomach from its hunger pains. I crave
The juicy cutlets you so well prepare,
Charred on the outside with the inside rare.
Your mother'd have me eating only fruit
And dried-up figs. Bring me what you can shoot!
Then, after I have eaten bounteously,
I'll pass my father's blessing unto thee."
So Isaac spoke and patted Esau's arm.
The thought of eating steak worked like a charm
To rouse his scant-toothed mouth to watering.
Indeed, that thought had served enough to bring
Some glimmer of his youth, fresh as the day,
Into his wizened mind. No more to say,
The elder son arose and took his leave,
Assured then of the blessing he'd receive
Before the close of day. Remember how
He traded off his birthright claim, made vows
To hand it over for a bowl of food?
That all had been his choice, but still he viewed
That whole thing with contempt. It shot a pang
Each time he heard its melodies or sang
The tune of memory. He put it out
Of mind, his great mistake. He wouldn't pout
About it now or cry that Jake had robbed
It from his hands with clever words and swabbed-

Up stew. He had the plate to show for it.
How foolish he had been, he knew. Legit
Was all the shame he felt. The blessing would
Be different. He wouldn't sell that good
Thing off for just a bowl of stew. Oh, no—
He'd cherish that, and that way he could go
And bless his own sons then in turn. It was
A comfort Esau had, more so because
That blessing came today. So, he would hunt,
Content and self-assured. The wily stunt
His brother pulled before was in the past.
A blessing would the birthright more outlast!
Rebekah watched as Esau left. She watched
Him prep his gear; she watched as Esau splotched
His ears and eyes with mud as if he'd paint
His face for war, some rugged patron saint
Of beastly men. With bow in hand, he hit
The field. Rebekah didn't waste a bit
Of time. All Esau's hopes she knew as myth.
She'd neither stand on ceremony with
Accepting attitudes of what would come
Nor keep her silent tones beneath Man's thumb.
She knew to set the stage, was not delayed
To weave her will. Rebekah, unafraid,
Saw duty was to Jacob, not her sire.
And so, against her husband she'd conspire
For grander plots. That girl would not recant
Till younger did the older one supplant!
But such a plan commanded tactful haste
Before Esau returned. No time to waste,
She found her Jacob busy knitting quilts
And seasoning his soup. The blade and hilt
He wielded was a spoon, not any sword.
"Get up!" his mother yelled. "Now, by our Lord,
Your father wants to pass the blessing now
To Esau's hands. By God, I won't allow
This thing without a fight!" So Bekah spoke.
In turn, she did her anger more provoke.
"Right now?" her son replied. "Is Father ill?"

"Don't think upon that, son," she said. "Go kill
A little goat or two and bring them here.
I'll make the meat myself. Be quick! I fear
Your brother will be back before we get
This done." But Jacob, stopping short, then met
His mother's eyes and said, "I'll never pass
For him! He's hairy as an ox, and crass,
And grim. And though that oaf might be my twin,
I can't pretend the peach fuzz on my chin
Is like his beard or like his arms. Our dad
Will know the difference. Then ironclad,
Instead of blessing, he will speak a curse!
So, your great plan for me will work reverse."
Rebekah thought, and quickly she replied,
"Just trust your mother, son. Beef up your stride
And kill those goats for me! I'll make a stew,
One that your aged father's jaws can chew.
I'll also make the slaw he loves with dates
Mixed in. It helps him go. At any rate,
For you, you'll set to work in skinning off
The fur of those two goats. Now, do not scoff;
This plan will work." So she assured her son,
And off to work they went to see it done.
Rebekah made the food, and Jacob scraped
The pelts of flesh. And then Rebekah draped
The parts of fur on Jacob's neck and hands,
Securing them with leather twine—the strands
She tucked beneath. Oh, now he looked the part—
A motley piece of vivisected art.
Then Bekah took a cloak ('twas Esau's best)
And wrapped it round Jake's shoulders and his chest.
It smelled of sweat and Esau's armpit stink.
"We're almost done," his mother said. "Don't shrink
From off the goal!" She handed him the meat
And all the rest. Then both of them, discreet,
Gave one good, thorough glance across the field.
But what their thorough glance had not revealed
Was that the elder was already back
And making quick the work to cardiac

His flint to flame. For Esau had success
In his great hunt! He only had to dress
The deer and make a couple sides; he might
Just sauté onions, too. Just something light
To go with it. But Jacob and his ma
Both thought the coast was clear. Jake took the slaw
And tender meat—the bread and wine, as well—
And headed for his father's tent. He'd sell
A lie and see if Isaac's mouth would bite.
Then Jacob knocked, not to seem impolite,
And knocked again when there was no reply.
He stood there for a moment, wiped his eyes
From all the sweat that dripped his skin and stilled
His breath. Just then a voice rose up and shrilled,
"Who's there?" old Isaac asked. "Who's at my door?"
"It is your elder son," the younger swore!   (Genesis 27:19)
"I brought some bread and meat that I just killed;
There's coleslaw also here and wine I've chilled."
"Come in," old Isaac said, "my life and death!
It's time you got the blessing father Seth
And all our other fathers ever gave.
I'll eat, and then I'll bless your line. The grave
Can have my bones when I am done." So spoke
The son of Abraham, and Jacob broke
The distance and approached his father's bed.
The bloody fur he wore and leather thread
Were caking stiff and sticking to his hands
And neck. He reeked of blood and sweaty glands
And Esau's stinking clothes. But odd enough,
His father caught no whiff of all that stuff.
He only smelled the food and licked his lips.
Jake set the tray on Isaac's lap while strips
Of leather thread became dislodged and danced
Around the tray like puppet strings. They pranced
Atop the steak until young Jacob found
They had come loose. That liar quickly wound
Them up and held them in his palms. "It smells
So good!" old Isaac faltered out. "But tell
Me this: You must have had a timely hunt,

·203·

To kill and prep the food you've placed in front
Of me like this?" "Oh, yes," young Jacob said,
"God favors me! Please eat your meal. I dread
To see it's getting cold." Then Isaac stopped
And held his sightless gaze, and then he propped
His head and squinting said, "Are you my son,
My elder born? Tell me you're him and none
But him you are." The old man smelled a rat.
Yes, something rotten on his nostrils sat.
"My boy, I am the victim of my years,
For not just eyes but also now my ears
Are playing tricks, for you like Jacob sound.
Give me the truth and not the runaround.
You really are my elder born—no scam?"
Then Jacob answered him and said, "I am!"
Old Isaac touched the fur and smelled Jake's clothes.
"Your voice is Jacob's voice, but still—who knows?
I guess my ears no longer work, for these
Are Esau's hands. This puts my mind at ease."
The old man laughed and ate the food. "Strange, though,"
He mused. "Son, if I didn't better know,
I'd say it tastes like what your mother makes."
Jake fidgeted while Isaac ate the steaks
And coleslaw, too. When Isaac had his fill
Of food prepared by bride, not Esau's skill,
He turned his heart to benedictions passed;
He knew his pilgrimage was done, at last.
"Come here and kiss my cheek," the old man said,
And smelled again the fur and leather thread.
"My son, dressed in the spoils of wilderness,
May your life's path be clothed in blessedness.
Let God who reigns, the heaven's dew to give;
On wine and fatness of the earth you'll live.
May people and may nations come to serve,
And may our God eternally preserve.
Among the nations may you wear the crown!
And may your mother's sons, to you, bow down.
To all your efforts, God will grant success,
And those who prosper you He'll also bless.

But those who trip you up He'll reimburse
With constant visitations of His curse."
So Isaac let his benediction close,
And Jacob (like an elder brother) rose
To stand a little higher than before;
He, fast as anything, was out the door
And making tracks—excoriated suit
Left in his wake. Just then, in walked the brute—
Paul Bunyan of a man, the elder son.
He said in his resounding voice, "I've done
As you have asked! I've made my hunt, my kill,
And I have cooked a meal that you can fill
Your belly with. I'm ready for that bless-
Ing now." Like so, the elder spoke, no less
Than confident and ready to receive
His father's words. "Oh, how my ears deceive
Me now again, or maybe it's a dream."
Old Isaac was perplexed—so great the scheme
That made him play the fool! Then Esau said,
"It is your elder son. I have the bread,
And you will love the steak I made, or should.
I tried a piece before I came—it's good!"
Now Esau's voice, those deep and brutal tones,
Did well to rattle Isaac's ancient bones.
His stature was already frail and weak,
But now he shook to hear the elder speak.
"Another meal?" his father asked and hoped
In vain. Deep down, he knew that Jake eloped
With Esau's blessing. It was sad but true.
There would be hell to pay, the old man knew,
When Esau caught the wind of it. "The first—"
Said Esau, feeling all the tension pursed
Up in the room, "The first since we had spoke
This morning, Father. Come, is this some joke
You're playing now?" A dread began to grip
The elder's gut. Old Isaac bit his lip
And said, "I fear—" but couldn't bring his tongue
To say the rest. A great malaise hamstrung
His words. "I fear—" he tried again, "I fear

A cunning fox I blessed instead." A tear
Burst out of Esau's eye and hit the plate
He held with force. It struck with such a weight
That Esau dropped it to the ground, the juice-
Y steak caked up with dirt. His cheeks ran puce
As anger welled, engulfing every beat
His heart pumped out. From head down to his feet,
He felt a pulse to kill, to strangle, break,
And to deform. He'd deal with brother Jake
In time. "There must be something you can give
To me!" poor Esau pled. But punitive
Was Isaac's slow reply: "To Jacob I
Gave all. It's down in stone, and by my thigh,
A blessing spoken can't come back again!"
But Esau couldn't get his mind to pen
The thought. "You're telling me there isn't one
Thing left to give?" Then Isaac said, "My son,
I told you that I gave it all away.
There're only scraps. But if you want, I'll say
A blessing for these things. It is your call."
"I'll take it," Esau said, "if that is all
That you have left." Old Isaac cleared his throat
And spoke these words as postscripts later wrote:
"My son, by sword you'll live and also serve
Until that time you get what you deserve.
I mean, you'll get his foot from off your back,
And all that weight he holds on you will crack."
And that was it! Not much but meager scraps—
Young Jake took gold, and Esau held the crap!
In spite of this, old Isaac blessed the both
His sons in faith. Still, Esau swore an oath
Unto himself that, once his father died—
After he mourned and all his tears were cried—
He'd kill his brother Jacob, dead and gone.
He'd nothing left to lose. So every dawn,
In thinking Jacob would rule over him,
He soothed himself by chanting out this hymn:
"Oh, after Father's death, this much I pledge:
I'll serve my brother well on dagger's edge."

CHAPTER 20

Better Wives

The wives that Esau took from Hittite soil
Had vexed his mom and dad! Those gals might spoil
The hope that God had given them and kin,
For surely such a mixture would unpin
The promised blessing from their future seed.
They all but missed the point; it was not breed
Of tribe or race that made God's favor pour
But trust in what He said He'd do—no more.
Rebekah wasn't standing idly by
To see it all play out. She set her eyes
Like flint; sleeves rolled, she stepped up to the plate.
Her cunning tact again would demonstrate
How able she had always been among
The men who to their head-of-household clung.
She knew too well the evil that will rest
Within man's heart; it wakes when time is best
To strike a blow of death. She knew that wrath

Was in her elder son; she did the math—
The fury that lay dormant would be loosed
As soon as Isaac ceased to breathe. Reduced
By age, that old man's time was near. She went
To harp her husband's sleepy ear, hell-bent
To see her chosen son removed from harm!
She went up close, her hand upon his arm,
Her pageant words well-tuned to sing. "I hate
My life!" she wailed on the old man. "I rate   (GENESIS 27:46)
All my achievements only dung. Just look
At me. Just look what I've become! You took
Me from my home for this!" Through sobs, she spoke,
And Isaac from his midday nap was woke.
He jostled from that snooze. "My sisters cried!"
His wife went on, "All so I might abide
With you and with your father here. But now
I reap a rotten crop upon the plow
Of poor decisions made." He was distraught
To see his wife in such a state. He'd caught
About the half of what was said and craned
A more attentive ear as she complained.
He hoped it'd seem as if he hadn't missed
A moment of her speech and gently kissed
Her through her blubbering. "There, there—don't weep,"
He said to her and wiped the crusted sleep
From out his eyes. "Why are you so upset,
My love?" he asked with care. "Why do you fret?"
Then Bekah sniffed and asked, "Am I your love?"
"You question that?" he gasped. "By God above,
None other gives me pleasure, only you!"
He swore, "And for you anything I'd do."
That his concern was real must be confessed—
'Twas chivalry, not chauvinism dressed.
She squeezed another tear: "How can you say
You love me when our sons are free to stray
Amid the women of the land?" A bit
Confused by such a question poised, he knit
His eyebrows tight and tried to comprehend
How loving her could oddly then amend

Into the topic of their sons. "Be clear
With me, Rebekah," Isaac pled. "I fear
Your meaning will get lost in being coy."
She had him butter-basted for the ploy
And leveled out her feline gaze. "The girls
Our sons are mixing with will all but hurl
Them into pagan ways." Old Isaac scratched
His head; it was an egg and would be hatched
With dispositions of the hen. "Come near,"
She said, to sprinkle season in his ear,
"My sisters, long ago when I had left—
Though they were sad in their lament, bereft
Of any joy—still thought to bless me with
A mother's creed, forged stronger than the smith
At heaven's forge could ever beat upon
The amber steel. There, in the morning dawn—
Their virgin cheeks still soft with callow hope—
'World without end,' they prayed. Oh, what a scope
They had in mind for all who would be blessed
From out my loins and off my milking breast.
But now, it seems there shall be no increase—
That thousand generations, here, will cease!"
Her tears began to flow again. "How so,
My dear?" the old man asked. "How do you know
The girls of Heth are not the ones our God
Will bless us through?" Disgusted was the nod
She gave and tucked her lip. "So you are done?
A no-good Hittite hussy for my son?
That's what I have in store?" Old Isaac raised
His hand to calm his wife. It barely grazed
Her shoulder when he felt her cold receipt.
How quickly warmth is stifled when it meets
The frosty chamber of a woman's scorn!
Old Isaac understood, but he was torn.
He didn't want to send young Jake away
Since he was close to death; his final day
Was not far off. The man could hardly hear
Or even see at all; another year
Would be a miracle. But even still,

How worse to live with women when the chill
Is all you ever feel! Old man or not,
His implement of manhood would see rot
Much sooner from a frigid lack of use.
Oh, call it what you like, but it's abuse
When women tyrannize or even trade
Their warm advantage for some favor paid!
Old Isaac bit the bullet on the point
And said, "Tell me the course, and I'll appoint
The means for it." Rebekah didn't gloat
Above her kill; she loved her man and smote
Him cordially, but love of husband does-
N't close compare with love for child. That buzz
Is louder in the ear, and she would see
Her Jacob safe. That meant he had to flee
The older twin—that meathead of a man,
That lout. It all was up to her! The plan,
The secret will of God, was told to her!
She'd run the show and wouldn't soon defer
To chance. "Jake has to go," she said to him.
"He cannot stay with us. Things here are grim,
And he will surely die by Esau's hand
If he stays here. He'll travel to the land
Of Ur, and there I'm sure that he could stay
With brother Laban, honest as the day."
All this had Bekah said. She knew the balm
Of time would bring indifference and calm
The open wound that Esau had, still red
And swelling sore. Some passing time would bed
That hate with clemency. So, Isaac then
(That noble patriarch and head of men)
Called for his son, the younger twin, advised
Him of the plan his lovely wife devised,
And sent Jake on his way. When all were gone,
When wife and child had left, he thought upon
The words he gave his son and hoped they'd stay
Fresh in his mind while on he made his way.
"The LORD is pleased to make you very strong;
His favor is your banner and your song.

In fullness let Him keep you and your seed,
And on His table's plenty, you will feed.
May He be so inclined for nothing less
Than blessing you, and blessing in excess."

CHAPTER 21

Stairwell

The makeup artist then was on the lam
(From Esau, anyway). Theatric scams
And blatant lies had earned that fleeing crook
A set of shaky nerves, and now he'd look
With wary eyes at anyone he met
By day. The rustle of a leaf would set
That thief on edge. That swindler, *yep*, had known
His brother would then Michael Corleone
Him if he could. The criminal would have
To watch his six each time he used the lav
Or started up his car. *Well, Fredo should*
Have seen it coming, dear. He understood
He'd need to hide awhile. He had his fake
Identity, new passports in the wake
Of masqueraded heists. He'd posted bail
And skipped the town, but you can't hide that jail-
House ink, still glossy with its Vaseline.

His dirty paws were nowhere close to clean,
And tells were on his face. In turn, he ran—
The pirate with his pot of soup, con man
And thespian about to find a sneak
No better than himself. He'd go and seek
His uncle out, a penny-pinching cheat
As Laban named. That man will fail to meet
A chapter of his own, no compliment
Or commentary shown. We'll represent
Him in the least! That character would waste
My scissor snips and globs of Elmer's paste.
A menstrual cycle fools the likes of him!
We'll name him not again by pseudonym
Or monikers that might our fancy strike.
Let's leave him here to rot impaling spikes
And press them deep into the muddy ground
Of halfway points. For I am sure you've found
We've reached the summit of our little trek
Through Genesis. So, give or take, we'll check
And count our chapters later if you wish.
Or do it now. I'll chew my licorice
And wait until you're done. I couldn't care
An ounce and gladly sit the thoroughfare
While you go leafing through your leather gen-
Uine. Or holster up that fountain pen
And pad of college ruled; we're somewhere close.
Just trust me, friend! For what should more engross
Your mind is that we've gone and painted three—
Yes, two-plus-one the patriarchs we'll see.
And of these men, I'd have you make a note
That each a liar was. Still, God had wrote
A blessing on this crooked line of men,
Determining He would, both there and then,
Keep blessing them. Like so, God kept His rule
In spite of their intents to play the fool.
It's common knowledge, friend, that candid words
Do no injustice to nor make absurd
Our great exam. It's how they viewed themselves!
I'm only using terms pulled off the shelves

Of ancient scribes—the very terms they used
When they described their fathers and accused
Them of realities. And I am not
The least bit different. In fact, I've got
These sentiments you're reading from the books
They wrote. Or maybe you think Balaam took
A quill and metered out his little song
All by himself. And then he searched, both long
And hard, until that man had found, by luck,
One Moses named—the one whom God had stuck
With jotting down the lengthy Pentateuch.
Then Balaam, after he received rebuke
From such a man of God, had named a price
And sold his ditty for a song. How nice.
What is the going rate for tunes on dried-
Up cattail weed? I'm sure he must have cried,
Though, in the end—that such a thing was penned.
Your ignorance would readily defend
This group against themselves! I'm telling you,
They understood how comical, how lu-
Dicrous the tale of their own history
Had seemed to anyone who'd look and see,
Without a biased eye, the anecdotes
For what they were. They're simply petticoats
Beneath the more important dress and serve
To highlight this alone—that God preserves
Them just because He went and said He would.
That's what the ancients knew and understood!
Perhaps you'd bake another cake from what
You read—a fruit-topped dainty, delicate
And sitting in the glass where it can rot
In peace, untouched. Or go and keep it hot
In Grubhub bags until you've dropped it at
Another's door. I'll mind the thermostat
That hangs outside my smoking house. I'll cure
My meat and cheese with proper care and sure-
Ly pour an ale when they're enjoyed. You keep
The cakes. Let's rest these arguments and steep
Ourselves within the text; aperitifs

Are done for now. We'll pick up where our thief
Was on the road—yes, on to Haran went
Until he found a cozy spot and spent
The night. He gathered up some stones by day
To make a pillow, stiff, then down he lay.

A man will nod to sleep when all the day's
Hard chore is done. He's wearied from the blaze
Of beating sun and rests the afternoon
Upon his couch. His thoughts grow less attune
To worries of his toil, to daily strife
And woe. So dies another day in life,
When eyelids bat the light away. Then blind
To fact, a dreaming logic rules his mind,
And all's acceptable within that world.
But sometimes fear comes on, his safety whirled
And frightened by the thought of death. He jerks
Awake; belief that he was falling lurks
Within his mind. He cannot separate
What's feigned from fact and only gets them straight
When what is plausible becomes more clear.
But in those moments, what is real seems queer.

So nodding sleep on Jacob took its grip,
And when its dreaming nectar hit his lip,
He saw the empty black of night reborn
With morning rays. Above, the sky was torn
From one end to the other; it was rent
With light. There in the gulf, to represent
A bridge between two worlds, a ladder dropped
And cut the sky till at his pillow stopped.
In riddles twisted heavenward that stair.
Jake saw ascending and descending there
God's angel messengers, no less—and yet
With manners of mankind they were beset.
Still closer on the visage Jacob glanced
On features that appeared to be enhanced
By some Divine—some everlasting—youth.
Not one looked haggard down by age, in truth.

But still, by shape or form Jake couldn't tell
From those who earth and those who heaven dwell.
He traced the snaking stair till he had found
The zenith height, and at the top was crowned
The LORD on high. He sat there in the clouds,
Suspending weight and glory that, unbowed
To any other in this world, would make
Each stiffened knee and hardened back to break
In half! Though strange it must have all appeared—
A stairway from the earth to heaven tiered—
Young Jacob thought he'd climb. And so, he raised
His foot and touched the bottom stair. It grazed
The first of many steps; he flattened it
And brought his other up. They seemed to fit
That sturdy structure well enough. He let
His foot to stomp down twice, wanting to vet
And test the stair that seemed like rock. But straight
His feet felt heavier than lead, the weight
So much he could not lift his foot to grip
The second step. He started then to slip
Down off the first, for then the whole began
To shake from side to side, the weight of man
Too much for it to hold. He thought egress
The safest course, his climb of no success,
And stumbled more than stepped back to the earth,
The dusty origin of Man's first birth.
Then loud, resounding tones above him roared
As though there were a thunderstorm. The LORD
On high was speaking from His throne and said,
"Get down! Your strength could never climb unwed
To faith." Jake held quite still to not provoke
That voice and mutely listened as it spoke—
Unveiled transcendence reaching out to dust
Through forest winds and animating gusts.
"I Am the God your fathers served before,
And on the land where you now sleep, I more
Will give to you and to your seed that be
As grains of sand and waters in the sea.
From out your loins, I'll bless the corners four!

My favor on all tribes and tongues will pour.
In stranger lands, I'll keep you through your chain
And guide you to this very land again.
And I will not depart from you until
My word is kept! This is My steadfast will."
Then Jacob woke, the beads of sweat were cold
Upon his back, and restless panting told
Of all his fear. For such a dream seemed real
Enough, and all that man could think and feel
Was terror then, so much so that he said,
"O holy ground, O house of God I've tread!"   (GENESIS 28:17)
So, Jacob sat in stillness on the ground
And took some bread from out his bag. He found
Some oil there, too; he'd make his morning meal,
And troubled mind, by nourishment, would heal.

A man will spend his strength against his work
To see his chore complete. He doesn't shirk
That effort, but he pushes on to match
It with his flagging energy, dispatch-
Ing out his vigor till it's all but spent.
Then body calls for sleep; his back is bent,
And arms are sagging at his sides. He rests,
And when he wakes, and after he has dressed,
He thanks his God and then partakes of food.
He feels his strength return, his life renewed.

Young Jacob felt renewed when he had ripped
A handful of his bread apart and dipped
It in the oil. This mix contained a scent
That fed his soul and body's full extent.
Then Jacob took another piece of bread
And broke the thing in half. But then, instead
Of eating it, he rather took to swab
At all the oil until he had a glob
Of mushy bread. He held it in his fist
And squeezed. Like so did Jacob then persist,
Until he got out every drop of oil,
Completely soaking with it, then, the soil

Around his feet. And then he took the stones,
The dreaming pillow whereby he'd been shown
The throne of God and stairwell to the sky.
With these he made a pile, not very high,
Atop the oily ground. Then, oily palms
Were placed upon the stones, and rather calm
He made a vow to God, as firm as stone:
"If you will keep, preserve my flesh and bone,
Then to my father's house again will guide,
And worldly needs of self and kin provide,
Then You, my God, forevermore shalt be.
This oath I swear, by oily stones, to Thee."
The place where Jacob slept and where he trod
Was Bethel, rightly called the House of God.

CHAPTER 22

Stones

The clouds, in some tenacious march, strolled by
And showed their bleak indifference. The sky
Had been completely filled with storming arm-
Ies led by thunder calls—the chant and charm
Of battle cries. They'd come to penetrate,
By thrusting bolts and rain to saturate,
The verdant muff of earth. Her moistened lips
Were open for that kiss, and censorship
Could find no leaf. In turn, the seed was cast
Repeatedly. Like so, the day had passed.
The husbandman, the one called Afterward,
Had stood there in the rain. He wasn't stirred
But felt himself then pressed into the earth.
No questions filled his mind. He knew his worth
And knew he had a purpose to fulfill.
With resolution and his plow, he'd till
The fields that numbered four—his rightful claim,

The fields that numbered four, each one a name,
The fields that numbered four, each one a bride—
The fields that promised offspring they'd provide.
All tender frame, in luscious youth then clad,
And none his fertile tillage had forbad.
The first was Grief, demeanor only grim,
And this one came by trickster ways to him.
Then to Calamity, for she was next.
This field, much like the first, was duty vexed.
The third, as thunder clouds, called Dripping Pour—
The tears of heaven's endless reservoir.
The final field was Silence, which keeps mute
Before the knife of slaughter, no dispute.
From all his fields, in gray-eyed wisdom, hauled
Twelve rocks. A rustic house was to be walled
Where each the fields connected. With his spade
And sweaty back, a rugged structure laid.
He stacked his stones, which numbered ten plus two—
The elements and glass of murky view.
For what he thought the end-all was a hint,
A clue left at the crime, a fingerprint
That told of something more. But how could he
Have known of Cornerstones? He couldn't see,
Nor could he ever glimpse that far ahead.
No eye has seen nor ear has heard, it's said,
What God has planned behind His curtains hung.
But still, he set those rocks to earth, those tongue-
Less tattletales when blood is wrongly spilled.
The structure he had laid had later killed
The owner of the fields. That's when the rocks
Were tumbled down; the toddler with his blocks,
Who sees not one atop another stand,
Then, by that same capricious little hand,
Will have another built. Who'll grant that types
Are not just simple things when stripped of hype?

CHAPTER 23

Grapple

A young ephebe will sow his oats, both wild
And tame, in distant lands and shores. The child
Becomes a man away from home, forgets
His precious motherland as more he gets
A taste for life abroad. The paths he had
Been so familiar with go dark and sad-
Ly fade from out his mind. But men-at-arms
Will catch their passage home, and simple charms
Of places long forgotten then return.
He looks upon the trees and can discern
How much they've grown, and even his own feet
Will find their way along the roads and streets
His mind let slip from thought.

So Jacob marked
The landscape of his youth as he embarked
Upon his journey home. It made him smile

To overview that place, his juvenile
And adolescent land. Some twenty years
He'd been away, and now the souvenirs
He'd gained within that time would come along
With him. Despite his fears, he would prolong
Reunions not a moment more. He'd need
To face the music finally, to plead
Forgiveness from the brother he had wronged.
He couldn't run forever; he belonged
Beside old Isaac in his closing days.
Like so, Shame squares the debts, and Piper pays.
But troubled news then reached our Jacob's ears
About his brother's clan—seemed yesteryears
Were fresh as morn in Esau's mind. In fact,
That brute and some four hundred men had packed
Their bags and saddled up, and now those men
Were charging near. Then Jacob, mother hen
And maker of the soup, let fear take hold.

A whitetail buck will see his doe be strolled
Upon the field ahead of him. He stands
Along the forest edge, the hinterlands
Then out of sight, and watches as the doe
Feeds open ground. He waits until he knows
It's safe before he goes and joins her side.

So Jacob sent his children and his brides
Ahead to meet his brother Esau's rage.   (GENESIS 32:23)
He sent some gifts, as well—thought he'd assuage
That hairy ruffian with sheep and goats.
He hoped it'd be enough to sugarcoat
His actions of the past. That night Jake spent
Across the Jordan's edge; the distance lent
His mind a sense of some security—
Alone and out of reach he seemed to be.
But still, his mind was troubled there. He gave
A large amount of all his goods to wave
The hand of Esau off, and now he felt
Much like he had when he first left and knelt

Before an oily pile of rocks. It was
A humble feeling, and it came because
The man was being shaken to his core.
His goods could pass away; he cherished more
The promise that his God had made. Perhaps
He hoped another stairwell would collapse
From out the sky, assuring him of some
Great blessing in the future yet to come.
But as he sat and tended to the flames
His fire had brought, he noticed then a frame
Upon the dark of night, a silhouette
That watched without a word. There was no threat
Expressed, but neither were there cheers a friend
Might speak or offer helping hands to lend.
The more as Jacob watched the Man (for man
It seemed to be), the more He other than
A man had seemed to Jacob be. The great
Supplanter worked to squint his eyes, dilate
Those orbs against the black. He'd looked too long
At flame, and all proportions had been wrong
And even seemed to lie about the size
And shape of He who'd come. At last, his eyes
Could see the Man; Jake felt a terror swat
Him in the mouth.

A Sumo wrestler squats
Upon the line and waits. His balance strains
But holds his massive bulk. And then he cranes
His head, prepared to throw his volume at
The man across from him.

So Jacob sat
And measured up the figure on the night;
He also felt a looming urge to fight!
At once, Jake stood and dropped his cloak around
His feet. The Stranger then, without a sound,
Had pulled from out a simple haversack—
The bag he wore around his brawny back—
A wineskin and a leather cup. He filled

The cup with glowing liquid. Nothing spilled,
And then He held the cup and spoke these words
To Jacob: "For your stone-heart sepulchered."
While Jacob tried to wrap these words with mind,
The stranger rushed the void of night, entwined
And tackled Jacob, ill-resisted bound,
And pinned his flaying limbs against the ground!
He held the cup above poor Jacob, smote
And poured it bottoms up down Jacob's throat.
Rejuvenation was the liquid's goal,
And vigor-fueled combustion charged Jake's soul!
Then Jacob would consider no restraint;
He'd found new life. With strength no longer faint,
And putting then aside his stewing pan,
He'd grapple with a God, as man to Man.
A naked man to Man, if true be told,
For when each one had sought to grab a hold
Upon the other, clothes were torn to shreds—
And birthday suits were all they had for threads.
Soft Jacob had surprised himself, that he
Could hold his own with agile Deities.
The losing grip that slipped his brother's heel
Found muscle tendons tight and tense with zeal.
They clashed with panting heat and sweaty brows
On through the night, and neither would allow
Defeated wills to have a say.

A cramp
Will hold a twisted leg in place; it clamps
A painful spasm with an awkward pose
Till muscles can relax. Sometimes it throws
One off his couch of rest, sees him contort
Beneath a knotted pang, a panicked sort
Of squeeze that makes him roll around the ground.

So Jacob held on like a cramp and bound
The Man beneath his grip. He wouldn't let
Him go! But when the eventide had set
To close, when dawning day was soon to make

A show, the Man who'd come worked hard to break
The hold of Jacob off His arms, to free
Himself from human hands. But seeing He
Could not, for Jacob was a scrapper in
The end, He grew annoyed and took to pin
That Jacob down. And then, He touched his hip,
And out of joint did bone from socket slip.
A cry of pain was echoed in the dark,
For Jacob screamed in pain! That patriarch
Had never felt the stab of agony
That way, but still he wouldn't quit or free
The Stranger from his pertinacious hold—
In deeper purposes was Jake enrolled.
The Stranger saw this, too, and even said
These words: "You need to let Me go! The red
And rosy hue of dawn is coming near."
But Jacob would choose death, for any fear
He had of seeing God (that is, his God
Then face to face) seemed nothing but a fraud
That paled compared to Godly blessings passed.
You see, the ancients held that if one cast
A human gaze on God, that one would die.
The Greeks believed this, too, and testify
Of it in myths of Zeus. They say that dunce
Would change his form before a dalliance
With mortal ladies and with mortal boys.
For if Olympians were to employ
Their true and given form, the mortals would,
On seeing gods in flesh, then burn like wood
Upon the hearth. Well, Hebrews felt the same:
To see God's face would mean consuming flame.
And so, for Jacob then to hold his God
On through the night and even when the broad
And wide-eyed sun began to wake, it shows
He didn't care if he would die. He knows
He needs a blessing from his God. And so
Jake spoke these words: "I will not let You go
Until You speak a blessing over me."
God questioned, for the most part sociably,

"What is it you are called?" He asked this thing—
A subject you would not expect to sting
The mind of God, but let that go. He asked,
And Jacob then, with such a question tasked,
Did say, "I'm he who follows afterward."
The God of heaven smiled when He had heard
This thing, for irony amused His mind.
And then He spoke these words to Jake, "I find
That you are one who fights with God and men,
And you prevail upon us both. So when
You give your name again, say this—that you
Are first among the nations now." He drew
The mortal close to Him and kissed his head.
Like so, God blessed the man. But then Jake said,
Or rather asked, "And won't You tell me what
Your name is, too?" By then the sun had shut
The door of night, and visages were clear
As crystal day. Jake looked on the appear-
Ance of his God,

complexion like the dew
With features soft and fresh as if they drew
Upon some wellspring of eternal youth—
As humble and as pure as sister Ruth,
As clean as brass that sounds the turret walls
And rings across the chilly heights to fall
Upon the slated roofs below.

Like so,
The rising sun had labored then to show
The face of God to Jacob's mortal eyes.
God gave reply, and not to jeopardize
Some wonder in the future yet to come,
Then spoke these words: "It isn't bothersome
That you would ask My name, but who We are
Is what We do." So, cryptic and bizarre
Had God responded to the son of dust.
Then fast as anything, as if He must
And couldn't help but leave, the LORD was gone.

So, Jacob stood alone. The kindled dawn
Was warm against his naked skin, the calls
Of hunger sounding off his stomach walls.
He stood awhile that way and watched the morn-
Ing multiply. He knew and would have sworn
That he had just seen God; he even said
These words: "How strange it is that I'm not dead!
I've seen God face to face, and I'm alive!"   (GENESIS 32:30)
For, like I said before, to then survive
A meeting with our God was not thought pos-
Sible. Well, that is, face to face. To cross
The path of God and see Him in His pure
And unadulterated form would sure-
Ly mean your speedy death. Perhaps you've heard
This argument before? A little bird
Has told you how this was an angel Jake
Had met. It wasn't God at all! Go take
A look; one little search your engine runs
Will bring you copious returns and tons
Of jargon why this wasn't God. Oh, for
The love of hoops and logic blocks! There's more
Than making little pieces fit your grid.
This isn't paint by numbers, friend. Amid
Your great and grandiose—your bold campaign
At which you work so hard to now maintain
That contradiction fits infallibles—
You wrongly work to make agreeable
Those texts that never asked of you for help.
We prove ourselves not alpha males, but whelps
Who chase their tails and nap with bloated bel-
Lies full of soggy chow—the pimpernels
Of causes wrong in head. Just trust me, friend.
Your faith does not rely on dividends
Acquired by false and underhanded means.
That stock will pay, at least and so it seems,
Us dirty money now. Just leave it off.
Our God is not reliant and would scoff
At how you twist. But back to Jacob now,
That brawler whom the LORD thought to endow

With dislocated hip. *That looks as if*
It hurts, or maybe he's just really stiff
From fighting all night long. Oh, no—that man
Would limp the rest his life. In fact, the clan
Of Hebrews, even to this day, will not
Eat sinews joining hip and thigh. It rots
Or it is burned, but it is never chewed.
That pretty fact our text does not exclude.
Yes, all his days Jake hobbled from his hip,
A blatant mark like clefts upon the lip.

CHAPTER 24

Below the Belt

Well, here is not a tale found in the lines
That Sunday school Crayola might assign
With Dixie cups of punch to keep us mute.
There's Nilla wafers, too. All these they scoot
Across the table with a tattered box
Of broken crayon sticks (the orthodox
Explained with tinted wax). We concentrate—
Protruding tongues and half our bodyweight
Then pressing down in one gyrating force
That shakes our neighbor's work of art. *Of course,
We'll put the coat of Joseph on the fridge.*
How indispensable that tutelage
Had been for me, the chilly classrooms made
Of painted cinder blocks. And there, betrayed
By Mom who'd like to sing her hymns in peace,
I suffered shoes that better served to crease
My ankle bones than cushion budding soles.

Yet never in those cleric cubbyholes
Of Father Kirk had I been handed such
A page to color with my lurid touch
Of some flamboyant hue. Yes, no such page
Was handed me to teach or to engage
Me on the story next our list. That said,
We'll give accommodation—king-sized beds
And presidential suites with ocean views—
To house a tale so destitute with flu
And cough. He's standing on the corner now,
His cardboard sign more suited as a plow
Against the cars. Or maybe it's a shield,
And waving hands do nothing more than wield
An unseen sword. Our little knight is at
The pan and handle trade, and butterfat
From windows cracked will be his holy grail.
But let's get into it, I mean the tale
That's been reduced to beg on streets. You might
Agree to have this sewer socialite
Assigned to trench a ditch, at least so kept
Beneath the Persian rug where he's been swept—
But I would ask my audience to hear
The narrative from me before you smear
It from your minds with some eraser pad.
We'll have it showered up and dressed in plaid,
The woolen jackets hanging on the hooks
Behind my study door. They have the looks
But also have the feel we're going for—
I mean the touch, the flair to reassure
Our skeptic selves of one's ability
To teach. Yes, put on one of these, and see
You wear a scarf. *It isn't even cold.*
It's all in what's perceived and how it's sold.
The dynasty of Jacob might have proved
A noontide soap, an opera approved
By housewives, all. I ought to know; I've had
My share. These jilted women sit and pad
Their chairs with pillow-plush and there command
A life vicarious, the secondhand

Of feelings long forgot. Who else is fit
To judge our play? The men? Those hawk and spits
Who'd rather crack a brew and cut the grass?
Oh, I think not! That meathead ruling class
Is better left outside or off to store
For milk and eggs. But on this, I'll no more.
I say this tale is like a soap—a show
You'd watch on boob and tube, in stereo
On Monday afternoons—because it has
The elements of drama there, the jazz
Of rising conflict, climax, and the fall.
There's love there, too—the cannon and the ball
Of any story ever told. But we
Should cue the music now and let you see
It for yourself. Just keep in mind this gem
As we go on, for surely you remem-
Ber Jacob is our theme. But think of this:
That saint esteemed could bed, and bed in bliss,
The four his wives he had around the house.
For those with planted seed I'm calling spouse.
And bedding, not just one, but make it four,
Whenever he so pleased—and even more
When he had felt his man's biweekly itch,
Producing children everywhere, and which
In turn established one unhappy nest.
For twelve his eggs were male and thought it best
To squabble as if toughness would divide
The brothers by the faux and bona fide.
Four wives to take to bed? It's not all fame
And glory, dear. Four kittycats to tame
And to declaw, four kisses to goodnight,
Four lists of honey-do's, and, if I'm right,
Four anniversaries. But like I said,
There's trouble more, the more you take to bed.
Think on the strife a single wife can pour,
And multiply those headaches into four.
No wonder he was not around to raise
The kids. Or maybe you would render praise
For how he reared? Now, that's a bold campaign!

Go write a book and tell how to abstain
From any wit or commonsense, or pull
Examples from (I know not where) some bull,
Then bullet-point me down to yawning sleep.
Raise children right, and when they're old, they'll keep
The faith. I'm simply not convinced. Review
The text and, what you will, you will construe.
The fact remains that Jacob was a fail-
Ure when it comes to raising sons. Impale
Your doting eyes upon a spoon and call
Things what they are. For all his charms, for all
His running after God, still Jacob flunks
The test of fatherhood. His sons were punks;
That's multiform. I'm speaking of the sons
That Leah gave to him. They were the ones
Who pushed their weight around, so write the scribes,
When Canaan's land was served among the tribes.
And now we've hit the nature of the beast,
What drove the politics, what made a feast
And famine from the lottery of land
When conquests were complete. The upper hand
Was always with these sons! They really felt
They held the rightful claim, the title belt
To Jacob's hand-me-downs. But let this go—
Just keep it in your mind now that our show's
About to start. We have a daughter, ripe,
A nubile lass of seventeen, the type
Who catches looks with callow eyes and child-
Less hips. You know, the stuff that gets men riled
And randy for a taste. But who has turned
His head? Was it an older man, one burned
And burning for a look, one wishing at
The unattainable, for pussycats
Now always out of reach? These ones, like Faust,
Would trade their souls to have those thighs be doused
In drool. Alas, it was not these who caught
The eyes of our young lass. *You're sure it's not*
The other way around? Perhaps it was
The lass who caught the eye, who made one pause

Midstride. But he who's watching her, turns out,
Was next in line for king—an eagle scout
And prince, no less, a Pyramus who peered
Beyond the wall for love. Now, by my beard,
Our Thisbe loves him back! She's making eyes
And flirting with him, friend; she'll advertise
Her something not for sale. I cannot know
Another explanation here. And so
We're crystal—Dinah was the lassie's name.
(But for our purpose, D will work the same.)
Two star-crossed lovers who could never love,
Then sorely strapped to death-marked fate. Oh, shove
Your Shakespeare to the side, for here and now
(In fair Verona, if you like), I'd vow
We have the Romeo and Juliet
Of Bible times. But reader, don't forget:
Our D has older brothers who will fight
And will protest what suitor has the right
To bed their sister down. They think a spouse
Can only come from Ur, be of the house
Of Abraham. I'd ask them of the wives
They took or ask them if they think the lives
Of women dance to other tunes. No mix-
And-match was good enough—the politics
Of white supremacy. *Of Jew suprem-*
Acy. Such knuckle-draggers would condemn
A man for what is not in his control.
At any rate, our D loves, heart and soul,
This Shechem who is not of Jacob's kin.
And girls will talk, as free as West Berlin,
About their escapades with men. Suffice
It so to say, she had her share of spice
With someone from the town, and then she talked.
The news had traveled fast and even knocked
On Jacob's ears. *I think she's pregnant, dear.*
They never say, but that to me seems clear.
Well, either way, she talked, and sewing cir-
Cles threaded through the camp, the whisperers
For minds that would inquire. It wasn't long

Before each ear was filled up with the song
That birdie sang. In fact, the only ones
Who didn't know were all of Jacob's sons
Who then were working in the field. *What's this?*
I just heard someone call it rape! Well, kiss
The civil courtesy goodbye. This will
Get ugly quick! When day began to spill
Into the night, the brothers had returned.
They read the bulletin, and each one burned
With rage to hear their sister was defiled!
The dad stayed calm and would have reconciled
The whole affair, but Leah's sons were hot
To act. They let their hatred further knot
Into a mania of sorts, consumed
With wrath, dressed up to kill, and so perfumed.
It's all they thought about, so when the dad
Of Shechem had arrived to plead the lad's
Undying love and offer what seemed fair
And principled, they worked a lie to snare
The honest man. *I thought they said he sacked*
The girl against her will? But now he'd act
Affectionate and kind and even wants
To marry her? He has to sense he taunts
With death. It isn't adding up, I know.
The brothers heard and even saw the show
The king had made and that it had been done
Then good in faith. This father wants his son
To get a bride. But older brothers have
A reputation to uphold, and cav-
Alcades of kings are futile in their face.
These brothers then, without the slightest trace
Of any guilt, did say unto the king,
"We cannot mix with you. But if you bring
Yourself, your son, and all the men within
Your palisade, and let us cut the skin
From off your penis tips—yes, circumcise
Each male—it's then, you see, within our eyes
You will be fit to wed. And we will mix
Our girls with yours." Such were the wily tricks

And words of Leah's sons! But they went on,
"Just do this thing—just snip your little johns,
And then your son will have our sis for wife.
But do it not, we swear by death and life,
We'll take her and we'll go the way we came."
(So much for rubs to crutch our bogus claims.)
The old man Hamor then seemed oddly pleased
With all these words. He reached down and he seized
His cup and, lifting it to heaven, spoke,
"By God above the earth, and dirty jokes
Aside, we'll do this thing and make your sis-
Ter bride!" He drank and said he would dismiss
Himself. But when each gave a hearty hug
And final wave goodbye, the brutal thugs
Of Leah set to sharpen up their shears.
There'll be a shotgun wedding now. No tears
Were shed that night; those Barbers of Seville
Would go to work in morrow's morning chill.
Just take a little off the top. You mean
The tip, a pinch and pull and then a clean-
Ing snip. *He must have really loved her, dear.*
Seems obvious. Who else would volunteer
For such an act? Now all they had to do
Was wait. They'd wait three days, till black and blue
Had swelled upon their manliness—three days   (GENESIS 34:25)
Till Shechem's men had not the will to raise
Themselves from off a pillowed couch. They'd wait
Three days until they went to decimate
Those men, like barreled fish, to slaughter them
By tribal genocide and stratagem.
They let their throats taste vengeful, bitter steel.
A slaughter of the helpless was ideal.
Well, that's below the belt, a sturdy kick
Upon the nads and mushroom-headed dick!
Yes, Simeon and Levi did the deed.
Oh, Levi—there's a one. His sons would feed
The altars when it all was said and done.
The bloody butcher shop of God he'd run
In tabernacle times. But think on this:

Just two from four had gone to kill and sis
Retrieve, two cannon cockers set to fight.
But when the day had passed, and in the night,
The other brothers came like birds of prey;
They hauled the widows-made and gold away.
For men and wealth of Shechem, no escape—
Hard price for love and statutory rape.
They took their wives? It's double standard shit!
And punishment comes nowhere close to fit
The crime. Well, Jacob wasn't pleased, to say
The least! These sons of Leah filled each day
With worry and anxiety. He said,
With all the ruckus tucked away to bed,
"God told me I'd be great, but you've brought stench
Upon this house. It stinks! Your acts will drench
Us all! The scavengers will smell the reek
And come for their revenge; my life they'll seek.
You're nothing but a bunch of brigands now;
You are not sons to me." This didn't cow
The boys into a penitential mood.
They knew how Jacob felt; his attitude
Was little more than simply laissez-faire.
They had to think about themselves, take care
To guard their interests. Forsaken by
A hateful dad, their burning battle cry
Would ever be for mom! And so, they said
To Jacob then—the man who hung his head
In shame—they said it then, still bloody-gloved:
"This was for Mom, the one you never loved.
This action was an answer to a deed,
And your neglect had fertilized that need.
So, maybe you should care a little more
When daughters of our mother play the whore."

CHAPTER 25

The Other Two

Poor Leah, voiceless wife dismissed. That ten-
Der-eyed and ample-hipped, that fountain pen
Of effortless fertility had done
The best she could. She gave to Jacob sons—
Not one, but six of twelve—and of these, four
Made up the first-string batch. They came before
The rest. *Blue ribbons on the effort, dear.*
But let us not forget their world premiere,
Quartet of mama's boys. So many flaws,
What does our text explain about their paws?
That two had bloody hands and two had hands
That copped a feel. In fact, I'd say it stands
To reason that our text is getting filled
With sex and murder, thanks to them. I'm thrilled
To write this verse! *It's rated R, my dear.*
Well, be that as it may, I'll never fear
To hang the dirty laundry out to dry,

To flap the open air and catch the eye
Of all at Sunday sauntering. It's what
I do! But like I said, these brothers glut
Their wants in other ways, yet all and each
With his own sword. Some cut a throat; some breach
A father's wife. I think a field day Freud
Would have with all of this, but let us void
The checks to therapy for now. Suffice
To say that sex and murder serve as vice
And victual for Man. With that, let's bring
Our Reuben to the stage. This man will sing
About the appetites of lechery.
That's lust, my dear. That's funny now to me—
To have our Reuben sing of appetite.
Corned beef with Thousand Island—oh, and might
I have a little extra kraut? *You may.*
But 'fore we hit on lust, I have to say,
For manly men, our Reuben seems complete.
Oh, he's a man, alright, and even eats
His pumpernickel swabbed with bacon fat.
There were no kosher laws as yet. And that
I've seen with my own eyes, the ones who'd swipe
A piece of bread in bowls of lard and wipe
It down their throats for appetizing bliss.
You'll call me to the carpet now, dismiss
My soft urbanity for clubs and grunts.
Okay—I will admit that once, when stunts
Of reckless youth were more my thing, I tried
The stuff. I heard the call and so replied
A hearty bite's consent. It was some time
Ago, a quirky custom of the clime
Where I had been. Not wanting to offend
That powder keg, my virtue thought to blend
As much as possible. I may have dipped
It twice. *It's just white butter, dear.* I skipped
Dessert, if that means anything. My point
Is that our Reuben is a knuckle joint—
Yes, one tough cheese, of twelve the eldest born.
He wore the sibling pants, the brother sworn

To lead and to protect. Imagine then
What Jacob thought when Reuben took a hen
From out his house to rooster her. *He took*
A wife from Jake? A queen, and moved his rook
In close to mate. Tell me she's concubine;
I dare you, make the case! You'll break your spine
In bending reason back. But riddle sense
When 37:2 would soon dispense
A concubine as wife. The fact remains—
He shared his father's bed, and both their stains
Were on the sheets. Then Jacob heard of it.   (GENESIS 35:22)
One sees the shaking head, the eyebrows knit
Up tense with angst. He couldn't catch a break!
His sons would be the death of him, and Jake
Would go into the grave and know his brood,
His troublemaking Godless multitude,
Would be in charge when he was gone. It's strange
He didn't yell about the interchange
Of wife and in-law made. Or what if she
Were pregnant then—would son or grandson be?
Or Reuben would have brothers for a son.
At least the family pictures would be fun.
At any rate, our Jacob doesn't voice
A peep concerning it. It was his choice
To let it go, not worth a word's address.
He'd bide his time until the time to bless.
But what of Judah now, the last our four?
On this account, I may just need to pour
A glass. Our Judah likes the ladies of
The land, a hypocrite who goes and shoves,
With judgments down, so he can do the deed
He has condemned. I like him too! But read
The text another way, and what is it
I mean? I mean that we can retrofit
This tale to mount our understanding's wheel.
For stale perspectives flatter us and steal
The sweetest juice. So, let a play be sung,
And it will see our dirty laundry's hung.

Cast

Judah—fourth son of Leah and Jacob
Hirah—an Adulamite and friend of Judah
Shua's daughter—a Canaanite wife of Judah
Tamar—widow for Er, woman for Onan, whore for Judah
Er—eldest son of Judah and husband of Tamar
Onan—second son of Judah and surrogate for Er with Tamar
Shelah—youngest son of Judah with a girly name
Servant—slave in the house of Tamar's father
Chorus—women of the towns

Act I

It is the funeral of Er. Judah's wife and Tamar are standing near a chilly grave. Tamar has an elaborate black veil strung round her face to hide any tells of uncertainty concerning her future. It's early morning, and the bleating and the stink of goats is somewhere close.

> Shua's daughter {*Weeping over the grave*}.
> > He was my firstborn son! It's hard to think
> > He'll sleep in earth and sand.   (GENESIS 38:7)

> Chorus. Life is a blink
> > Of any eye and not a given thing.
> > What blesses us today may go and fling
> > Us to the side when next tomorrow comes.

> Shua's daughter. I wish I had more time with him. It numbs
> > Me at the core to look upon this sight.

> Chorus. They're necessary tears, a mother's right
> > To mourn her son. But what about his wife?
> > Poor Tamar wears a veil to hide the strife
> > She feels. A childless widow now without
> > An heir to family blood. She feels the drought
> > Of barren days before.

> Shua's daughter. A mother's pain
> > Is other than a wife's, but still—it's plain

She suffers too. Her sorrow may be worse
Than mine, though each of us can feel the curse
Of death. I have two sons when only one
Was lost. The same loss leaves her now with none.

Chorus. It's right what you have said. But tell me this:
    What's Judah's plan for her? He can't dismiss
    Responsibilities; the patriarch
    Must act.

Shua's daughter. He must decide; he bears the mark
    Of caring for the girl now that my son
    Is dead. It falls to him, and he's the one
    Who knows.

Chorus {*To Tamar*}. Sad girl, your grief is hard to bear.
    Your veil can only hide so much.

Tamar. I'll wear
    This veil to hide my tears but also hide
    My face from men. Men hold or cast aside
    A woman as their whim demands. We wait
    Upon their fickle moods.

Chorus. It's as you state.

Tamar. A woman's contribution is with child.
    We hold that one, that pure and undefiled,
    That right from God to bear a child for them.
    But when that right, that one and only gem,
    Is taken from our hands, we're useless in
    Their sight. A child is how a woman pins
    Her feet to worlds of men.

Chorus. Your husband's gone.

Tamar. The wretched truth, I know.

Chorus. You cannot spawn

A child with someone dead.

Tamar. One can't, nor would.
    And this is all my grief, my widowhood
    Made worse, to have been plucked when I was ripe
    And in my verdant youth, when rosy stripes
    Were on my cheeks. And yet, I wasn't picked
    To be devoured, as one might well predict
    Of younger men, but picked to lay the grass
    And rot, no seed for other trees. Alas,
    Who else will want me since I've lost my flower?
    I'll live now like a slave, when every hour
    I will recall the chance I had and lost.
    For Er, that wicked husband who'd exhaust
    The patience of a God, gave not a child
    To me.

Chorus. We've seen him round. He was a wild,
    Unruly man.

Tamar. He never really cared
    To be at home, and worse, he never shared
    The bed with me.

Chorus. Your pain is heavy now
    Because of it.

Tamar. The heavier from how
    He ruled his life.

Chorus. So, consequences live
    Long after death arrives. But look and give
    Attention here, for Judah comes, the sad-
    Dened father of the dead. His eyes are clad
    With grief and shame.

Enter Judah.

Judah {*Casting dirt into the grave of Er*}.

Great God, come gather up
My son into Your fold, and let him sup
Upon the meat that all Your pastures give,
To roam with sun upon his face and live
Another life that's free of pain.

Chorus. Our prayer
Is with yours now, and we will gladly share
This grief with you.

Judah. My eldest son is dead—
A truth that I would soon deny instead
Of just accepting it. For I've been told
From youth that God would bless my line, consoled
That I had stars and sand within my loins.
But now my firstborn son is laid to join
The earth, to decompose without a son
Himself.

Chorus. Death causes pain for anyone
Who eats the bread of earth.

Judah. Death should have come
To me instead.

Chorus. It comes to all whose sum
Of days is filled.

Judah. My son has died too soon;
His life cut short before the harvest, hewn
To fall against the earth.

Chorus. Why was he killed?

Judah. A wicked deed.

Chorus. We all erect and build
The gallows that we hang ourselves upon.

Judah. His crime was more specific, though, for on
    The hour I gave a bride, he swore that day
    He had despised the girl. He wouldn't pay
    The debt a husband owes his wife because
    He didn't like my choice.

Chorus. You think there was
    Another girl he loved?

Judah. Perhaps.

Chorus. You should
    Have asked.

Judah. I wouldn't hear his pleas but stood
    In arrogance that day.

Chorus. Poor boy.

Judah. My Er. {*To Tamar*}
    He's dead and lies in earth because of her!
    She could have been the bed for him, but now
    His bed is dirt! No woman's warmth to plow
    And sink himself inside, and so he turns
    To sink himself in clay.

Tamar {Aside}. My grief returns
    To me.

Judah. What woman can't entice a man
    To bed?

Tamar. He had me for the ask. No ban
    Was on my favors, sir.

Judah. And yet he's stiff
    And sunk in deep to muddy ground. He sniffs
    At roots and licks the dust.

Chorus. Beware! You make
>   A greater wrong, for words can also take
>   A life. You have a duty now to care
>   For her. No son was given her to share
>   That load.

Judah. I make no wrong; I'm just upset!
>   And don't need some reminder of the debt
>   I owe the girl. I'm head of my own house!
>   And since she has no heir, at least from spouse,
>   I will have one provided by a son.
>   My second son, my Onan, he's the one
>   Who will provide the heir for her.

Chorus. Your sec-
>   Ond son will do this thing? Will this not wreck
>   His hopes for his own family and home?

Judah. He'll do as I have said, or he can roam
>   Away from here. For this is now my will!
>   I'll have him sleeping with the girl until
>   She has a child, a son.

Chorus. But any son
>   He has with her, by rights, will not be one
>   That is his own. 'Twill be his brother's child.

Judah. The customs of our people have been styled
>   This way, and all that you have said is true.
>   But this is what our duty says to do.

Exeunt.

Act II

Five years have passed. The second son of Judah, Onan, who had been provided as a surrogate to Tamar, was also killed by the LORD for similar reasons as the first brother, Er. Childless Tamar is in her father's house and waiting on word from Judah. The patriarch has promised to give his youngest son, Shelah, to be another surrogate and provide Tamar with an heir. But it seems this promise has gone cold. The boy is old enough, and yet Judah is making no effort to fulfill his duty to the girl. Tamar is told that Judah is making a trip to Timnah, the very place he met his first wife. Knowing Judah is more concerned with his own progeny than hers and that he likely will never fulfill his vow to her, Tamar determines to trick Judah into keeping his word.

> Tamar. In helplessness, a woman waits on men.
>   This station God saw fit to give, to pen
>   Upon their fates. Our bodies have been made
>   To bear the load men can't. And still, it's weighed
>   Our chests like bricks. It heaves within and makes
>   Us feed a child on sorrow's milk, the lakes
>   And oceans poured from motherhood. But worse
>   For those with heavy loads who cannot nurse
>   A child! They carry weight without reward,
>   No blessing smiled upon that beauty stored
>   In youth. For age must come and hollow out
>   A woman of her ripened juice; its snout
>   Will suck us dry as does the bear who strives
>   To lick the dripping honey out the hive.
>   So, God gives lavishly to all those girls
>   In youth! It blushes at their cheeks and twirls
>   Their hair to fall about their necks. It twines
>   A coronet of velvet-petaled vines
>   Upon their breasts. And all this to entice
>   A man to marriage vows. It seems the price
>   We pay for men to wed is fronted by
>   Our God, a dowry that's Divine. But why
>   Are we to spend it in our youth? And what
>   Will be our currency when age has cut
>   The wrinkles on our face?
>
> Servant. A woman acts
>   Before her beauty's spent, before the tax
>   Of age has come to call. It's common so
>   For girls to marry when the afterglow
>   Of childhood starts to ripe.
>
> Tamar. So I thought, too!

When Judah picked me for his son——a true
And honest thing for fathers who would choose
A bride for sons——I didn't think I'd lose
My female charms to lips that wouldn't taste.

Servant. You say this of your husband Er?

Tamar. He chased
    For pleasures that my charms would not provide.
    My sheets went cold; he never occupied
    The bed with me.

Servant. What man would have a wife
    Without a single taste?

Tamar. And now the strife
    Of childlessness is mine to bear.

Servant. Poor girl,
    Now widowhood is sitting on your pearl
    Of youth. But what about your dad-in-law?
    Does not he have a duty now, a raw
    And basic role he should fulfill? He must
    Provide an heir for you.

Tamar. I placed my trust
    In this. And so, he gave his second son
    To give me such a child. Had Onan done
    The work his sole commission had required,
    Our God would have been pleased and not retired
    That man from what is life.

Servant. He's dead?

Tamar. Yes, killed
    For always pulling out and semen spilled.
    He'd lose his rights to any son he gave
    To me. You see?

Servant. He'd till your field but save
    It from the seed.

Tamar. It's as you say.

Servant. What now?
    Does Judah plan to keep his word, his vow
    To you?

Tamar. He has another son, his last,
    As Shelah called. When Onan died, I asked
    Of Judah if he would provide this son
    To be a surrogate to me.

Servant. This one
    As Shelah called?

Tamar. That's right. And Judah said
    He would; he said that when the lad had shed
    His youth, he'd send the boy to me.

Servant. And so
    You wait on Shelah now, this boy to grow
    Into a man?

Tamar. I've waited now for five
    Years' time. The lad is grown by now, and I've
    Not heard a single thing from him.

Servant. That's not
    A hopeful sign he'll keep his word.

Tamar. He'd blot
    Me from his mind. I think he blames me for
    His loss of sons. That I'm at fault. What's more,
    He only has but one son left.

Servant. You think
    He fears this son will also die?

Tamar. I shrink
    From such a thought. But still, he only pays
    Me service with his lips, and promise stays
    Without an act. His sons were in the wrong!
    He blames me for their loss, but all along,
    His parenting should answer such a charge!
    But we are women here, and men will barge
    Themselves around and in our pliant frames,
    To plunder in our fields and stake their claims.
    The only tools a woman has are lost
    With age. And still, I'm waiting here. I'm tossed
    Aside, forgotten and betrayed. Each year
    That passes by me now confirms my fear:
    I'll die a widow in my father's house.
    And yet, in Judah's eyes, I'm still the spouse
    Of his dead son. No husband could I take.
    I am his prisoner, one he would make
    To feed on empty promises and words.
    My vital fluid's drying up; it curds
    Within my veins. The longer now I wait,
    The more I feel I have to act!

Servant. The weight
    You bear is breaking you.

Tamar. All women bear
    Such loads.

Enter Chorus.

Chorus. We hurried over here to share
    The news we heard.

Tamar. What words have reached your ears?
    Does Judah send his son to me? For years
    I've waited for that news.

Chorus. That isn't it.
    We've heard that Judah's wife is gone; she's quit

This life. Yes, Judah's wife is dead.

Tamar. Hard news!
Poor Shua's daughter gone; it leaves a bruise
Upon my ears. My mom-in-law is dead.
She welcomed me into her nest and spread
Her wings to cover me. Sweet lady gone.
My tears are for you now.

Chorus. It bears upon
Us all a heavy grief.

Tamar. But what will come
Of Judah now? Poor wifeless man who plumbs
The depths of sorrow's well. What woman now
Will give this man more sons? It's shameful how
He's lost already two. And, surely, he
Will want more than a single heir.

Chorus. But we
Have heard another thing about the man.

Tamar. What's coming next?

Chorus. We've heard he's made a plan
To head to Timnah's plains. He goes to shear
His sheep.

Tamar. There's something in these words. It's clear
He goes to find another wife. The first
He found the same, poor Shua's daughter cursed
With death.

Servant. Another wife would mean more sons.

Tamar. And yet, I'm childless still, and not a one
Has come to me in years of waiting on
His promises. My waiting days are gone!
He cares more for his own affairs than mine.

He's left me little choice, and I am fine
With what will be my course ahead.

Servant. What will
    You do?

Tamar {*Holding up the veil she wore at Er's funeral*}.
    I'll work the tools I have, what still
    Remains of female charms. I'll play the whore
    For this devoted dad-in-law. He swore
    To give me children in the day and light.
    I'll see that promise kept in deeds of night.

Exeunt.

Act III

Tamar is sitting at the gates of Enaim, which is on the road to Timnah. She's covered herself with her veil and waits for Judah to pass. Judah and Hirah are headed to Timnah to shear their sheep. They pass Tamar and, thinking the veiled woman a prostitute, Judah goes into her and makes love to her, leaving several personal items as surety of a future payment for her services.

Hirah. Too many sorrows you have had in life:
    Two sons that you have lost, and now your wife
    Is also gone.

Judah. My father always said
    We'd have more sons than stars above. I fed
    Upon those words. But now with two sons gone,
    I wonder if those words are true. My spawn
    Is down to one; yes, only one of three
    Remain.

Hirah. What of that boy? I've heard that he
    Has grown into a strapping man.

Judah. Like so.
    And ready for a marriage bed to know.

Hirah. So Shelah now could take a wife?

Judah. He could
     And will. I've always thought it right and good
     For men to take a wife, and now that mine
     Is gone, I know that thought is right in line
     With truth.

Hirah. What of your first son's wife, the one
     As Tamar named? Did you not say your son
     Would be a surrogate for her?

Judah. Oh, I
     Regret that promise made! I'd rather die
     Than see my word fulfilled. That woman's like
     A spider, widow-black, and she would strike
     My third with death, as well. She strings her net
     And catches men. She's tainted water, wet
     With blood from two my sons. I know her kind
     And won't with such a girl again be twined.
     {Judah notices a prostitute sitting in the gates}

Hirah. But still, your word was given her.

Judah. I know,
     And some day I might have it done. But go
     Ahead of me. I see a girl who's caught
     My eye.

Hirah. I will, my friend.

Exit Hirah.

Judah {To veiled Tamar}. It's awful hot
     For veils.

Tamar. Some treats are better covered up.

Judah. Some treats may spoil if one can never sup
  Upon the things.

Tamar. And is that what you want,
  To sup upon my treats?

Judah. And you would taunt
  The hungry man? But what if I would pay
  To give your treats a taste? What would you say
  Could be the proper compensating price?

Tamar. Name that which both my need and want entice.

Judah. The best goat I can find from out my flock!
  I'll send it back to you. I have to walk
  To Timnah first, but you will have my word.

Tamar. I've had man's word before; by same I've heard
  A promise left for dead. I'll need a guar-
  Antee you'll pay the promised fee.

Judah. What are
  Your terms?

Tamar. You'll leave your staff and signet ring
  As pledge to wait with me. And when you bring
  Me what you said you would, I'll give them back.

Judah {*Handing her the items*}.
  Here are my things. Now give me what I lack
  And more desire.

Tamar. We both will give and get
  Today. Come sir, {*leading him off*} it's time to pay a debt.

Exeunt.

Act IV

In an attempt to save face, Judah has sent his friend Hirah to deliver the payment of a goat to the veiled prostitute. He returns to Judah with the goat and explains he could find no such woman, and the people of the town know nothing of the girl. Judah resolves to let her keep his personal items to avoid a scandal. He later hears that his son's widow, Tamar, is with child. Enraged by such news, he demands the girl be brought to him to answer and to suffer death for infidelity. The girl appears and provides the items he left with the prostitute. Judah repents.

Judah. What do you mean, she wasn't there?

Hirah. I tell
  You what I saw—no woman there who'd sell
  Her body for a goat.

Judah. You'd have a laugh
  At my expense? She has my ring and staff.
  What if she talks?

Hirah. Who would she tell? Just let
  It go. There isn't any kind of threat.

Judah. This has a bitter taste and turns my gut.

Hirah. It's something that you ate.

Judah. But tell me what
  Has happened to the girl; I need to know.

Hirah. Perhaps she had to move or had to go
  And get some sheep from other customers.

Judah. I'll let her keep my things and call them hers.
  It's better just to let this die. I don't
  Want all this getting out.

Hirah. My friend, it won't!
  And if it does, just say that you had got-
  Ten robbed.

Enter Chorus.

Chorus {*To Judah*}.
 Good sir, we've come, and we have brought
 You news about your first son's wife.

Judah. What of
 That woman, Tamar called?

Chorus. Immoral love
 That girl has known. But more, for now it seems
 She's pregnant by the same.

Judah. Dishonest schemes
 Behind my back! That wretched whore! I knew
 That girl should not be given trust. But do
 You know the man who's done the deed?

Chorus. She would
 Not say.

Judah. We'll find it out and have him stood
 Beside her in these crimes! Go bring her here
 To answer and to die!

Chorus. We will.

Exit Chorus.

Judah. To hear
 These words is music to my ears. Of course,
 She'll have to suffer death; I won't endorse
 Such acts with passive eyes. But knowing that
 Her death will now absolve me from the mat-
 Ter of providing her a son—that I
 Can breathe a sigh of some relief, whereby
 I know my word no longer needs be kept—
 That part is sweet. But still, she went and slept
 With one outside my line. She only had

To wait! I would have sent my son and glad-
Ly kept my word. I said that I would do
The thing; she should have trusted me. It's true,
I do regret I ever found her for
My firstborn son. She's been a thorn, a sore
Within my mouth, the vinegar that turns
A tongue, the smoke that clouds the eyes and burns.
Two sons I've lost because of her! Two sons
That I cannot get back. So, there are tons
Of those regrets, but now I'll go ahead
And marry Shelah to a wife instead
Of risking my last son with such a whore.
She ended two my sons and would have bore
Me childless in the end. It is a joy
To have her go! But where's the lover boy,
This rake who'd bounce the bed of my son's wife?
Oh, bring the man! I swear we'll have his life,
And then the girl will pay.

Enter Chorus and Tamar.

Chorus {*Handing Tamar to Judah, her hands bound with her veil*}.
    We've brought the girl
    As you have asked.

Judah. You have my thanks. This churl-
    Ish bitch will answer for her crimes!

Chorus. It's right
    To answer, lord.

Judah {*To Tamar*}. Speak up, you Canaanite,
    You whore who's brought this shame upon my house.
    Perhaps you have forgotten that your spouse
    Was my own son—forgot your vow, the word
    You gave? You haven't followed through, preferred
    A moment's passion to a promise kept.
    You lowlife dog! I spit on you! You've stepped
    Across the line. I see the way you bulge

A bastard. Is it one or two? Divulge
Your lover's name! I'll have it from your lips.

Chorus. The patriarch is right; his parentship
    Rules over you.

Tamar. It does. At least it should.

Judah. What does your insolence suggest? Or would
    You have me held responsible? I gave
    My son to you, and now he's in the grave
    Because you couldn't get him into bed.
    And so, I gave another son. He's dead
    Because he wouldn't seed your garden row.
    I promised you the third my sons, although
    He could just end up dead himself. And all
    You had to do was wait until the ball
    Had dropped.

Tamar. Your boy is grown; no word was sent.

Judah. I would have sent the boy! Your malcontent
    Has brought this shame on me. But tell me who
    You have deceived to fill his place, what clue-
    Less fool was duped to share your lethal bed?
    Perhaps he didn't know that he had tread
    Upon my house? Perhaps he didn't know
    That you were in my care? Well, now you grow
    With child. It was my place to see you had
    A son, not yours!

Tamar. It's as you say.

Judah. Don't add
    Another wrong to such a nasty deed!
    I'll have his name.

Tamar. You will. But first I need
    To keep my word before I die, just one

Last thing I need to do.

Judah. So, have it done.

Tamar. I told my lover once he came and kept
    His word to me, when I could then accept
    His word fulfilled, I would return his things
    To him—some simple items like a ring
    And staff. Well, now his word is kept. He gave
    Me sons; his promise is made good. {*Motions to Chorus*} And they've
    The things that were collateral.

Chorus {*Handing staff and ring to Judah*}. It's as
    She said, my lord.

Hirah {To Judah}. That ring is yours. It has
    Your name upon the seal.

Judah. My reprimands
    Have turned to shout at me, and charges stand
    In judgment on the judge. {*To Tamar*} You wore the veil?

Tamar. The same by which I'm bound.

Judah. Sweet girl, I'm pale
    With shame! And what was vehemence has cooled
    Into regret. I let myself be ruled
    By arrogance and pride, and every word
    I spoke was true of me alone. I've blurred
    The roles; you are the one who's fit to pass
    A judgment unto me. I have a crass
    And wicked way. Forgive this man for how
    He's treated you, for all my wrongs are now
    Made clear.

Tamar. I do.

Judah. So, what's inside of you
    Is mine?

Tamar. It is, and they inside are two.

Judah {*Kneeling before Tamar, undoing her bounds and placing hands on her stomach*}.
    God has returned my sons to me! I lacked
    In faith and didn't trust my God. This smacked
    Of arrogance, as well. Oh, wicked self!
    This girl was wronged, sweet girl who has herself
    Now shown my wrongs to me. From this day on,
    I'll treat you as a bride. You'll meet the dawn
    Within my house, and I will care for you.
    But let all people hear, for this is true!
    Her acts were righteous when she had been wronged,
    And all my judgments on myself belonged.

Lights down. Exeunt.

Was Judah not like Creon in our play?
When hubris runs amuck, it makes us say
Some unabashed rot! So, twice give thought
Before you stitch a scarlet A, and knot
Your tongue before loose words can rampant run.
What of the heroine, that Gatling gun
Of innocence? I love this girl's mystique!
Both bed and grave were part of her. And speak-
Ing of a grave that's shared, good John Donne said
Of graves that "They have learned that woman head,
Which is to more than one a bed." But toast
Your Ultra Lite in Diva cups, or host
A party where the hats are red. We'll end
On this, and optimistically I'll send
You packing with a treat. What of the thread
They wrapped around the first of twins, that red
Reserve around the wrist, there tied to mark
The older of the two? Well, it should spark
Your interest for this and this alone:
The arm was pulled back in, and then the groan
Of labor made the second one emerge.

At least our barren wife won't sing a dirge
Of childlessness again. But she had twins—
That thing that happens when the fertile grins—
And baby one was pulled back from his burst.
Again, the second overran the first.

CHAPTER 26

Back to Basics

God said to Jacob then, "Why don't you go
To Bethel now and dwell; I think you know   (GENESIS 35:1)
The place I mean, the very spot you went
Before to flee a brother who was bent
On killing you. Now, go there once again
And build an altar to the One who reigns
On high, the One who showed Himself to you."
So God had spoken clear, and rendezvous
At Bethel were in store for Jacob soon
Enough. And on that very afternoon,
He gathered up his daughters and his sons
And spoke these words: "Well, now that everyone
Is here, I'll speak, for what I have to share
Is meant for all of you. I know it's fair
To say I'm not the leader you deserve.
I've dropped the ball; in fact, I've let us swerve
Right off the tracks. So, what I'm sharing now

Is aimed at me more so than you. Somehow
We got off course; we have forgotten who
Our God has been to us. We've taken new
And idol gods that we can hold and touch.
We carry them around, and even such
Receive our prayers. We need to let these go!
They're earless little toys—a puppet show
And nothing more. I've seen our God; He's shown
Himself to me. He even broke my bone;
You've seen the way I'm limping through the camp.
So, trust me on this now, and rubber stamp
What I suggest. Let's put away the gods
Of wood and clay. Each one of us is flawed,
And none of you is worse than me in this.
But bring me all your gods, and do not miss
A one. Come clean, and leave them at my door."
So Jacob spoke, and they did not ignore
His words, but as the patriarch had said,
They left their idols at his tent for dead.
Then Jake went on, "Now get cleaned up and scrub
Behind your ears. Put on new clothes and rub
The wrinkles out, for at tomorrow's dawn
We're moving camp." Those were his words. But on
And in the morning light, before the rest
Of camp had even packed, the old man dressed
And gathered up the pile of idols left
Beside his door, not there by any theft
But brought by willing and repentant hands.
He gathered all these up, and in the sand
Beneath a cashew tree, he dug a pit.
Much like a celebrant, he did commit
Them to the earth; they would return to dust.
(So much for gods of earth and wood.) He thrust
His palms in hard and packed it tight. Then Jake—
That spur upon the heel, that bellyache
Within the gut, that cheat at cards—became
A weeping willow of a man, and shame
Would mark the rest his days. His flimsy knees
Were cratered in the sand as morning breez-

Es rustled through the leaves and tossed his beard
About his face. He stood, his life veneered
With wrinkled skin, and felt the wobbly state
Of life on earth—a role he'd abdicate
Or Mickey Finn, if chance would so allow.
But he could not. Life is a sacred cow
And wanders, quite untouchable, between
Those fences made of years. What intervenes
Is death by other hands, and down our steaks
Are set in freezers of the ground. Old Jake
Had known all this, but even more, he knew
That God had pledged His word. He'd carry through
Until the blessing had been made a fact.
Jake stood beside the tree, his idols packed
In dirt, and felt the wind begin to blow.
It shook the leaves and then began to throw
His beard around his face. And then he said,
Like one who just some heavy weight had shed,
"Your animating breeze is all my breath."
So spoke the prince of nations, son of Seth.

CHAPTER 27

Dreamer

Now Joseph was the child of Jacob's age.
A second chance of sorts, for at that stage
Of life, one tries to right the failures of
Their first attempts. Jake loved the boy above   (GENESIS 37:3)
The rest! And in that vein of love, he made
The boy a coat, and on it was displayed
The colors all his dyes could muster out—
A painted peacock pelt, without a doubt.
The brothers saw the way their father prized
This late arriving lad, and they despised
The younger boy! They never had a peace-
Ful word concerning him and wouldn't cease
Their vehemence of hate. What made it worse
Was Joseph always seemed to intersperse
The conversation with the dreams he had
And insult unto injury would add.
He'd say things like, "You won't believe the dream

I had last night!" And then with eyes agleam
Would Joseph prattle on, "The reapers came
With heavy scythes and narrow necks to claim
A harvest bulging at the seams. The tuft
Of each the stalks was golden brown and stuffed
With wheat. Then each of us, my brothers, tied
Our own into a sheaf. But then I spied
That mine was in the center of them all
And standing higher than the rest, a tall
And grander sheaf than each of yours. At once
Your sheaves were kneeling down in deference
To mine." Like so, the green-eyed lad would share
His dreams, oblivious and unaware
To how they were received. He lived apart
And didn't know what cankers human hearts.

A squirrel makes a home among the heights,
Precarious his leaps and grips, and fright
Has not a footing in his mind. He sim-
Ply runs along the branches, and from limb
To limb, he jumps, insensible to cares
Of earthy humankind. He more so shares
The mindset of a feathered bird than those
Now bound to dirt.

So Joseph wore the clothes
Of one who didn't know his own restraints.
His mind just wasn't held to earth, a saint
Among the devils with their stomachs on
The ground. But add another straw upon
The camel's back, for Jacob went and made
This boy the boss, a little accolade
For being one the man could trust. That's right,
Young Joseph was the boss and also quite
A stoolie for the dad. Remember, though—
Old Leah's sons would cook the books and go
Beneath the counter for a deal. They did-
N't need this Dudley Do, brown-noser kid
To rat them out. It happened, though, one day,

That Jacob sent young Joseph on his way
To gather such reports and bring him word.
The boys were camped near Shechem then; Jake heard
That was the case. The clan was south of there,
In Hebron's hills, and quite the hike to where
The brothers were supposed to be. Joe stuffed
A bag and left, his colored coat then cuffed
And pressed. *You'd see the boy a mile away.*
He came to Shechem then, and on a day
Of wandering the fields so he could find
His brothers there. A man appeared and, kind
Enough to help, told Joe his brothers went
To Dothan then; they'd pasture fields and tent
Up there awhile. And sure enough, Joe found
The brothers there on northern Dothan's ground.
And seeing from afar his colored coat,
The brothers then conspired to cut his throat!
They said, "Oh, look! The dreamer comes. Let's kill
Him now and throw him in a hole. We'll spill
His blood and say we found him torn to bits
By animals. Let him get close—we'll blitz
Him all at once." The oldest brother then,
As Reuben called, the calmest of the men
That day, did say, "Just throw him in the hole,
But don't you spill his blood. Who would console
Our father with him dead?" The plan was nixed,
But Simeon's and Levi's minds were fixed.

A tiger gets a taste for human blood
When it's been spilled. The salty memory floods
His mind for days on end and drives him from
The forest brush to seek it out, his gums
Still salivating at the thought.

Like so,
The bloody brothers licked their lips to throw
A thought like death around. They grabbed the lad,
A welcome more abomination clad,
And threw him in a pit. They'd need to stew

A proper subterfuge, a what-to-do
With him they hated so. But Judah said
To Sim and Lee, alone (he had a head
To make a buck), "How does it profit us
To simply kill the boy, to make a fuss
About his bloody robes? Let's sell him to
The traders now, the Ishmaelites, to do
What they do best." And so, those three agreed,
And when the oldest (Reuben) left with speed
To make a coffee run, they pulled the boy
From out the depths, ripped off his coat with joy,
And sold him to the traders passing by.
They'd take the lad to Egypt then—to die
Or be a slave; they didn't care. They sold
Their brother's life for silver, not for gold—
Yes, twenty silver coins. They didn't know
That evil deeds can greater plans still show,
Or that in sending Joe to Egypt's land,
He'd be the first of seventy to stand.

CHAPTER 28

Riot Act

Then Levi, bloody man for bloody chores,
Rose up. That leather apron ran the store
Of bleeding things, and he was more than apt
To kill a goat. And so, with knife unstrapped,
He drained its vital fluids on the ground.
When coasts were clear and no one was around,
They dipped the coat—that dandy little pelt   (GENESIS 37:31)
That Jacob gave to Joseph—yes, they dealt
With it as such: they swabbed the coat in red,
And many colors down to one were bled.
A crimson rag and more a clotted mess
That coat had then become—so, more or less
A mockery of something once so bright.
The deed was done and, in the morning light,
The brothers started back for what was home.
A couple weeks it took, no doubt, to roam
From Dothan back to Hebron's plains. I'm sure

They took their good old time to more ensure
They had their stories straight. They knew they'd hear
The Riot Act, and Jake would commandeer
What little trust he'd given them if he
Did learn the truth. So, Reuben had to be
On board; he had to play along with their
Charades. They'd meet their father, and they'd swear
A single story from the mouths of four.
And so, they did. They met the man and swore
They came across a garment in a field,
And happy accidents will sometimes yield
A precious find. On all the land between
Low Hebron's hills and northern Dothan's scene,
They just so happened on a bloody robe
Against the ground. Who wouldn't think to probe
A story such as this? They held the coat,
The crusty crimson rag that smelled of goat,
In Jacob's face. And then they said, "We came
Across this robe. It looks to be the same
You gave to Joe. It could be anything,
But tell us, do you recognize the thing?"
Then Jacob, prince of nations, was undone!
"I know this robe!" he cried. "It was my son's!
Some beast has gorged itself upon my boy!"
He took the bait, a lie for real McCoy.
They watched the vintage man then as he went
And tied some burlap round his groin and spent
The next few weeks in ash and hunger pains.
He held poor Joseph's coat within the reins
Of both his hands and tried to wash it clean
With tears.

A mother tiger works to preen
A lifeless cub with constant licks. Her tongue
Will press against the ribs until its lungs
Can take a breath.

So Jacob's tears were pressed
Against that coat, as if they'd fill a chest

With air, the lifeless son he'd never hold
Again. That grieving man was not consoled
By anything his daughters or his sons
Could do. Of all his clan, there wasn't one
To help. He wanted to be left alone,
And cheering efforts failed to work. "I'll moan,"
He said, "the rest my days on earth, and then,
In Hell, I'll also mourn." A broody hen
The man became and sat upon his grief.

And as King David couldn't find relief
From chills when that man's life was set to close,

So Jacob also felt (for less he chose)
His state of mind. Imagine, though, the verse
That jingled from the walls of Judah's purse.
What if old Jacob heard those silver coins,
His burlap undies strapped around his groin?
What if, just for a moment, that man heard
The clanking of the coins that had referred
His son to Egypt's land? I'll bet he did.
And at that very moment then, his kid
Was being sold in Egypt's market trade;
A slave to Potiphar was Joseph made.

CHAPTER 29

Aggressive Woman

Well, there she is—your wife, that strumpet of
A lass. When did you make your puppy love
The ball and chain you'd carry round? Yes, I've
Forgotten, too. But let us dumpster dive
And rummage through the half-chewed bits of meat,
The apple cores and such—a trick-or-treat
Where costumes aren't required. Perhaps we'll find
Regurgitated things that might remind
Us of the feast we once enjoyed, the spread
That we partook in years ago. It fed
Us for a while. *If milk is free, why buy
The cow?* It's never free. But pacify
My curiosity, and tell me when
You knew your wife was hot to trot for men
Apart from you? The cougars of the earth,
What discontent presided at their birth?
Don't act as if they don't exist or pay

Them service with an eye that winks. They sway
Upon stiletto pumps, like circus stilts,
And give the world a peep. Their satin kilts
And garter straps are on display. They know
The game; they have a carpetbag they tow
Around with tricks inside. They'll teach a class
On country matters down the hall. You'll pass
If extra credit is complete. Grow fat
Upon the show, O younger boys, for that
Will be your final supper, as it were—
And you can stuff yourself as you prefer,
Like pigeons at a wedding when the guests
Are throwing rice. No Pepto could arrest
What's coming next. You see that rock upon
The finger, friend? A princess cut she'll pawn
When things go south. Beware her needles and
Her ball of thread; she weaves a web to land
Another rich one in her lap. Eight legs
And jaws, she'll see you drained to lay her eggs.
But in the meantime, though, she'll need some ex-
Ercise. Those yoga pants do more than flex
The glutes. They hide the T-string bar and make
Things more accessible, your piece of cake
At noon. Her pants are glue, and eyeballs stick—
The dehydration stuff that has you lick-
Ing blocks of salt. She'll give you just a sniff,
Her milk and honey loaves, to get you stiff
Upon her trail, and then she's hunting you.
That wise composer of the Proverbs knew
These girls and said, "They lead to death, the ox
To slaughterhouse, the idiot to stocks
Of tutelage." It's gonna cost your life!
But anyway, let's get back to your wife,
That lovely crown upon your head. Oh, she's
A gem! When she's not mining gold, she'll tease
The staff with batting eyes, Egyptian lash
And feline gaze—call Hammurabi trash,
And set the pyramids ablaze. This girl
Could wreck a home. But you know that. The pearl

You plucked from out the mouth of clams had fangs.
Tread lightly, friend; your very life now hangs
From slender threads. John Edwards comes to mind!
But let that go. I'm not the least inclined
To have this conversation run about
In tweed damnation suits, the cancel out
That has us thankful for judgmental moods
And toasty warms of holy altitudes.
But tell me of the going rate you paid
For such a slave. What was the price? You made
A killing on this purchase, friend! The boy
You bought can handle things, so go employ
Your oversight to making meals—to what's   (GENESIS 39:6)
For dinner and dessert. *The leeks and nuts*
Were overcooked! His God is blessing all
He sets his hand to do. He'll overhaul
The way your house was run before. I mean,
He'll see it's now a proper-oiled machine.
He'll trim the fat and have you wondering
What you could do. Your plans for snorkeling
The Nile need not be put off anymore.
Or take your wife—go get some petit fours
And doppio; take in the sights and spark
The flames you've left to cool beneath the dark
Of many nights. Of course, I understand.
You're married to your work, and you had planned
To spend the extra time with longer hours
At office chores. But milk and honey sour
When left to sit the burners in the back,
And young Adonis gentlemen—sixpack
And pecs—are called to meet a need. I see
Her watching him, your idle devotee
Of marriage vows. She wants to feel her youth
Again. She thinks this slave might help, in truth.
For spicy love can palpitate a heart,
Excitement to the day's routine impart.
And you are hardly home, O Potiphar,
The captain of the guard, a commissar
Of Pharaoh's troop. So, what is she to do?

She feels the flutters anytime her view
Is on this boy, for Joseph is a stud—
A specimen who more than heats her blood
To blush. The locks of hair, the shoulder span
And eyes—this new kid on the block, this man,
Has turned her oven on, and tarts are hot!
Now sex with Joseph is her food for thought.
But just ignore her looks and go to work,
My friend. I'll keep an eye on her. I'll clerk
The day's events and let you know how things
Play out. (Another tense in now I'll sing.)
But then the wife, the horny, hounded wife,
Took well enough and sprinkled in some strife.
She pestered Joseph with her lush advance,
Enticed erotica in constant dance,
And when her charms were on him closer pressed,
Revealing ample cleavage in her breasts,
Asked, "Am I not desirable to you?
Come show me what your skills in bed can do."
But Joseph said, "Withdraw your hopeful prod,
This sin against your husband and my God!"
Yet she would not let easy go the chase
And daily propositioned him in lace.
She showed him secret fruit; he could have had
A bite. Then on one day, when only clad
In velvet skin, fresh out the spa and rinse,
The wife grabbed Joe and, wanting to convince
(For she was feeling more the normal urge),
Said, "Come, our ripened bodies need to merge!
My husband gave you all; now taste of me."
Then soft, "Or don't you like what you can see?"
She pulled him close to feel her plushy smooth
And curving frame. Held tight, he couldn't move.
He knew she wouldn't let him go. Just then,
While feeling all the stiff that only men
Can feel, he twisted from the frenzied grip,
And Joseph's robe off Joseph's arms did slip.
This boy can't seem to keep a coat. Hightailed
That Joseph ran, and self-control prevailed

A shirtless king. What of the robe he dropped,
The garment from his back that he had swapped
For naked skin? The wife held on to it.
Her nose would catch the scent of one who'd quit
Her sweet advance so brazenly. She smelled
His Hebrew musk still on the coat and held
It close, and for a moment only let
Her wild imagination run. And yet,
That sweet intoxication turned to scorn.
Deep breath, and like a banshee with a horn,
She sang soprano tones that shook the walls—
For jilted women, standard protocols!
She squeezed some tears and shock into her face
And threw a stitch of clothing on. Disgrace
Was in her voice as she explained then to
The other servants there how that Hebrew
Approached her in her bath. She even said
He tried to have some sport with her in bed:
"A randy little laugh at my expense!"
The rest that afternoon, the air was tense
And sober-thick. Poor Joe was forced to wait
In just his skibbies then and contemplate
What might be said when Potiphar returned.
The wife had kept his robe. That woman spurned
Was sitting on it then, a harpy egg
She'd incubate into a powder keg.

A cat will wound a mouse before she takes
His life. She toys around with him and makes
Her entertainment from the rodent's angst.
There's no escape, for now the mouse is fenced
Within her grasp. She tickles him with claws
And bats him in between her heartless paws.

Like so, the wife held Joseph's coat to taunt
Him till the husband had returned, to flaunt
The upper hand her weaker sex would grant.
Repeating out her story in a chant,
She took and memorized her Trojan horse,

Each bending of the truth that girl would force
Into her husband's ears. Yes, she would say
That sneaky Joseph tried to have his way
With her when he was off at work. That was
The way it stood, and all of this because
A slave had left her pass to sail the wind.
Each person in the house had eyes then pinned
Against the door and waited for the mas-
Ter to return. They heard him on the grass
And up the stairs; they heard the key insert
And turn; they heard the creaking hinges blurt
That doors were open wide. Yes, every ear
Within the house could hear the door, could hear
The keys tossed down as in the master walked,
The "Honey, I am home," the rear-end docked
Against the best recliner in the den.
The moment had arrived. For that was when
The wife got up and, taking Joseph's coat,
Did toss it in her husband's lap. Her throat
Was cleared—this Trojan horse would need some grease—
And then she sang, gave of her mind a piece!
"That slave you love, the one who you entrust
With running things, he looks to quench his lust
Upon your wife, as if I were a whore!
What sort of woman does he take me for?"

The January wind will paint a frost
On windowpanes and easily exhaust
The heat within a home. When morning rays
Of light arrive, announcing then the day's
Hard chore to meet, reluctantly one turns
From blanket warmth to make the fires return.

So Potiphar looked up reluctantly
And knit a frown. He'd learned to referee
Such things by being captain of the guard.
What's more, he knew who stamped his ration card
For peace of mind; he knew his wife was not
To be ignored if he had ever thought
To have a moment's peace again. He stared

And tried then not to look annoyed, prepared
To lend appearance some concern. He sighed
And lifted up the coat. "You say, he tried
To have some sport with you?" "Some sport!" she yelled.
No reason would hysteria see quelled.
She grabbed the coat. "He watched me in the bath,
Just like a perv! And then that psychopath
Took off this robe to bathe with me. As if
I'd let another man to have a whiff
Or taste of what is yours." (Let's shift the tense
To present now.) Theatrics and pretense,
I'm sucker for the blubber and the tears.
They call this being hood and winked, my dear.
But tell me you're not buying it, this spiel
About the Hebrew kid. Her sex appeal
Is powerful, but Joseph never gave
The least impression that he cared. That slave
Is occupied with managing your house—
No time for love. But still, she is your spouse,
And lies or not, her case will need addressed.
If not, I'll guarantee you'll never rest
In these four walls again. I know it's not
An easy choice, for who had ever thought
A house could run this smooth? You only had
To wonder what to eat; that canny lad
Would handle all the rest. But come to think
Of it, there's nothing cooking now. The sink
And stove are bare of bones. *No need to fret,*
For sweet old Mother Hubbard went to get
Some takeout, dear. But what are we to do
About the wife? We know her words aren't true.
My captain of the guard is way too sharp
To let himself be duped. But she will harp
On this till kingdom come. That doesn't mean
We have to buy her propaganda scene
And tabloid trash. It's like the wicked witch
From out the West had said: one needs to hitch
Her wagon on the train of delicate.
(Switch one last time.) Then said the wife, to cut
Into the chase, "You think I'm lying now?

At least your face would seem to say. But how
Do you explain this coat? He left the thing
Behind and ran when I had yelled to bring
The other servants to my aid. Explain
That one to me." Then Potiphar, in plain
And soft, sagacious tones: "Perhaps it's just
An innocent mistake. I have to trust
He'd never try what you suggest. As for
The coat, he might have left it on the floor
In haste to flee your naked loveliness."
The wife then worked her face into a mess
Of petulance—her cheeks a tawny hue,
Said, "Oh, I see there's nothing you will do
About this now!" Dismissal told her all
She needed know. "Let each our slaves come ball
Your wife!" The husband closed his eyes and held
His hands in front of him, the more compelled
To dam her words and shield his tender ears.
But on she went, emasculating shears
About to snip, "You'll either sacrifice
This slave you love or never have a slice
Of me again." She let these words sink in
Her husband's ears then whispered with a grin,
"Not only will you never share my bed,
I swear by Set, I'll tear this house to shreds."
The husband all but jumped from out his chair
And looked his wife straight in the face, "How dare
You threaten me!" The man had blown a fuse!
But calm, his wife replied, "You need to choose."
But what choice did he have? He'd need to rid
His house of Joseph then, this flawless kid
Who managed things so well. But then he had
A thought, a simple thought both ironclad
And safe, a thought alone that made him smirk:
"If Joe can't run my home, take him to work."
His anger simmered down into a brood,
And then he said, to have his wife subdued,
"Let Joseph rot in prison and be barred!"
Wise Potiphar, the captain of the guard.

CHAPTER 30

Overseer

And so it came to pass in time that two
Of Pharaoh's men—that is, the servants who
Had been in charge of baking bread and bear-
Ing cups—had been entrusted to the care
Of Captain Potiphar. For so it seems,
They'd been accused of crimes, and these extremes
Had landed them in Egypt's finest clink.
Now both these men, the one who poured the drinks
And he who baked the bread, were given to   (Genesis 40:4)
The oversight of Joseph then. *I knew*
They'd put that boy in charge. When many moons
Had passed and days were covered up with dunes
Of those forgetful sands in Egypt's ar-
Senal, when common place gives seminars
On what is out of place, our Joseph was
To notice something odd. This all because
These servants in his care looked out of sorts.

Yes, something bothered them. Our text reports
That each one had a dream—that each those dreams
Had its interpretation, too—and themes
Were not the same. When Joseph saw that both
These men were stressing out, he wasn't sloth
In his response but quickly asked of them,
"Your faces mop the floors, my friends. What hems
The heavy circles round your eyes?" They saw
The boy was all sincere; in turn, their jaws
Were quick to blurt, "We both had dreams last night—
Odd dreams they were, and strange. And now, despite
Our best attempts, we're lost on what they mean."
Well, Joseph thought it apt to intervene;
His repertoire was not devoid of rid-
Dles and of crazy dreams, and so he bid
The men to share with him. He said, "Do not
Interpretations rest with God? I've got
Some time, so tell me of your dreams. I'd like
To hear." So Joseph spoke. The first to strike
The air with words had been the bearer of
The cups. He said, "Well, in my dream, above
My head, there was a vine. And from this vine,
Three branches grew. And then at once, these bines
Were filled with buds and blossoms coming next.
And then the clustered grapes—so large they vexed
The vines to bend beneath their weight—those grapes
Were ripe and succulent. I took to traipse
The vineyard then, to smell the dew and touch
The vine. But then, I noticed in my clutch
The cup of Pharaoh's house. And so I took
And pulled a cluster close; the pruning hook
Had been my hand. I pressed the grapes and squeezed
Them into Pharaoh's cup. So I was pleased
To fill that cup again. With eyes agleam,
I gave it to the king." This was my dream.

Think of a reckless boy who runs the trails
He's made in forests near his home. He scales
The fallen limbs with ease, the aftermath

Of storms a week before. It is a path
He's come to know by heart. But something sparks
His interest one day, for off the bark
Of some grand maple on the path, there drapes
An oddity, a spongy bulb whose shape
Appears to be some large and swollen bean.
The boy picks up a stick and, not so mean
As curious, he swings the stick and smash-
Es it against the thing. At once, it splash-
Es colors out, a splattering that stains
The bark with green and blue—the loud remains
Of secret things. It makes the boy unwell,
Afraid of what the oozing colors tell.

Like so, the bearer of the cups had gazed
On secret things. But Joseph was unfazed
By any riddle such as this and said
Unto the bearer of the cups, "I've read
Your dream and have interpretations now.
Three branches are three days. And this I vow
To you: in three days' time you'll be returned
Unto your post—that is, you'll be concerned
With filling Pharaoh's cup again. But I
Would ask that you remember me, the guy
You met in prison here, and mention me
In Pharaoh's ear. I pray he'll come to see
That I have wrongly been accused and know
I suffer from a falsehood's undertow."
So spoke the man who didn't have a coat.
But when the baker heard these tender notes
Of good reports, he also thought to share
The dream he'd had. Like so, with little care,
This baker of the Pharaoh's royal bread
Went on, "I dreamed of baskets on my head—
Three baskets, each upon the other stacked.
But of the highest one, it had been packed
With bread and bagels, muffins, cakes, and pies.
At once a terror came, for all the skies
Were black with wings; a great cacophony

Of birds arrived! Bereft of modesty,
They filled their beaks with all the baskets held."
So spoke the baker of the bread, compelled
To give his dream to Joseph's sage regard.
Joe didn't hesitate, despite the hard
Interpretation Captain Bake would get.
Joe looked at him and said, "You'd better bet:
Three baskets mark the days. In three days' time,
You'll be released, but only so a crime
Can suffer death. You'll hang upon a tree,
And birds will come to dine, rapaciously.
Yes, that is how you'll serve your final feast;
Your flesh and bone will feed the bird and beast."
In three days' time, Joe's words were rendered true,
For bonds of both did Pharaoh then undo—
Restored the goblet lord to wine and tea
While baker served his supper on the tree.

CHAPTER 31

Seven Lean

When numbers were not even worth a count,   (PSALM 105:12-22)
When all their fame was simply tantamount
To those who wander round on camel backs,
The LORD preserved their path, and so their tracks
Were not oppressed by any man. The LORD
Rebuked the kings on their account, His sword
On standby then. He said things like, "Don't lay
A finger on anointed ones." He'd say,
"Yes, do My prophets not a bit of harm."
When famine had been summoned, when His arm
Had stripped the land of bread, He sent a man
Ahead of them. Yes, one from out that clan,
As Joseph called, was sold to be a slave.
He spent his days in pits so that he'd crave
The light of day, his ankles locked in bands
Of steel, his neck in chains. And in that land,
He heard a language that he didn't know,

A tongue he didn't understand. By slow
Degrees, it came to pass, the LORD had test-
Ed him; by God's own word he was oppressed.
But Pharaoh noticed him, and so that king
Undid his chains and took the metal ring
From off his neck to set him free. He made
Him ruler of his house and goods, arrayed
Him with a judge's robe, so he could bind
The princes at a whim. No more confined
To sit the depths and rot, he learned their speech,
And elders, in his wisdom gained, did teach.

We're getting near the end—that is, the end
Of our initial book, the book we spend
So many Januarys by. For who
Has not made New Year's resolutions to
Defeat the wide expanse of New and Old
Within a year? Such resolutions hold
A conscience for a while, at least until
The lunges of Leviticus turn Will
And Want into those lovers now estranged.
It happens more than not—that we've exchanged
The worm and early bird for pressing snooze.
I'm guilty as the rest and would accuse
The me, myself, and I before I'd dare
To point condemning fingers or compare
My measly merits to your own. But steer
Us back on course, and let those mutineers
Jump ship if they desire. Yes, let them sweat
Like pigs in Circe's barn, grow heavyset
On lotus chips, and barbeque the cat-
Tle of the Sun. But we've a pussycat
At home; she's waiting for us there. She knits
By day, undoing it at night. Our pit
And stop at sweet Calypso's bed must end.
We're sons of Laertes and can't pretend
We don't have suitors to confront. All this
To say, let's finish strong! A drive's remiss
When it has petered out on some fatigue.

But speak of Pharaoh now, the man in league
With sayers of the sooth—you know, the Ides
Of March and all that stuff, the homicide
Foretellers in the flesh. And yet, they weren't
So good at reading dreams. They'd gone and burnt
Their guesses on the themes of dull clichés.
Not one of those foretellers then could say
What dreams had meant. But wait! We've skipped a part.
It's better that we stop, or rather start
At the beginning of our tale. And so
We shall. Two years had passed since Captain Dough
And Captain Cup had been released from chains.
Two years on top of theirs, Joe felt the reins
Of prison life. And finally, this guy
That Joe had asked a favor of (the why
Is obvious) just happens to remem-
Ber that he owes the man a square. Condemn
Him if you must, but it seems fair to give
The benefits of doubt. We should forgive
The bearer of the cups; it slipped his mind.
Or think what you'd forget were you assigned
To filling Pharaoh's cup. But anyway,
Let's get into the text and let it say
The things it must. It happened then, in time,   (GENESIS 41:1)
That Pharaoh, king of Egypt, made his climb
From out of sleep, more troubled than he could
Remember being in the past. He stood
Beside his bed and there recalled the scene
With fear and dread—a dream of seven lean.
The nightmare started out with just a walk
Beside the Nile. The leaning cattail stalks
Were bending low and kissing, with the sedge,
The current's sway. As Pharaoh paced the edge
And took wide Giza's wonders in, he saw
Then rising from the riverbed a flaw-
Less breed of kine. Yes, seven pudgy cows
Ascended from the Nile. Mind not the hows,
For dreams reveal much stranger things than this.
But pay attention, friend, or you will miss

The main event. These seven cows then stood
Upon the river's bank. No likelihood
Could then dismiss what Pharaoh saw within
The dream. He saw those seven cows, not thin
But thick as thieves, in fattened fleshy health—
Some seven kine to image Egypt's wealth.
He stood and watched the seven start to graze
The pastures of the Sun. But dwindling rays
Were quickly overcast by darkened night,
And seven ghastly kine moved into sight—
These also from the navel of the Nile,
Yet plagued and gruesome, sickly, ill, and vile.
Their hides pulled tight against their ribcage bones,
And shoddy flanks let fly the hunger groans.
This second batch of sickly cows then went
To stand beside the seven good, intent
On eating more than just the reeds. They moved
In close and showed their teeth, which all but proved
Their appetites carnivorous. Accursed,
That second batch of cows consumed the first.
But then the man who paced the river's shore
Went further in his dream. He would explore
A cultivated field producing corn,
Upon one stalk were seven large ears borne.
These golden-kerneled ears, a ready feast,
Were followed by another stalk. The east-
Ern wind had blasted it to shreds. The skin
Or husk was burnt up to a crisp. These thin-
Ner, sicker ears then started eating up
The healthy ones. They didn't stop their sup-
Per till the first had been consumed. Of such
Were Pharaoh's visions made, at least so much.
Then Pharaoh woke! It was a nasty dream!
He splashed his face, applied some shaving cream,
And brushed his tarnished teeth, but dream still plagued
His waking thoughts! It's like that dream had egged
His mind, and fear was smearing down its walls
To cake up crusty in the sun. For all
His efforts then, he couldn't rid the thing

From out his brooding thoughts, nor could he bring
Himself to think it didn't show a deep-
Er truth for him to know. He tried to keep
Composure as he called for those who read
In dreams. And so, they came, but poppy seeds
And bags of bones were impotent to show
A meaning that made any sense. Just know,
The seers didn't have a clue to what
The dreams had meant! In time, the scuttlebutt
Had reached the ears of those in Pharaoh's court,
For no one could make long or could make short
Of Pharaoh's dream. But then it was that he—
The man who bears the cups, the maitre d'
Of beverages, the Krups of Pharaoh's hall—
Remembered that he knew a guy, a tall
And handsome lad without a coat, a youth
Who had some skill in reading dreams, in truth.

A promissory note will rest a vault
Until disaster strikes. Then one will halt
Their daily cares to find the key that o-
Pens up the safe where it's been hid. They know
No rest until that little key is found
And hands upon a banknote are around.

Like so was Joseph rooted from the pit   (Genesis 41:14)
In edgy haste, fast-tracked a work permit
And given razors for a shave. No more
He'd wear the cloaks of prison life's décor.
The peach fuzz of his youth was gone for good.
Zest-fully-cleaned and in a tux, he stood
In front of Pharaoh then, and Pharaoh said,
Like one whose time was running out, "In bed
The other night, I had a dream. There's no
One here who can interpret it. I know
We've never met, but I have heard that you
Can hear a dream and then say what is true
Concerning it." So Pharaoh spoke to Joe,
And Joe replied, "I really only know

What God will speak to me. But I believe
He'll tell me what they mean and so relieve
You of your fears." The Pharaoh then was pleased
That one might puzzle out his dreams and seized
The moment then to share. He said, "I had
Been standing by the Nile, without a tad
Of worry in my mind, but then I saw
The strangest thing. I simply watched in awe
As seven cows walked straight from out the Nile
And fed upon the reeds. It made me smile
To watch these cows. They all were plump and fat
And healthy too—attractive cows, at that.
But lo from out the murky water came
Then seven other cows. They weren't the same
As those that came out first, for these were thin
And grossly gaunt, not much but bones and skin.
These seven sickly cows came up and stood
Beside the seven healthy ones. I could
Not then believe my eyes; the seven lean
Ate up the seven strong. Their plates were clean,
And not a crumb of healthy ones remained.
What's really weird is—after they had strained
The first ones down their throats—the seven sick
Appeared then just as thin, not any thick-
Er than they were before they ate. I had
Another dream right after that; it adds
More questions, though. But of this, you will hear.
I saw a stalk of corn with seven ears
Upon the stalk. These ears of corn were plump
And ripened full. But then, from out a clump
Of dried-up clay, there grew another stalk
Of corn. It also had—as if it'd mock
The first—it also had but seven ears
Of corn. This second stalk was in arrears
And blighted by the eastern wind—a scant
And sickly show. The ears upon this plant
Then gobbled up the seven better ones.
These are the dreams that I have had, and none
From all my seers can explain the things

To me." So Pharaoh made an end of bring-
Ing dreams to Joseph's ears. Then Joseph said,
Some comprehension to confusion wed,
"These dreams are one, presented here as two,
And speak to what my God will shortly do.
Moreover, they are doubled up to show
That God won't change His mind. That much, I know."

Physicians tap a hammer on the knee
To check a tendon's deep retort, to see
If nerves respond. There's not the least delay
Between the tap and jerking knee display.

So Joseph didn't hesitate to give
Interpretations of the dream, to live
As vessel for the mouth of God. And so
He spoke in Pharaoh's ears, "This you should know:
That seven healthy cows are seven years;
That's true of both the cows and of the ears
Of corn. The healthy seven are the same.
The seven ugly cows and ears that came
Up afterward are seven years of want
And famine too. I won't mince words or taunt
You with some ambiguity. It's as
I said to you before, that God now has
Shown Pharaoh what He'll do. He plans to give
Abundance here. For seven years you'll live
With more than more enough. But then there'll come
The seven years of want when you'll succumb
To famine and to undernourishment.
The second seven years will then be spent
Forgetting that you ever knew a time
When things were ever good. I know that I'm
Not bringing you the best of news, but you
Should know it's set. It's what God plans to do!"
So Joseph spoke to Pharaoh's ears. The king
Of Egypt didn't say a word; the thing
Was hard to get his hands around. But then
The coatless man went on, "Select some men,

Discerning ones and wise. Put them in charge
Of running things for you. Then, by and large,
You should pull through. But also set some ones
To oversee the storing of the tons
Of excess in the years of health. One-fifth
Should be enough. You'll have to make do with
The rest; just tighten up your belts a notch.
You'll have a good reserve if they don't botch
It up." So Joseph gave his sound advice.
Then Pharaoh spoke, "Now, who could put a price
On hearing words of God? Does not this make
One wise? In fact, I'd say without mistake,
A man who hears from God is king to men."
So Pharaoh spoke, and all his councilmen
Agreed. But further he went on to say,
"I'm putting him in charge, right now, this day!
There's no one in my kingdom more equipped
To handle this; he reads the manuscript
Of God." Then Pharaoh stepped from off his throne
And put a ring on Joseph's hand, a stone
To image Pharaoh's rank and rule. He placed
A robe on Joseph, too, and then encased
His neck with gold, a yoke of luxury.
Then Pharaoh said, "Each one shall take a knee
When you are passing by, and none will move
A pinky finger or a toe if you've
Not shown consent. When you say jump, they'll ask
How high. But all these gifts aren't so you bask
In power's lap but so my kingdom knows
That you're in charge. You're gonna run the show,
And only I will ever be above
Yourself!" So Pharaoh spoke, disposing of
Those flickers of a doubt that might exist
Concerning Joseph then, this man who'd kissed
The filthy pit for thirteen years. Those days
Were done! And Joseph then, without delay,
Had set to work. He oversaw the stock
And pile of grain when seven years did knock
A healthy tune in Egypt's fields. And when

The seven sickly years had come, when men
And women got the worst of it, the doors
Of that reserve were opened wide to pour
What had been wisely set aside. They found
That hoard was more than they would need—a mound
Of grain so large that it could clearly feed
The world and wide. Then Joseph said, "Indeed,
All lands are starving now, but we have bread."
And so, they thought to market it, to spread
The word that Egypt had its grain for sale.
And all the earth took note and didn't fail
To bow at Egypt's—rather, Joseph's grace—
A king then for each tribe and tongue and race.

CHAPTER 32

Governor of Grain

The famine came. The seven kine who sucked
The life from seven healthy cows had shucked
The better corn and gorged it to the cob;
A greedy guest to guzzle down and swab
Its dripping mouth on people's shirts. He stayed
And overstayed his welcome out, delayed
Departures seven years, demanding mints
And fresher towels and turndown fingerprints
Upon the sheets. But Egypt had its store
Of grain, thanks to the slave who answered for
The wrongs of everyone he ever knew.
He got a wife out of the deal and two
Young strapping brats. The wife was from the line
Of On—a priest, no less—the spit and shine
Of Egypt's royal class. That kid had gone
From rags to riches overnight, a swan
Among the ducks, a coatless man to wear

The lengthy robes of those who rule, who bear
The weight of nations on their backs. He took
It all in stride, exchanging shepherd crooks
And prison bars for scepters of a king.
But horns of plenty dangle down and sing
Their empty echoes for the other lands.
They have no store of grain and wring their hands
At how they'll feed a flock. Old Jacob's there
Within the crowd, a hoary head of hair
He wears from countless bowls of soup. His days
Are stacking up and weighted with malaise
Of parentship gone wrong. How could he leave
With so much left undone? His wrinkled sleeve
Of skin had made the grade and showed no signs
Of slowing down. But no one undermines
Their date with Death! *I think he has cajoled*
The Ferryman to put his job on hold,
Trade busing souls for gigging frogs. At least
He has a boat to do the job. He'll feast
On lily pads and legs when they've been peeled,
The sweet cuisine the river Styx could yield.
Old Jacob knew his end was near. He'd held
Departures off as any man impelled
To not go gentle into that good night.
Who knows how one would act? Perhaps you might—
As sweet Miss Emily E. Dickinson—
Be so preoccupied with death, so done
With social nonsense and with petty talk.
Go pull all curtains closed and further lock
Yourself within the attic boards and there
Produce the poetry of lords. I swear,
That's one appealing thought! At any rate,
Old Jacob neared his death, so contemplate
What that would mean. A neat and tidy end
Was on the mind. It wasn't only bend-
Ing truth and trickster ways, not only that;
I'm sure he did hard labor, too—and fat
He'd grown. Both work and guile had earned the guy
A hefty sum. For who could quantify

The beasts he had to feed? But legacies
Were on the line when famines came to seize
The milk the land would lend. There was no food!
Old Jacob knew he'd lose his multitude
Of beasts to hunger pains before too long.
His people also started singing songs
For meat five times a week. They'd eat him out
Of house and home. But there was talk about
The town; they'd heard that Egypt had some grain
To sell. At least that's what the ad campaign
Was running in the *Times. He's gonna make*
A trip just like old Isaac did and shake
The hand of Pharaoh, too. But Abraham
Had done the same and worse. Think of the sham
He sold when he had lied about his wife!
Oh man, here comes the sister part. By life
And death, these guys can't get it straight. Perhaps
His wives are ugly, though—no need to wrap
Them up in lies. We know they had more kids.
That's true enough. Well, anyway, amid
The famine Jacob heard that Egypt had
Some grain to sell. So old man Jake—the dad
Of twelve, *eleven sturdy boys*—then spoke
To Progenies of Promise he could choke.
He said, "Get off your butts! Why are you sit-   (GENESIS 42:1)
Ting round and staring holes in walls? Go hit
The road to Egypt's land. They've grain for sale.
Go purchase it before it's gone! Derail
Your apathy and try to act as if
You care that we don't die!" So Jacob's tiff
Was verbalized unto his loving sons.
The brothers did just that, except for one—
The youngest lad called Benjamin. So, ten
In all had made the journey down; ten men
Before the man in charge would stand. But Joe
Was overseer of the grain, and no
One bought the stuff without him there. Now all
Of Canaan felt the sting of Hunger's call,
And many made the trip to buy some grain,

And surely Joseph monitored that train
To see if Leah's sons had hitched a ride.

A dragonfly adjusts its speed and stride
To match its prey, foreseeing where the thing
Will fly, anticipating moves to bring
A meal between its jaws.

So Joseph could
Predict his brothers' moves. He understood
It was a simple waiting game, that soon
Enough they'd come. Well, on one afternoon
Young Joe saw them approach, the brothers who
Had threatened him with death, the mobster crew
That left the kid for dead. And he, in wit-
Ness and protection programs now, could sit
Aloof, clean shaved and robed with twenty years
Of age to change a face. And yet, to hear
Them speak his native tongue, the voices he
Identified with hate and perfidy,
It chilled the marrow of his bones. They bowed
Themselves to Joseph then, both awed and cowed
By wonders of the Nile. Unrecognized,
The seller of the grain went on and sized
Them up, this dirty brood that smelled of goat.
So much had changed since they had torn the coat
From off his back.

A boy will fish the streams
Beside his home when summer heat and beams
Of light are in their strength. His line runs straight
Into the murky pool where squirming bait
Awaits a hungry mouth. The line goes taut—
A bluegill or a catfish has been caught—
And out it's pulled to drip against the shore,
To batter up its sides with dust the more
It flails around. The boy then works the hook
From out its jaw, deciding if he'll cook
It or just throw the gasping fish back to

The rolling stream.

So Joseph then could do
Much as he pleased. But when he saw them there,
All bowing down as if to say a prayer,
He thought about his boyhood dream—the one
That had eleven stars, the moon and sun
All bowing down to him. It left an odd
And acrid taste to march his mouth and plod
Its way on down his throat. That boy had seen
His dream made flesh! The dream he'd had when green
With youth, some twenty years before, was play-
Ing out. But it would be a lie to say
He didn't feel a tinge of anger too—
An anger mixed with wonderment. And who
Could blame the kid for being rude to them?
For that is what he was! He cleared the phlegm
From out his royal chest, and in his best
Egyptian learned, he greeted then his guests.
Yes, in another language Joseph spoke
These words: "Who are you, and why do you poke
Your nose into our lands, and where's the place
That you call home?" They stood there face-to-face
With him they'd sold to be a slave, although,
That man from Adam they would never know.
Translations heard, the brothers said, "We are
From Canaan's fields, and we have traveled far
To buy the grain that Egypt has to vend."
Those brothers softly tread, not to offend
But simply state the facts. But Joseph then
Did say, "You look like spies to me, like men
Who've come to see if we are weak!" He spoke
These words in foreign tongues to shrewdly cloak
The fact their language was within his reach.
To them he seemed illiterate of speech.
But when translations had been done, a shock
Then worked to stupefy, to stun and knock
The men from any coziness they might
Have felt. Repulsed by such a charge, in fright

They blurted out, "My lord, you've got it wrong!
We're only here for food!" But Joseph's song
Was still the same; repeating it, he said,
"No, no. I've got it right. And you have tread
Our land to scan for any weaknesses."
Then said the men, intent their grievances
Be heard, "My lord, please hear us out. We've come
To buy the grain, and that is all! We're from
The land of Canaan, lord, and brothers too—
All from one man, as Jacob called. It's true!
Twelve brothers all from him. We left but one,
The youngest one, at home. Another son
Has died some time ago. So, we are ten
Who stand before you now, and honest men,
At that. The truth is, we are here for grain."
But Joseph didn't miss a beat; again
He said, "The truth is, you are here to spy!"
But softer then, the lord went on. "But I
Will give to you a chance, a chance to prove
Your story isn't lies. I will approve
That one of you can leave. The other nine
Will sit in jail. Let me be crystalline!
Unless your little brother is produced,
Then death on each your heads will come to roost!
You'd better hope that boy exists. Or if
You've sold him as a slave so you might stiff-
En out your purse, then search both long and hard.
I swear by Pharaoh's heel, you will be barred
And suffer death if he's not brought to me!"
So Joseph spoke, and that the men would see
That he was serious, he let the ten
Then spend some time in Egypt's finest pen.
That time was three whole days. *The same that saw*
One Jonah take his ambergris to spa
Before a date with Nineveh. The same
Amount of days that labored long to frame
The earth in dark, the number nine of plagues
That had descended from the Heaven's Hague
To black Egyptian skies. Three days did he

Named Abraham then trek so brazenly
Across the sand to find a place that looked
Much like a skull. When Moses went and booked
A conference with Pharaoh and then asked
For leave to put away their burdens cast-
Ing bricks to worship in the wilderness,
He asked for three days' time. When nothing less
Than three days' time was passed, the throbbing dudes
Of Shechem found that barber fees include
A knife in each their backs. A three-day march
Had worked a hefty thirst, did more to parch
The throats of Israel at Marah's sink.
That bitter pond converted to a drink
By Moses and his wood. When Josh was fixed
On crossing Jordan's wet, before they mixed
In Canaan's feud, they waited three days' time.
It was three days those seers then did climb
The hills of Jericho to find him famed,
The gristly prophet as Elijah named.
It took Jehoshaphat a three-day span
To plunder out his enemies, the clans
That saw each man against the other turned.
When David was then more and more concerned
That Saul was out to slit his throat, he asked
Then of his friend called Jonathan and tasked
That man with tracking down the truth. He wait-
Ed out three days within the fields, the weight
Of worlds upon his mind, until the news
Had reached his ears and arrows, not just two
But three, had missed their mark. When Rahab had
Advised the spies to hide behind the pads
Of hilly ground, it was for three days' time.
The Philistines had tried to guess the rhyme
And riddle Samson told for three whole days.
When Saul of Tarsus waited for his gaze
Of sight to be restored, it was for three
Days' time—poor Ananias, appointee
To such a job. The Israelites were told
They should abstain from sex, put that on hold,

For three long days and nights, until they met
With God on Sinai's cliffs. Do not forget
That Nehemiah spent three days beside
The temple walls before he did decide
To start his great campaign of reconstruct-
Ing them. Because they feared one might abduct
The body of our Lord, they posted guards
Beside His tomb for three days' time. When hard
And urgent tribulations brought that one
Egyptian slave to David's feet, he'd none
To eat for three days' time. Some figgy cake
And raisins were provided for his sake.
When Saul had lost his donkeys for the span
Of three whole days, he ran into the man
Who would anoint him king. One had three days
To eat the meat of sacrifice or blaze
It with a flame until it was consumed.
When all of Israel had then resumed
To marching desert sands, their thumbnail stop
At Sinai done, the first and foremost prop
Of that parade had been the ark for three
Days' time. When Joshua had learned that he
Was duped by men of Gibeon, it was
When three of days had passed. That great faux pas
Delivered water boys and lumberjacks.
Sweet sister Esther then could not relax
The three days leading up to when she'd speak
Before the king. That nightingale would leak
The news and sing of Haman's little planned
Pogrom. When thousands in a crowd did stand
And sit Jesus' feet, they'd gone three days
Without a meal. Church fish fries underway,
They soon were fed. It's when young David told
Amasa to assemble Judah, hold
A meeting then in three days' time. He failed
To do the king's command and so exhaled
His last on Joab's blade. Three days had marked
The time between two births, the births that sparked
A meeting with old Solomon the wise.

For sudden infant death had claimed its prize
On one, and arguments suppressed the true;
They'd split the last surviving kid in two.
When Ezra had returned from Babylon,
He and the elders camped from dusk till dawn
For three days' time beside a river that
Unto Ahava flowed. When Jesus sat
With all the elders in the temple halls,
His parents searched three days for him, their calls
To no avail for all that time. That Son
Of Man had also claimed he could be done
With building up the temple in just three
Days' time. Vast Nineveh was said to be
So large that one could walk for three days' time
Before they'd cover it. When paradigms
Of kings were soon to swap, the seer Gad
Told David he could choose between the bad,
The worse, and terrible. He had three days
To make that fateful choice. The census stays
Dave's greatest goof! (Some trust in horses, some
In chariots.) When Israel had come
To Rehoboam and had boldly asked
If he had planned to stop that tactic tasked
With wrongful tax—the missîm of misuse,
A nasty little practice of abuse—
That king had told them, "Wait three days and see."
When that great ship that carried Paul at sea
Had foundered on the rocks of Malta's base,
He stayed with Publius there at his place
For three days' time. And so, it was the same
For Joseph's brothers, then. They scratched their names
Upon the walls of Egypt's jail for three
Whole days and nights, the very lock and key
Where Joseph stayed. But that was years before
He got the job at Egypt's Grains and More.
Yes, on the third of days those men were brought
From out the pit, the grave, the hell they thought
Would be their end. Their hands were raised to shield
Their eyes, and dirty clothes had not concealed

The stink of death that followed them. They stood
Before young Joseph then, the brotherhood
Before the second son. And Joseph said,
"I'm not a vicious man, nor would I bed
You all in prison on a whim. That seems
A little harsh to me, and such extremes
Don't bring me any joy. For all I know,
Your story might pan out. I'll let you go,
Because I am a man who fears Almight-
Y God. That's right, I'll let you go, despite
My reservations on the case. You say
That you are honest men, the attachés
Of Canaan's land who've come to buy the food?
If so, then hear me out; the certitude
Of what you've shared depends on it! Just one
Of you will stay, and nine will leave. I'm done
With keeping all of you, so nine will leave
And take the grain. I want you to relieve
Your starving family members back at home.
But one of you must stay behind; he'll roam
A prison cell until the rest return.
You'll need to bring this youngest son to earn
My trust. Yes, bring your youngest brother here
So I can know if you have been sincere
With me." Such were the words of Joseph in
His brothers' ears. And then, in their chagrin,
The sons of Leah had a whispered chat.
And Joseph, that bilingual diplomat
Caught every word. They said, "This trouble comes
As tardy punishment. We all were numb
When Joe was crying for his life. He pled
With us for mercy, but we went ahead
And sold him anyway. That's why we're in
This mess, because of what we did, our sin
Against our brother years ago." And then
The eldest Reuben spoke, "Remember when
I told you not to touch the boy? I knew
That nothing good would come from it. But you
Just tuned me out, and now we have to an-

Swer for his blood." Their conversation ran
To Joseph's ears, and that man had to leave
The room. The tears were coming, sobs and heav-
Ing chest. He'd sell his tough advantage for
A ditty of lament, a thing he swore
In therapy he didn't want to do.
He couldn't let them see, and out of view
He ran to cry. But when the man was done
With blubbering, he'd gained one megaton
Of confidence. He marched into the room
Just like he owned the place, his poise a plume
To grace Egyptian garb. He gave command
For Simeon to wear new bonds, to stand
In chains—the bloody brother Joseph felt
Was most responsible in what was dealt
Him many years before. The other nine
Were told to hit the road, and by design
Their sacks were filled with grain and with the coins
By which they paid for it. *Did one purloin
The stuff? There's honor among thieves, my dear.*
How had it gotten there? Conjecture, fear,
And not a little misery had sat
Upon their minds. They said, "What is it that
Our God has done? He's torturing us now!"
Well, when the men were home, when every brow
Was lifted with the sight of ample food,
The nine had told old Jacob how the rude
And spiteful keeper of the grain had called
Them spies, had argued with them, and had stalled
Their journey three days' time. They told old Jake
How Simeon was left, his life at stake
If they had failed to bring young Benjamin
For show-and-tell. So Jacob said then in
Response, "My youngest son will not go down
With you. Two sons I've lost—first Joe, whose gown
Was bloody death. But if that loss was not
Enough, my Simeon will also rot
Egyptian prison cells. No way in hell
I'd give my youngest son to go and quell

Some madman with a pile of grain!" And so,
The bloody brother Simeon would go
And take one for the team. But let's not shed
Too many tears for him; the man had wed
Himself to violent ways, and those who live
By swords will find a life on swords will give.
In time, the hungry mouths of Jacob's clan
Had eaten all the food, and baking pans
Accumulated dust. *They have to make*
A run for borders, dear. And then, old Jake
Had gathered Leah's sons and spoke, "Go buy
Some grain. We're out!" But Judah wasn't shy
To tell his father how things stood; he said,
"The man was clear! Said if we ever tread
On Egypt's sand again, we better bring
Young Benjamin with us. We can't just fling
His words aside or have his rules dismissed!"
Then Jacob cut him off; the man was pissed!
"How could you be so stupid to parade
The fact another brother hadn't made
The trip? You should have held your wagging tongues!
But now I have to jeopardize my young-
Est son!" The brothers answered Jacob then
And said, "He was inquisitive, and when
He asked about another brother back
At home, we told the truth." Such words were slack
In bringing any comfort to the man.
So Judah followed up: "We have no plan
For food apart from this; we have to leave.
Don't act as if you'll only have to grieve
The life of Ben. For our whole clan will die
If we don't go. In turn, we must comply
With what the governor of grain required.
That is, to bring young Ben with us. I'm tired
Of begging here! I have some sons like you,
Young sons from Tamar's womb. Now, should these two
Be made to starve and suffer death because
Of Ben? We don't have time to lose; to pause
The trip is asinine. We could have made

The journey twice by now!" Then Judah laid
His anger down and said, "I'll keep the lad
Beside me every step, and nothing bad
Will come to him."

A sky runs black with storms
That ride the southern winds of spring. They warm
The air and strip the trees of budding leaves.
The frenzied rain and tempest one perceives
Engulfs the heavens with despair, the scope
Of it made larger by our fear. Yet hope
Returns when rays of sun can pierce the clouds
Of emptied rage.

So Judah cut the shroud
Of gloom his father wore. Assured they would
Return with Ben (at least the likelihood
Seemed pretty good), old Jacob gathered gifts,
A couple thoughtful presents that might lift
That mood of his, this Governor of Grain.
Some almonds and pistachios might gain
Some favor with the man, and honey, too,
And balm. Let's not forget the balm, the goo,
The scented stuff that pats us in the buff
For smoother skin, so much the huff and puff
Of Jacob ramping up to grease a palm.
He felt it was expedient to calm
This man who held their futures in his hands.
Jake said, "Perhaps he's one who understands
Complexities, that it was some mistake—
That silver coins, you'd never meant to take."
So Jake, at last, consented to the need
Of such a trip, reluctantly agreed
To let his youngest also go—an act
Made less of faith than necessary tact.
Then Jacob said, "Let God on High afford
You favor in this rash man's eyes, this lord
Of Egypt's grain. And may he grant that all
My sons return." So Jacob spoke; he'd stall

His sons no more. They took then twice the coin
They had before, the gifts, and there to join
That motorcade was Ben. They made the trip
With speed—all pell and mell and buggy whip
And dinner bell stampede—to buy some grain.
They stood in front of Joe again, the brains
Behind the hoard, and Joseph saw young Ben
With them, the kid he hadn't seen since when
He'd been a tot. Joe felt a giving mood
Come on, an altruistic attitude
That had him passing invitations out.
He'd have them come for lunch; some sauerkraut
And roasted ox were on the grill, and all
Of Joseph's brothers then received a call
To come. Joe wanted them to play some Clue,
A game of murder mystery where who
Is dead and gone turns out to be the host.
The seats had been assigned; they went from most
Of age to least, from Reuben down to Ben.
And Simeon was there, fresh out the pen
And on parole. There was an open bar,
And Joe would get the tab. He went so far
To see that no one's cup was dry, and drunk
Each man became before they hit the bunk.
But when the morning light had come, Joe went
To work at planting evidence. He sent
The brothers off with swag, the very coins
They used to pay were smuggled in to join
The mouths of each their sacks of grain. But more
A dirty trick was played on Ben. He wore
Within his little sack the master's watch,
A Rolex made of gold and not a Swatch
You'd buy on markets black. Yes, they were framed!
In turn, it didn't matter when they claimed
Immunity through ignorance. The hounds
Of Egypt's guard were at their heels, and sounds
Of clinking cuffs were sure to follow suit.
And back to Joseph they were brought, the brutes
Before the brains. Joe looked at them and said,

Still harping in Egyptian tongues, "I spread
A meal for you, and then you go behind
My back and steal from me? You think I'm blind
Or that I wouldn't notice when you took
My watch? Or don't you know I read the books
Of God, that I divine the mind Divine?   (GENESIS 44:15)
You really thought you'd pull the wool?" The nine-
Plus-two just looked at him, for none could make
The heads or tails of how, without mistake,
The silver was again within their bags.
Then Judah spoke—said it was not some gag
To stuff a mouth with inexpensive laughs.
He further said, "Bring out the polygraphs;
I swear by God above, we're being framed!"
His face was grim as he went on and named
The only explanation in his mind.
"I fear," he said, "that all this was assigned
As punishment for actions years ago.
God's stumbled on our crimes; He lets us know
He's found us out." So Judah spoke into
The ears of him he'd wronged. But Joe, who knew
The truth, in fact, had orchestrated all,
Saw fit to put the pressure on and call
His terms. He said, "Here's what I'm gonna do.
My mind's made up. I'm keeping one of you,
The one who had my watch. He'll be my slave.
The rest of you can clear on out; go pave
The road for Canaan's land." So Joseph spoke.

A fugitive will hide a temple, soak
The altar with his tears and grip the horns
To plead his case.

Like so had Judah torn
His shirt and gripped at Joseph's knee. He held
The governor and said these words, compelled
By his concern for what he thought would cause
A father's death: "My lord, Ben's here because
Of your demands. You said that if we came

Again to bring the lad. We've proved our claim;
He is our brother, as we said. But more
Than this is now at stake. You see, I swore
To bring Ben home. I gave my word unto
A dying patriarch, a father who
Has had his share of grief. This boy you want—
My father's youngest son—he is the vaunt
Of all his age and from his sweetest love,
The dearest wife he had. By God above,
She only had two sons. The first is dead
Some time ago, as we have aforesaid.
Now Ben's the only thing my dad has left
That ties him to his love, for he was reft
Of her when Ben was born. She died that day.
You see, he needs the boy. I mean to say
You cannot keep the lad, for that will send
My dad to death." So Judah made an end
Of words but added one last thing: "Take me
Instead." Young Joseph squared him up to see
If he was serious, and then he asked,
"You say this brother's dead, that he has passed
From out this life? What makes you sure; how do
You know he's dead?" And Judah, that man who
Was weighted with remorse, returned this script:
"I'm sure of it, my lord, because I stripped
Him of his coat and threw him in a pit.
I further sold him as a slave to knit
His days with servile threads. You see, I know
He's dead. God lets me know he's dead. He shows
Me in this suffering. But this was years
Ago." And Joseph then, before his tears
Could start, had uttered out, the best he could
In Hebrew tongues that Judah understood,
"I've been reborn."

Imagine, now, a boy
Who climbs the monkey bars, how he employs
His energy to reach the platform op-
Posite. His friend is waiting there to prop

Him up when he's arrived. But then in play,
For boys are imbeciles in countless ways,
He thinks to push him when he's reached his side.
The boy upon the bars is mortified
To find his friend has shoved against his chest.
Grip lost, he falls until his back's confessed
Its weight against the solid earth, a slam
That empties air from out his diaphragm.
The boy can't take a breath; his lungs are locked.

So Judah had the wind from out him knocked
When he had heard these words, and fear began
Its hold. Indeed, the four of Leah's clan
Were more than riveted with mortal dread!
They couldn't speak, for confidence had fled
Their mouths. But Joseph said to all of them
(His masquerade was done), "I don't condemn
You for what's in the past. Your acts were wrong—
That's true. But still, we had to play this song
And dance until I knew that I could trust
You all again. But tell me this: I must
And need to hear about our father's health!"
But Joseph's brothers then still nursed their wealth
Of disbelief; they asked of Joe, "It's you?
It's really you?" And then, like one who knew
The weight of words and worlds, "It is," said Joe.
"But listen to me now, for this I know:
God sent me on ahead of you so that
We'd be preserved. And we are only at
The second year of famine, friends. There're five
To come. Go tell my father I'm alive,
That I am Egypt's glory now. Go tell
Him he should come to me, and you can dwell
In Goshen's green. Tell him the famine has
Five years to go. He'll be safe here, whereas
He'll lose all he has gained in Canaan's land."
So Joseph spoke these words, the High Command
Of Egypt's means. But further Joe went on:
"I know you're scared. You fear I'll come upon

You for some sly revenge. But understand,
It wasn't you who sent me here; your hand
Was just a tool. And though your acts had ill
Intent, our God saw fit to work His will."   (GENESIS 45:8)

A Foucault pendulum will swing upon
A predetermined plane. The simple brawn
Of gravity propels the bob across
The floor. Suspended on a string, it toss-
Es back and forth to compass out the day.
To human eyes, the bob appears to sway
A circle round as to and fro it's hurled,
And yet, the only spinning is the world.

So Joseph's brothers then had not perceived
How, through one's wrong, God's will could be achieved.
But Joseph saw the deeper plan, and off
His brothers went to get their dad, to cough
Up truths about their acts before, come clean
About their lies. But Jake could not convene
His mind to meet belief and, more than this,
He couldn't bring himself to simply kiss
Goodbye to Canaan's land. The promise swore
Unto his dad and to his dad before
Was that the land of Canaan would be theirs.
How could he leave? But God, Who knows the cares
Of human minds, told Jacob he should go
To Egypt's land. God said to him, "I know
That you're concerned. But I will go with you.
And know this much, that I will follow through
To bring you out again." The words of God.
So, Israel did more than step; they trod
The balminess of Goshen's open mouth,
From northern plains to bellies in the south.

CHAPTER 33

Seventy Down

How many made descent to Egypt's land?
How many Hebrews heard the reprimand
Of Famine's jaws, a voice that patronized
An empty tum? How many cauterized
Their fears with need? For was it not a fear
They had of that Egyptian engineer?
And after all, it was a valid dread;
They'd sold him as a slave, left him for dead
Some twenty years before. Perhaps he had
Some trap in store for all of them when Dad
Was in the ground. Unease on hold, they packed
Their shepherd bags to go and interact
With those who hated shepherd stink. They chose
To make a home among that crew, dispose
Of comforts so they might be strangers in
A stranger land, the nomad Bedouin
To live with those of picket fence, the ones

Who take a bath three times a day, who run
The razors dull for hairless skin, the prudes
Of horticulture life who seek a nude
Dependence on the Nile—their wonders made,
The phallic symbols weightily displayed
For girth instead of length. But let this go;
We started out to find if we could know
How many made descent into the pit—
How many Hebrews went to retrofit
Their lives in Egypt's luxuries. We'll call
It seventy. Yes, seventy in all
Had gone to dwell in Goshen's plush. And count
Our Jacob, even though, for his account,
He gets his body laid in Canaan's soil.
Well, so does Joseph, dear. You're gonna spoil
The next our books! At any rate, old Jake
Had made young Joe to swear that he would take
His bones to Canaan's land when he had died.
Yes, he had made him swear, and he applied
His hands beneath the thigh when it was done.
Beneath the thigh? Oh, yes—that is when one
Will grab the scrotum; squeezing balls, he'll swear
The promise such-and-such while he does bear
The family gems within his grip. *I've moved*
The codpiece to the side and found it's proved:
He goes commando, dear. Seems true enough.
Well, wipe the sugar off; we'll find the stuff
That studs a thoroughbred. But was it not
Their history where promises had sought
To gauge the plots of God? It is agreed
That oral lore sees promise guaranteed
Against the mind's neglect. But Godly jaws
Would chew on forty winks, a snoozing pause
To last four hundred years; a burning bush
Would serve to sound alarms in morning's push
Of waking dawn. Yes, God was ramping up
To hold His tongue, and Hebrews then could sup
On undernourishment and bitter herbs
Where mugwort and where coriander curb

A servile gut. But let us step away
From all of this, not see the trees that sway
All by their lonesome selves but rather see
The forest's grand expanse, the potpourri
Of scribe and bard. Let's grant and ever give
Our gratitude to those whose toil does live
Upon the page. For Genesis does read
As if it were some novelette. Thank Bede,
The Venerated one, and Justin, who
Has lost his head; thank Tertius, who drew
The letters up for Paul, and thanks to Luke,
In turn, and do not fail to thank Baruch,
That scribe of Jeremian thought. Of course,
We'll have our Ezra in the ranks, the source
Of more than we could know. But let us skip
A little further back—when penmanship
Was soft within the egg; we'll find our roots
In temple songs—the prophet on a lute,
The poet with a quill, the keeper of
The forests of the king. Yes, there above
The rest, let Asaph stand. All hail the bards,
The ones who spend their hours at avant-garde!
It's by their work we get a glimpse of God.
So, hold your tongues to let these pass; be awed
Before the presence of the great. Excuse
Them all their less-than-perfect words; their muse
Is what our faith is charted by. But now
The cream upon the cake, the dairy cow
Of what is final course, the utter last
Our stories for today, the grand amassed
Finale of our book: I hear the drums,
And in the stalwart twelve of Jacob comes.
Among that crew is one called Afterward,
The maker of the soup, the man interred
With grief. He speaks and says, "I've had few years,
And evil are my days. My souvenirs
Are suffering." The constant sorrows ring
Upon his lips, like Soggy Bottoms sing
In overalls. *Odysseus has noth-*

Ing on this guy. But clear the tablecloth
And pour the man a drink; we'll have his last
Hurrah before his body's gone and cast
The ghost aside. *In vino veritas,*
The blunted kind of speech where one can toss
The euphemisms out, the man will bless
His sons; he'll speak it out no more or less
Than they deserve. And so, he sits and bids
The twelve to hear his words. Like so, this rids
The room of joyful words' exchange. Each man
Attends, and Afterward begins, "My clan
Is strong, but Reuben is my first. You met
My gaze with fortitude and might, and yet
You're stable as the surface of a lake.   (GENESIS 49:4)
You also shared my bed, as if you'd take
My couch of climax for yourself. Because
Of this, you won't excel in life; your flaws
Will hamper up your feet. For Simeon
And Levi, bloody men, the pantheon
Of violent thoughts has ruled your minds. You will
Be scattered on your future paths, but still
You'll find a home on brutal blades of strife
And rest the shades provided by a knife.
O Judah, bathed in glory, golden flame,
Eternal generations praise your name.
From cub to king and crown and mighty claws,
You'll throttle enemies between your jaws.
The rod and scepter won't depart your line.
Be sage upon the throne, and from the vine
Of wisdom, may your cup be filled. As for
My Zebulun, you'll be a harbor—more
A haven for the ships that venture on
The raging seas. For Issachar, your brawn
Is like a bull that bends its neck in fields
Of rest. But when you lift your head, you'll yield
That neck into a yoke of servitude.
My Dan will judge with skill and aptitude—
A cunning viper, not deterred by hooves
Of mighty steeds. My Gad is frail and proves

Himself of weaker strength. Your foes will tramp
Upon your neck, but in the end, you'll stamp
Theirs in return. The bread that Asher kneads
Is fit for kings; your dainties go to feed
A crown. Naphtali, you're a stag by streams
Of morning dew. The sun will gild its beams
Upon your cup. Your speech has not been dressed
With words, but silence sounds your great request.
A fruitful tree is Joseph, sturdy bough.
The pain that you have suffered will endow
Your branches more with elegance and shade.
With blessings from beneath, you'll be repaid.
May blessing of the breast and of the womb
Continue till you're resting in the tomb.
Young Benjamin will conquer and will smite
His foes. For your rapacious appetite
Is like a wolf that hunts both night and day,
Forever gorging on its fallen prey—
Dividing spoils, when moonlight overhangs,
Between the bloody dripping of his fangs.
You are my twelve—the stones pulled from the fields
I had in youth when female charms appealed.
Be gathered now as monument, and stage
And mark what is the ending of an age."

A prophet? No, nor was my father one.
I only tend the figs beneath the sun.
(AMOS 7:14)

Made in the USA
Monee, IL
19 September 2021

77746445R00196